FIFTH EDITION

Focus on Grammar 5B

Jay Maurer

Focus on Grammar 5: An Integrated Skills Approach, Fifth Edition, Volume B

Pearson Education, 221 River Street, Hoboken, NJ 07030

Staff credits: The people who made up the ***Focus on Grammar 5, Fifth Edition, Volume B*** team, representing content creation, design, manufacturing, marketing, multimedia, project management, publishing, rights management, and testing, are Pietro Alongi, Rhea Banker, Elizabeth Barker, Stephanie Bullard, Jennifer Castro, Tracey Cataldo, Aerin Csigay, Mindy DePalma, Dave Dickey, Warren Fischbach, Pam Fishman, Nancy Flaggman, Lester Holmes, Gosia Jaros-White, Leslie Johnson, Barry Katzen, Amy McCormick, Julie Molnar, Brian Panker, Stuart Radcliffe, Jennifer Raspiller, Lindsay Richman, Robert Ruvo, Alexandra Suarez, Paula Van Ells, and Joseph Vella.

Text design and layout: Don Williams
Composition: Page Designs International
Project supervision: Bernard Seal
Contributing editors: Julie Schmidt and Bernard Seal

Cover image: Andy Roberts / Getty Images

Printed in the United States of America

ISBN 10: 0-13-413631-4
ISBN 13: 978-0-13-413631-8

9 2024

Contents

WELCOME TO FOCUS ON GRAMMAR

FIFTH EDITION

BUILDING ON THE SUCCESS of previous editions, *Focus on Grammar* continues to provide an integrated-skills approach to engage students and help them understand, practice, and use English grammar. Centered on thematic instruction, *Focus on Grammar* combines comprehensive grammar coverage with abundant practice, critical thinking skills, and ongoing assessment, helping students accomplish their goals of communicating confidently, accurately, and fluently in everyday situations.

New in the Fifth Edition

New and Updated Content

Focus on Grammar continues to offer engaging and motivating content that appeals to learners from various cultural backgrounds. Many readings and activities have been replaced or updated to include topics that are of high interest to today's learners.

Updated Charts and Redesigned Notes

Clear, corpus-informed grammar presentations reflect real and natural language usage and allow students to grasp the most important aspects of the grammar. Clear signposting draws attention to common usage, the difference between written and spoken registers, and common errors.

Additional Communicative Activities

The new edition of *Focus on Grammar* has been expanded with additional communicative activities that encourage collaboration and the application of the target grammar in a variety of settings.

Expanded Writing Practice

Each unit in *Focus on Grammar* now ends with a structured "From Grammar to Writing" section. Supported by pre-writing and editing tasks, students engage in activities that allow them to apply the target grammar in writing.

New Assessment Program

The new edition of *Focus on Grammar* features a variety of new assessment tools, including course diagnostic tests, formative and summative assessments, and a flexible gradebook. The assessments are closely aligned with unit learning outcomes to inform instruction and measure student progress.

Revised MyEnglishLab

The updated MyEnglishLab offers students engaging practice and video grammar presentations anywhere, anytime. Immediate feedback and remediation tasks offer additional opportunities for successful mastery of content and help promote accuracy. Instructors receive instant access to digital content and diagnostic tools that allow them to customize the learning environment to meet the needs of their students.

The *Focus on Grammar* Approach

At the heart of the *Focus on Grammar* series is its unique and successful four-step approach that lets learners move from comprehension to communication within a clear and consistent structure. The books provide an abundance of scaffolded exercises to bridge the gap between identifying grammatical structures and using them with confidence and accuracy. The integration of the four skills allows students to learn grammar holistically, which in turn prepares them to understand and use English more effectively.

STEP 1: Grammar in Context integrates grammar and vocabulary in natural contexts such as articles, stories, dialogues, and blog posts. Students engage with the unit reading and theme and get exposure to grammar as it is used in real life.

STEP 2: Grammar Presentation presents the structures in clear and accessible grammar charts and notes with multiple examples of form and meaning. Corpus-informed explanations and examples reflect natural usage of the target forms, differentiate between written and conversational registers whenever appropriate, and highlight common errors to help students avoid typical pitfalls in both speaking and writing.

STEP 3: Focused Practice provides numerous and varied contextualized exercises for both the form and meaning of the new structures. Controlled practice ensures students' understanding of the target grammar and leads to mastery of form, meaning, and use.

STEP 4: Communication Practice provides practice with the structures in listening exercises as well as in communicative, open-ended speaking activities. These engaging activities provide ample opportunities for personalization and build students' confidence in using English. Students also develop their critical thinking skills through problem-solving activities and discussions.

Each unit now culminates with the **From Grammar to Writing** section. Students learn about common errors in writing and how to recognize them in their own work. Engaging and motivating writing activities encourage students to apply grammar in writing through structured tasks from pre-writing to editing.

Recycling

Underpinning the scope and sequence of the *Focus on Grammar* series is practice that allows students to use target structures and vocabulary many times, in different contexts. New grammar and vocabulary are recycled throughout the book. Students have maximum exposure, leading them to become confident in using the language in speech and in writing.

Assessment

Extensive testing informs instruction and allows teachers and students to measure progress.

- **Unit Reviews** at the end of every unit assess students' understanding of the grammar and allow students to monitor their own progress.
- **Diagnostic Tests** provide teachers with a valid and reliable means to determine how well students know the material they are going to study and to target instruction based on students' needs.
- **Unit Review Tests, Mid- and End-of-Term Review Tests, and Final Exams** measure students' ability to demonstrate mastery of skills taught in the course.
- The **Placement Test** is designed to help teachers place students into one of the five levels of the *Focus on Grammar* course.

The Importance of Context

A key element of *Focus on Grammar* is presenting important grammatical structures in context. The contexts selected are most relevant to the grammatical forms being introduced. Contextualized grammar practice also plays a key role in improving fluent use of grammar in communicative contexts. It helps learners to develop consistent and correct usage of target structures during all productive practice.

The Role of Corpus

The most important goal of *Focus on Grammar* has always been to present grammar structures using natural language. To that end, *Focus on Grammar* has incorporated the findings of corpus linguistics,* while never losing sight of what is pedagogically sound and useful. By taking this approach, *Focus on Grammar* ensures that:

- the language presented reflects real, natural usage
- themes and topics provide a good fit with the grammar point and elicit the target grammar naturally
- findings of the corpus research are reflected in the syllabus, readings, charts, grammar notes, and practice activities
- examples illustrate differences between spoken and written registers, and formal and informal language
- students are exposed to common errors in usage and learn how to recognize and avoid errors in their own speech and writing

Focus on Grammar Efficacy

The fifth edition of *Focus on Grammar* reflects an important efficacy initiative for Pearson courses—to be able to demonstrate that all teaching materials have a positive impact on student learning. To support this, *Focus on Grammar* has been updated and aligned to the **Global Scale of English** and the **Common European Framework** (CEFR) to provide granular insight into the objectives of the course, the progression of learning, and the expected outcomes a learner will be able to demonstrate upon successful completion.

To learn more about the Global Scale of English, visit www.English.com.

Components

Student Books with Essential Online Resources include access codes to the course audio, video, and self-assessment.

Student Books with MyEnglishLab offer a blended approach with integration of print and online content.

Workbooks contain additional contextualized practice in print format.

Digital Teacher's Resources include printable teaching notes, GSE mapping documents, answer keys, audio scripts, and downloadable tests. Access to the digital copy of the student books allows teachers to project the pages for whole-class instruction.

***FOG Go* app** allows users to access the student book audio on their mobile devices.

* A principal resource has been Douglas Biber et al, *Longman Grammar of Spoken and Written English*, Harlow: Pearson Education Ltd., 1999.

The *Focus on Grammar* Unit

Focus on Grammar introduces grammar structures in the context of unified themes. All units follow a four-step approach, taking learners from grammar in context to communicative practice. Thematic units add a layer to learning so that by the end of the unit students will be able to discuss the content using the grammar points they have just studied.

STEP 1 GRAMMAR IN CONTEXT

Before You Read activities create interest and elicit students' knowledge about the topic.

Vocabulary exercises help students improve their command of English.

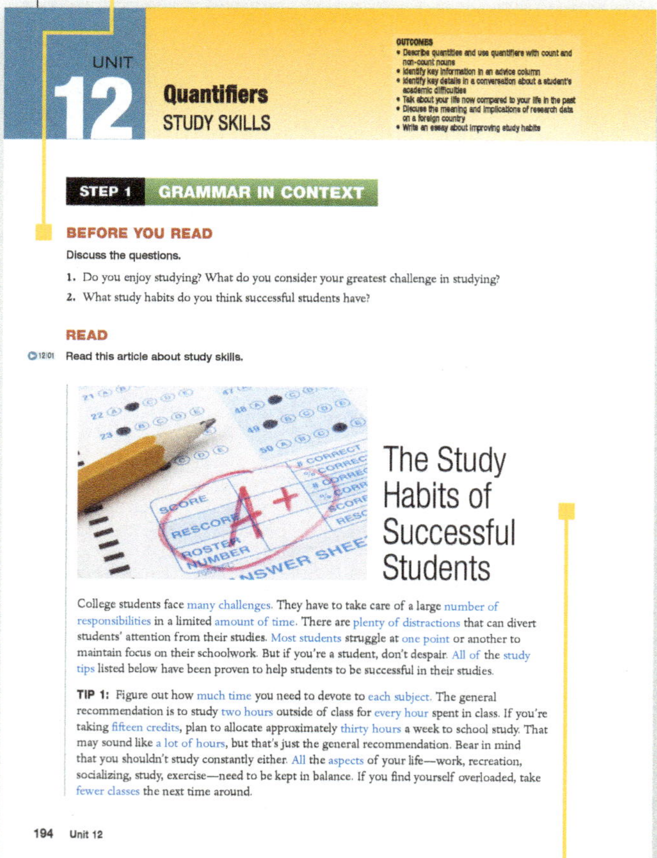

UNIT 12

Quantifiers

STUDY SKILLS

OUTCOMES

- Describe quantities and use quantifiers with count and non-count nouns
- Identify key information in an advice column
- Identify key details in a conversation about a student's academic difficulties
- Talk about your life now compared to your life in the past
- Discuss the meaning and implications of research data on a foreign country
- Write an essay about improving study habits

STEP 1 GRAMMAR IN CONTEXT

BEFORE YOU READ

Discuss the questions.

1. Do you enjoy studying? What do you consider your greatest challenge in studying?
2. What study habits do you think successful students have?

READ

12|01 Read this article about study skills.

The Study Habits of Successful Students

College students face many challenges. They have to take care of a large number of responsibilities in a limited amount of time. There are plenty of distractions that can divert students' attention from their studies. Most students struggle at one point or another to maintain focus on their schoolwork. But if you're a student, don't despair. All of the study tips listed below have been proven to help students to be successful in their studies.

TIP 1: Figure out how much time you need to devote to each subject. The general recommendation is to study two hours outside of class for every hour spent in class. If you're taking fifteen credits, plan to allocate approximately thirty hours a week to school study. That may sound like a lot of hours, but that's just the general recommendation. Bear in mind that you shouldn't study constantly either. All the aspects of your life—work, recreation, socializing, study, exercise—need to be kept in balance. If you find yourself overloaded, take fewer classes the next time around.

194 Unit 12

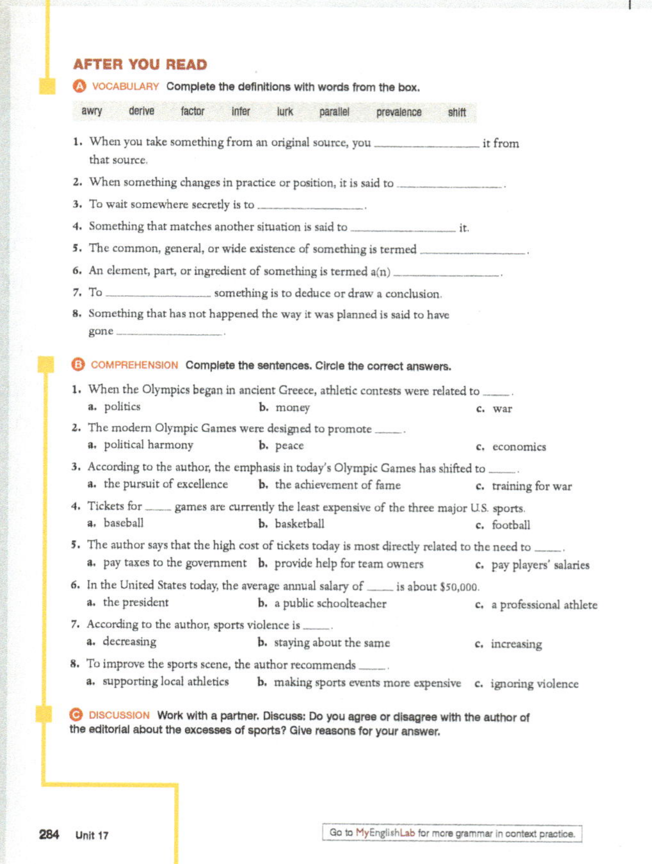

AFTER YOU READ

A VOCABULARY Complete the definitions with words from the box.

awry	derive	factor	infer	lurk	parallel	prevalence	shift

1. When you take something from an original source, you __________ it from that source.
2. When something changes in practice or position, it is said to __________.
3. To wait somewhere secretly is to __________.
4. Something that matches another situation is said to __________ it.
5. The common, general, or wide existence of something is termed __________.
6. An element, part, or ingredient of something is termed a(n) __________.
7. To __________ something is to deduce or draw a conclusion.
8. Something that has not happened the way it was planned is said to have gone __________.

B COMPREHENSION Complete the sentences. Circle the correct answers.

1. When the Olympics began in ancient Greece, athletic contests were related to ____.
   a. politics b. money c. war
2. The modern Olympic Games were designed to promote ____.
   a. political harmony b. peace c. economics
3. According to the author, the emphasis in today's Olympic Games has shifted to ____.
   a. the pursuit of excellence b. the achievement of fame c. training for war
4. Tickets for ____ games are currently the least expensive of the three major U.S. sports.
   a. baseball b. basketball c. football
5. The author says that the high cost of tickets today is most directly related to the need to ____.
   a. pay taxes to the government b. provide help for team owners c. pay players' salaries
6. In the United States today, the average annual salary of ____ is about $50,000.
   a. the president b. a public schoolteacher c. a professional athlete
7. According to the author, sports violence is ____.
   a. decreasing b. staying about the same c. increasing
8. To improve the sports scene, the author recommends ____.
   a. supporting local athletics b. making sports events more expensive c. ignoring violence

C DISCUSSION Work with a partner. Discuss: Do you agree or disagree with the author of the editorial about the excesses of sports? Give reasons for your answer.

284 Unit 17

Go to MyEnglishLab for more grammar in context practice.

Engaging, high-interest **readings** in a variety of genres present the target structures in natural and realistic contexts. As students read, they encounter the form, meaning, and use of the grammar.

Comprehension and **Discussion** activities focus on the meaning of the text and draw students' attention to the target structures. NEW!

STEP 2 GRAMMAR PRESENTATION

Grammar Charts present the structures in a clear, easy-to-read format.

STEP 2 GRAMMAR PRESENTATION

INFINITIVES

Infinitive as Subject

Infinitive (Subject)	Verb	Object
To procrastinate	causes	a lot of problems.
Not to go ahead	proved	a mistake.

Infinitive as Object

Subject	Verb	Infinitive (Object)
Not everyone	wants	to procrastinate.
He	decided	not to go ahead.

Infinitive as Subject Complement

Subject	Verb	Infinitive (Subject Complement)
His job	is	to motivate people.
Their real intention	is	not to succeed.

***It* + *Be* + Adjective + Infinitive**

It	*Be*	Adjective	(*For/Of* + Noun/Pronoun)	Infinitive
It	is	foolish	(for Alice/her)	to procrastinate.
It	was	wrong	(of Hal/him)	not to go ahead.

Verbs Followed by Infinitives

	Verb	(Noun/Pronoun)	Infinitive
They	decided	Ø*	to call.
	convinced	Steve/him	
	expected	(Steve/him)	

*Ø = When *decide* is used with an infinitive, it cannot be followed by a noun or object pronoun.

Adjectives Followed by Infinitives

	Adjective	Infinitive	
Hal is	reluctant	to complete	his work on time.
He's	careful	not to make	mistakes.
They're	happy	to hear	the test has been postponed.

Nouns Followed by Infinitives

	Noun	Infinitive	
He can always think of	reasons	to put off	studying.
It seems like	the thing	to do.	
She always shows	reluctance	to finish	a job.

Infinitives 143

NEW!

The newly designed **Grammar Notes** highlight the main point of each note, making navigation and review easier. Simple corpus-informed **explanations** and **examples** ensure students' understanding.

GRAMMAR NOTES

1 Passive Voice vs. Active Voice

A sentence in the passive voice has a corresponding sentence in the active voice. In an **active** sentence, the **subject acts upon the object** of the sentence. In a **passive** sentence, the **subject is acted upon by the agent**.

- active — The police **catch** ***some criminals***. (SUBJECT: The police; OBJECT: some criminals)
- passive — ***Some criminals*** **are caught** by the police. (SUBJECT: Some criminals; AGENT: the police)

The **subject** of the active sentence **becomes the agent** (preceded by the preposition *by*) in the passive sentence, or disappears.
Some criminals are caught **by the police.** (AGENT)
Some criminals are caught.

Transitive verbs are followed by an **object**. **Intransitive** verbs are not followed by an object. Many verbs can be used both transitively and intransitively.
They **returned** ***the clothes*** to the store. *(transitive)*
They **returned** home late in the evening. *(intransitive)*

BE CAREFUL! Only **transitive** verbs can be made **passive**. **Intransitive** verbs **cannot** be made **passive**.
Several people **died** in the accident.
NOT Several people ~~were~~ died in the accident.

2 Forms of the Passive

To form **passive** sentences, use ***be*** + past participle or ***get*** + past participle. They occur in **present, past,** and **future** forms, as well as in the **progressive**.

- present — Police officers **are** well **trained.** They **get tested** on the job almost daily.
- past — The suspect **was arrested** yesterday. He **got caught** committing a crime.
- future — He **will be held** in the local jail. He'**ll get charged** soon.

To make a **negative** passive sentence, place ***not*** after the first verb.
Cooper **has *not* been caught.**
The man **did *not* get killed** in the robbery.

To form **progressive passive** sentences, use ***being*** + past participle.
The prisoner **is** currently **being questioned.**
The suspect **is being held** in prison.

USAGE NOTE Use the **present progressive** and **past progressive** passives to describe actions **in progress** (= not finished) at a certain time.
The robbery occurred while the money **was being taken** to a bank.

90 Unit 6

NEW!

Clear signposting provides corpus-informed notes about common usage, differences between spoken and written registers, and common errors.

PRONUNCIATION NOTE

12|02 **Reducing *of* in Quantifiers**

Quantifiers containing the preposition ***of*** are often reduced in rapid speech and in conversation. The word ***of*** is often reduced to "a." This reduction often happens when the word following *of* begins with a consonant. When the word following *of* begins with a vowel, full forms are generally used.

a couple of → "a couple a"	We met **"a couple a"** new people at the party.
a lot of → "a lotta"	I had **"a lotta"** work to do tonight.
lots of → "lotsa"	There are **"lotsa"** great movies playing.
plenty of → "plentya"	There's **"plentya"** time to get there.
a number of → "a numbera"	I had **"a numbera"** problems with the homework.
amount of → "amounta"	The **"amounta"** traffic today was incredible.
a bit of → "a bitta"	He had **"a bitta"** trouble hearing the lecture.
most of → "mosta"	I was able to solve **"mosta"** the problems.

IN WRITING The forms *couple a, lotta, lotsa, plentya, a numbera, amounta, bitta,* and *mosta* are **not used in writing**.
We have **a lot of** work left to do.
There's **plenty of** food for everyone.
We had **lots of** fun at the amusement park.
The **amount of** money she earns is amazing.

NEW!

Pronunciation Notes are now included with the grammar presentation to highlight relevant pronunciation aspects of the target structures and to help students understand authentic spoken English.

STEP 3 FOCUSED PRACTICE

Discover the Grammar activities develop students' recognition and understanding of the target structures before they are asked to produce them.

Controlled practice activities lead students to master form, meaning, and use of the target grammar.

STEP 3 FOCUSED PRACTICE

EXERCISE 1 DISCOVER THE GRAMMAR

A GRAMMAR NOTES 1–6 **Read the sentences based on the reading. Underline the verbs showing future time and label the ways they show future time.**

1. So you're visiting some new countries this year? *present progressive*
2. You leave in exactly four weeks. ________
3. A month from now, you'll be relaxing in the sunshine. ________
4. I'm going to give you suggestions in five areas. ________
5. The suggestions will help you with your trip. ________
6. You'll have been flying for eight to ten hours. ________
7. When you land, it will probably be late morning. ________
8. By then, you'll have acquired nice memories. ________

B GRAMMAR NOTES 1, 3–4, 6 **Look at the underlined verbs in the sentences based on the reading. Check (✓) *Present Time* or *Future Time*.**

	Present Time	Future Time
1. So you're visiting some new countries this year?	☐	☑
2. You already have your tickets.	☐	☐
3. You leave in exactly four weeks.	☐	☐
4. When you land, it will probably be late morning.	☐	☐
5. You can get package deals that include accommodations.	☐	☐
6. Airbnb links owners with renters.	☐	☐
7. Find out about the countries where you're going.	☐	☐
8. You'll have learned a lot by the time you arrive.	☐	☐
9. Put yourself in the shoes of the people who live there.	☐	☐
10. So there you have it.	☐	☐

40 Unit 3

EXERCISE 2 SENTENCE ADVERBS

GRAMMAR NOTE 1 **Combine each pair of statements into one statement containing a sentence adverb. Use the adverb form of the word in parentheses. Vary your sentences so that the sentence adverb appears in different positions in the sentences: beginning, middle, and end.**

1. National service is beneficial. (obvious)
   National service is obviously beneficial.
2. Military service can be dangerous. (unfortunate)
3. I'm against the death penalty because I consider it cruel. (essential)
4. There's a lot more violence in movies than in the past. (certain)
5. Nuclear weapons can be eliminated. (hopeful)
6. A vaccine against AIDS can be developed. (possible)
7. The prime minister's position is wrong. (clear)

EXERCISE 3 FOCUS ADVERBS

GRAMMAR NOTE 2 **Complete the sentences. Circle the correct answers.**

1. Bill believes that women should not fight. He feels ___ in noncombat roles.
   ⓐ they should only serve b. only they should serve
2. Carrie thinks women can do most jobs men can do, but she feels ___ in combat.
   a. men should serve only b. only men should serve
3. Samantha is against gambling, but ___ the benefits of lotteries.
   a. even she can recognize b. she can even recognize
4. I'm in favor of higher taxes. ___ taxing food and medicine.
   a. Even I'm in favor of b. I'm even in favor of
5. My husband has some good reasons for supporting nuclear power. However, I ___.
   a. don't just agree b. just don't agree
6. My father ___ the military draft; he's a military recruiter.
   a. doesn't just support b. just doesn't support
7. My friend and I ___ $100 for the tickets, but the concert was worth the money.
   a. almost paid b. paid almost

Adverbs: Sentence, Focus, and Negative 273

A **variety of exercise types** engage students and guide them from recognition and understanding to accurate production of the grammar structures.

Editing exercises allow students to identify and correct typical mistakes.

EXERCISE 7 EDITING

GRAMMAR NOTES 1–5 **Read the email from Elena Gutierrez to her sister Rosa in Colombia. There are eight mistakes in the use of adjective clauses and phrases. The first mistake is already corrected. Find and correct seven more. Delete verbs, change pronouns, or add words where necessary. Do not change punctuation.**

TO: Rosa111@yoohoo.com
FROM: ElenaGut@gomail.com
RE: Life in L.A.

Hi Rosa,

I'm writing this in English because I think we both need the practice. How are you doing? Please say "hi" to everyone back there, ~~included~~ *including* all our friends in the neighborhood.

I'm still having a hard time here in Los Angeles, but things are a little better than they were. I'm not quite as lonely as before because I've met some people in my neighborhood, many of which are friendly, but so far I don't know anyone really well. I do have some friends who from my classes at the university, most whom are very interesting. I'm looking forward to getting to know them better as time goes on. The hardest thing is the food, most of it I just don't like very much. It's difficult to find quality food that's not too expensive.

I did do one really fun thing recently. One of my friends from school and I went to Universal Studios. We took a tram tour around the park and saw several actors working, some of that

STEP 4 COMMUNICATION PRACTICE

Listenings in a variety of genres allow students to hear the grammar in natural contexts.

STEP 4 COMMUNICATION PRACTICE

EXERCISE 9 LISTENING

16|04 **A** Listen to the radio call-in show. Overall, what does the caller think about human nature?

____

____

____

16|04 **B** Read each statement. Then listen to the talk show again. Check (✓) *True* or *False*.

	True	False
1. Capital punishment is used in every state in the United States.	☐	☑
2. The host of the radio show says that there clearly seems to be a worldwide movement to abolish capital punishment.	☐	☐
3. The caller is in favor of capital punishment, overall.	☐	☐
4. Capital punishment is apparently used in China.	☐	☐
5. Generally, the caller feels that people have gotten more civilized.	☐	☐
6. The caller believes that robbery is clearly a capital crime.	☐	☐
7. According to the caller, rehabilitation is clearly impossible for all criminals.	☐	☐
8. The caller hopes that the death penalty will not be abolished worldwide.	☐	☐

C Work with a partner. Discuss the questions. Give reasons for your answers.

1. Do you basically agree or disagree with the viewpoint of the caller in the Listening?
2. Do you believe that, overall, people have become more or less civilized than they were in ancient times?
3. Do you believe that, generally, criminals are capable of rehabilitation?

EXERCISE 10 HOW DO YOU FEEL ABOUT . . . ?

A SURVEY Work in a group. Ask your classmates for their opinions on the controversial issues in the chart on page 279. Then add up your group's responses, noting the number of students supporting and opposing each viewpoint.

EXAMPLE: A: How do you feel about making all schools coeducational?
B: I'm absolutely in favor of it. Boys and girls should go to school together.
C: I'm against it, overall. Coeducational schools are fine, generally, but some students do better in single-sex schools.

278 Unit 16

In the **listening activities**, students practice a range of listening skills. A **new step** has been added in which partners complete an activity that relates to the listening and uses the target grammar.

NEW!

Engaging **communicative activities** (conversations, discussions, presentations, surveys, and games) help students synthesize the grammar, develop fluency, and build their problem-solving skills.

EXERCISE 10 THE NOUN GAME

A GAME Divide into two teams. First, work with your own team. Look at the words in the word box. Match them with their definitions in the chart.

~~advice~~	a space	baldness	fast food	people	talk	work
~~a criterion~~	a talk	cancer	film	rice	the police	
a film	a tan	cholesterol	lightning	space	thunder	
a people	a work	criteria	news	sunblock	traffic	

a. ______: an art form that involves moving pictures on a screen	f. ______: a brownish color that the sun gives to the skin	k. ______: a cream used on the skin to protect it from burning by the sun	p. ______: a sudden electrical discharge in the atmosphere	u. ______: a movie
b. advice: an opinion about what could or should be done about a situation	g. ______: movement of people or vehicles along routes of transportation	l. ______: a substance found in the human body and in various foods	q. ______: people who are responsible for capturing criminals, etc.	v. ______: a booming sound that occurs with an electrical discharge in the air
c. ______: conversation	h. ______: a disease involving the abnormal growth of cells in the body	m. ______: standards, rules, or tests on which judgments can be made	r. ______: a grain that many people eat, grown in warm climates	w. ______: a particular ethnic group
d. ______: a condition that involves the loss of hair on the head	i. ______: a blank or empty area	n. ______: hamburgers, fries, and fried chicken, for example	s. ______: your job or activities that you do regularly to earn money	x. ______: the area beyond the atmosphere of the earth
e. ______: a painting, book, play, or piece of music, for example	j. a criterion: a standard, rule, or test on which judgments can be made	o. ______: information about events that have happened recently	t. ______: human beings	y. ______: a formal discussion

B Work with the other team. Take turns asking and answering *what* questions about each word or phrase in the word box. Then check your answers on page 435. Which team got the most answers correct?

EXAMPLE: TEAM A: What is *advice*?
TEAM B: *Advice* is an opinion about what could or should be done about a situation.
TEAM B: What is *a criterion*?
TEAM A: *A criterion* is a standard, rule, or test on which judgments can be made.

Go to MyEnglishLab for more communication practice.

Count and Non-Count Nouns 175

FROM GRAMMAR TO WRITING

A **From Grammar to Writing** section, now in every unit, helps students to confidently apply the unit's grammar to their own writing. **NEW!**

FROM GRAMMAR TO WRITING

A BEFORE YOU WRITE **Consider the personality categories that have been mentioned in this unit and choose the one that fits you best. Write a few sentences about why you believe you fit into this particular category.**

B WRITE **Using your ideas in A, write a five-paragraph essay about the personality type that best fits you. Remember to use identifying and nonidentifying adjective clauses. Try to avoid the common mistakes shown in the chart. Use the example below to help you begin your essay.**

EXAMPLE: No single personality type applies perfectly to a person, but for me one comes closer than all the others. The personality category that fits me most closely is Type B. First, Type Bs are social people who are basically extroverts. I've always enjoyed my friends, which is why I think this category fits me quite well. . . .

Common Mistakes in Using Adjective Clauses

Use ***who***, not *which*, to refer to **people**.	The neighbor **who** is the nicest is Mrs. Lopez. NOT The neighbor ~~which~~ is the nicest is Mrs. Lopez.
Don't use a **double subject** in an adjective clause.	I'm impressed by people **who** are kind and helpful. NOT I'm impressed by people who ~~they~~ are kind and helpful.
Don't enclose identifying adjective clauses with **commas**.	People who put others before themselves are admirable. NOT People, who put others before themselves, are admirable.
Don't use *that* to introduce a **nonidentifying** adjective clause. Use ***who***, ***whom***, or ***which***.	Hussein, **who** is my best friend, was born in Tanzania. NOT Hussein, ~~that~~ is my best friend, was born in Tanzania.

C CHECK YOUR WORK **Look at your essay. Underline adjective clauses. Use the Editing Checklist to check your work.**

Editing Checklist

Did you . . . ?

- ☐ use *who* or *whom* to refer to people and *which* to refer to things
- ☐ avoid using a double subject in adjective clauses
- ☐ enclose nonidentifying clauses with commas
- ☐ avoid using *that* to introduce a nonidentifying adjective clause

D REVISE YOUR WORK **Read your essay again. Can you improve your writing? Make changes if necessary.**

Go to MyEnglishLab for more writing practice.

Adjective Clauses: Introduction 245

The **Before You Write** task helps students generate ideas for their writing assignment.

In the **Write** task, students are given a writing assignment and guided to use the target grammar and avoid common errors.

Check Your Work includes an Editing Checklist that allows students to proofread and edit their writing.

In **Revise Your Work**, students are given a final opportunity to improve their writing.

UNIT REVIEW

Unit Reviews give students the opportunity to check their understanding of the target structures. Students can check their answers against the Answer Key at the end of the book. They can also complete the Review on MyEnglishLab.

UNIT 15 REVIEW

Test yourself on the grammar of the unit.

A **Complete the sentences. Circle the correct answers.**

1. Dr. Brand and Dr. Wang, neither of whom / which I've met yet, are well-known professors.
2. Professor Meemook, which / whose classes I enjoy, is originally from Thailand.
3. My two roommates, both of who / whom are from Nigeria, are experiencing culture shock.
4. Hamburgers and hot dogs, neither of them / which I like, are not popular in my country.
5. Rashid and Hussein, who / whom are both newcomers to this country, work in a grocery store.
6. Anyone interested / interesting in culture shock should attend the lecture.
7. Pelé, born / was born in Brazil, used to be a great soccer player.
8. You can do several things to get over culture shock, includes / including befriending local people and learning more about their culture.

B **Complete the sentences with words from the box. You will use some words more than once.**

that	which	who	whom	whose

1. I've met five new colleagues, all of ______________ I like.
2. I'm taking three new courses, none of ______________ are very interesting.
3. I made two friends, both of ______________ are teachers, this week.
4. I've lived in several countries, examples of ______________ are Chile and Mexico.
5. Two famous authors, both of ______________ books I've read, are here today.
6. I read a novel about a young man ______________ is caught in a dead-end job.
7. The country ______________ Emiko moved to is very different from Japan.

C **Find and correct five mistakes.**

MyEnglishLab

MyEnglishLab delivers rich online content to engage and motivate **students**.

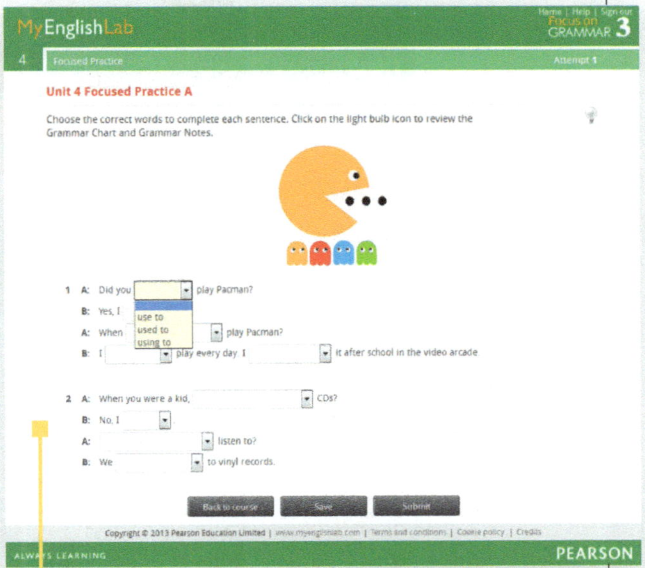

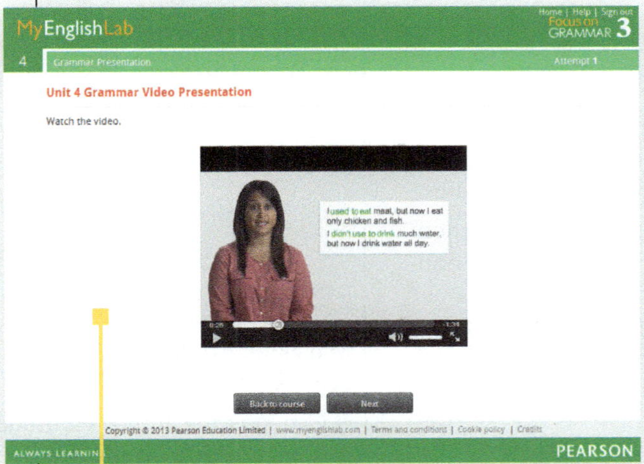

Grammar Coach videos give additional grammar presentations.

NEW!

MyEnglishLab provides students with:

- rich interactive practice in grammar, reading, listening, speaking, and writing
- immediate and meaningful feedback on wrong answers
- remediation activities

NEW!

- grade reports that display performance and time on task

MyEnglishLab delivers innovative teaching tools and useful resources to **teachers**.

With **MyEnglishLab**, teachers can:

- view student scores by unit and activity
- monitor student progress on any activity or test
- analyze class data to determine steps for remediation and support

MyEnglishLab also provides teachers with:

- a digital copy of the student book for whole-class instruction
- downloadable assessments, including the placement test, that can be administered on MyEnglishLab or in print format
- printable resources including teaching notes, suggestions for teaching grammar, GSE mapping documents, answer keys, and audio scripts

Scope and Sequence

	UNIT	GRAMMAR	READING
PART **1** **Present, Past, and Future**	**1** **Present Time** Page 4 THEME The Digital World	■ Can use the simple present for habitual actions and the present progressive for actions in progress ■ Can use the present perfect and the perfect progressive to connect the past with the present ■ Can correctly use action verbs to describe actions and non-action verbs to describe states ■ Can use adverbs with action words and adjectives with non-action verbs	Opinion Editorial: *Connected!* ■ Can infer the author's attitude in a linguistically complex text that contains the author's opinions
	2 **Past Time** Page 18 THEME Intercultural Marriage	■ Can use the simple past, the past progressive, the present perfect, and the past perfect to refer to past events ■ Can describe past habits and situations using *would* and *used to*	Magazine Article: *That Special Someone* ■ Can infer the author's attitude in a linguistically complex text that contains a narrative
	3 **Future Time** Page 35 THEME Travel	■ Can use *be going to* and *will* to refer to future events ■ Can use the simple present for scheduled events, and *be going to* and the present progressive to describe future plans ■ Can use the future progressive, the future perfect, and the future perfect progressive to describe future actions or states	Advice Column: *Get the Most Out of It* ■ Can infer the author's attitude in a linguistically complex text that contains advice or suggestions
PART **2** **Modals and Other Auxiliaries**	**4** **Modals to Express Degrees of Necessity** Page 52 THEME Cultural Differences	■ Can use *must*, *have to*, and *have got to* to show strong necessity ■ Can use *must not* and *don't have to* to show prohibition ■ Can use *had better* for warnings ■ Can use *should* and *ought to* to offer advice, and use *be supposed to* and *be to* to show expectations ■ Can make suggestions using *could* and *might (have)* PRONUNCIATION Reducing Modals and Modal-like Auxiliaries	Personal Narrative: *What We Should and Shouldn't Have Done* ■ Can infer the author's attitude in a linguistically complex narrative about a personal experience

PART **2** CONTINUES ▼

LISTENING	SPEAKING	WRITING	VOCABULARY
A conversation about identity theft ■ Can follow a group discussion on a complex topic such as identity theft	■ Can contribute fluently and naturally to a conversation about common uses of technology	■ Can write a detailed essay that highlights the benefits of an electronic device	access AWL associate (with) do without downside exposure AWL origin put things in perspective AWL undeniably AWL
A news broadcast ■ Can recognize important details in a news broadcast or interview about complex, unfamiliar topics	■ Can clearly and precisely offer opinions about past events or goals, agreeing or disagreeing with others' opinions	■ Can write a linguistically complex discursive essay about a past experience	acknowledge AWL ethnic AWL eventually AWL furthermore AWL priority AWL rely AWL sustain AWL unique AWL
A conversation about travel plans ■ Can recognize details in a fast-paced conversation about a schedule or itinerary	■ Can speculate and make predictions about future plans or events	■ Can write a linguistically complex discursive essay about future goals and aspirations	acquire AWL chart your own course excruciatingly hectic inevitable AWL maximize AWL minimize AWL out of whack
A conversation about suggestions ■ Can identify the suggestions that are being made in a fast-paced conversation between fluent speakers	■ Can discuss do's and don'ts in different cultures, using linguistically complex language	■ Can write a linguistically complex discursive essay, offering regrets, opinions, and/or advice about a past situation	albeit AWL colleague AWL etiquette gracious occur AWL odd AWL overall AWL reciprocate

AWL = Academic Word List item

UNIT	GRAMMAR	READING
▼ PART **2** CONTINUED		
5 **Modals to Express Degrees of Certainty** Page 69 THEME Mysteries	■ Can use *may*, *might*, *could*, and *may not* or *might not* + base form of the verb to convey the degree of certainty in the present ■ Can use *may have*, *might have*, *could have*, *must have*, and *may not* or *might not* + past participle to convey the degree of certainty in the past ■ Can use *should* and *ought to* + base form of the verb and *may*, *might*, and *could* + base form of the verb to convey the degree of certainty in the future	Academic passage: *Who Really Discovered America?* ■ Can infer the author's attitude in a linguistically complex academic text that challenges established ideas

PART **3**

Passive Voice

UNIT	GRAMMAR	READING
6 **Passives: Part I** Page 86 THEME Crime	■ Can use the passive with the past, present, and future tenses and modals ■ Can use the passive causative to talk about services or activities that people arrange for someone else to do	News Article: *Did He Get Away With It?* ■ Can understand and form opinions about theories presented in a linguistically complex news article
7 **Passives: Part 2** Page 105 THEME Legends and Myths	■ Can use stative passives to describe situations or states ■ Can use regular passives to report ideas, opinions, and beliefs	Anthropology Passage: *The Strangest of Peoples* ■ Can distinguish between literal and allegorical meaning in an academic text

PART **4**

Gerunds and Infinitives

UNIT	GRAMMAR	READING
8 **Gerunds** Page 124 THEME Friendship	■ Can use gerunds and gerund phrases in place of nouns, and as the subjects and objects of sentences ■ Can use a possessive noun or pronoun before a gerund to demonstrate possession	Magazine Article: *Friends* ■ Can infer the author's attitude in an expository text
9 **Infinitives** Page 140 THEME Procrastination	■ Can use infinitives as subjects and objects in the simple, past, and passive forms ■ Can use verbs with infinitives and/or gerunds ■ Can use an adjective or noun followed by an infinitive	Magazine Article: *Seize the Day* ■ Can infer the interviewee's opinions on a subject from an interview transcript

LISTENING	SPEAKING	WRITING	VOCABULARY
An academic discussion ■ Can follow a group discussion on an academic topic	■ Can clarify own points and ideas about an ambiguous event, using linguistically sophisticated language	■ Can write a complex essay about a mystery, using modals to speculate about clues and possibilities	cohort debris hypothesize AWL nonetheless AWL potential AWL specification AWL stem from theory AWL
An interview about a crime ■ Can identify key details in a fast-paced interview conducted by native speakers	■ Can critically evaluate evidence presented in an article to discuss and speculate about a crime	■ Can write a linguistically complex essay about a crime, using the passive voice to illustrate actions	diminish AWL equip (with) AWL inadvertently notwithstanding AWL presumably AWL proceed (to) AWL recover AWL reveal AWL
A news bulletin about a natural disaster ■ Can follow chronological sequences in extended informal speech at natural speed	■ Can contribute fluently and naturally to a conversation about an academic topic	■ Can write a linguistically complex discursive essay about a legend or myth from one's culture	devote (to) AWL focal obtain AWL participation AWL practitioner AWL predominate AWL repulsive ritual
A telephone conversation between friends ■ Can identify key details in a telephone conversation between native speakers, spoken at a normal rate	■ Can contribute to group discussions about personal topics, even when speech is fast-paced and colloquial	■ Can write a well-developed, grammatically varied essay about a personal experience	abandon AWL coincide AWL compatible AWL context AWL likewise AWL naive seek AWL vulnerable
A news bulletin about a prison escape ■ Can recognize key information in a news bulletin spoken by a native speaker and containing reported speech	■ Can contribute fluently and naturally to a personal interview, alternating between answering and asking questions	■ Can write a well-developed, grammatically varied essay about a personal experience	connotation illustrate AWL motivate AWL scenario AWL straightforward AWL syndrome widespread AWL

AWL = Academic Word List item

PART 5
Nouns

UNIT	GRAMMAR	READING
10 **Count and Non-Count Nouns** Page 160 THEME Health	■ Can use common nouns, proper nouns, regular and irregular count and non-count nouns, and nouns that are only plural ■ Can make certain non-count nouns countable by adding a phrase that gives them a form, a limit, or a container	TV Program Transcript: *Concerned About Health? Ask the Expert.* ■ Can infer the interviewee's opinion on a subject from a long and linguistically complex interview transcript
11 **Definite and Indefinite Articles** Page 178 THEME Disappearing Species	■ Can use indefinite nouns to describe things that are non-specific or general ■ Can use definite nouns to describe a particular person, place, or thing ■ Can use indefinite and definite articles in a variety of different situations ■ Can use no article with names of people, the names of most countries, and habitual locations	Scientific Article: *Going, Going . . . Gone?* ■ Can follow abstract argumentation, for example, the balancing of alternatives and the drawing of a conclusion
12 **Quantifiers** Page 194 THEME Study Skills	■ Can use a variety of different quantifiers with count and non-count nouns ■ Can use *some*, *a few*, and *a little* with affirmative statements, and *any*, *few*, and *little* with negative statements PRONUNCIATION Reducing *of* in Quantifiers	Advice Column: *The Study Habits of Successful Students* ■ Can infer the author's attitude in a complex text that presents advice or suggestions
13 **Modification of Nouns** Page 211 THEME Expectations	■ Can use participial adjectives, noun modifiers, and compound modifiers to modify nouns ■ Can put multiple modifiers in a fixed order PRONUNCIATION Modifiers of Nouns	Expository Article: *I Hope for It, but I Don't Expect It* ■ Can infer the author's attitude in a linguistically complex text that details different people's personal experiences

LISTENING	SPEAKING	WRITING	VOCABULARY
A conversation about health issues ■ Can identify important details from a fast-paced conversation	■ Can orally convey information from different sources, reconstructing arguments to present the overall result	■ Can write a well-developed, grammatically varied essay about personal attributes	advocate (v) AWL authority AWL category AWL deviate AWL hence AWL imperative (adj) in moderation offset AWL
A conversation about a controversial topic ■ Can follow a fast-paced conversation between fluent speakers well enough to form one's own opinion about the topics discussed	■ Can contribute to a group discussion about a controversial topic, using linguistically complex language	■ Can write a linguistically complex discursive essay about a topic of environmental or social importance	considerable AWL crucial AWL diversity AWL institute (v) AWL nevertheless AWL restrict AWL strategy AWL vanish
A conversation between a professor and a student ■ Can follow a fast-paced conversation held by fluent speakers	■ Can consult a variety of sources, using one's findings give a linguistically complex presentation about a country	■ Can write a well-developed essay that clearly states one's opinion about how to improve study habits	allocate AWL approximate (adj) AWL aspect AWL despair (v) orientation AWL precise AWL refine AWL ultimately AWL
A conversation about performance ■ Can follow a fast-paced conversation well enough to recognize key details	■ Can contribute fluently and naturally to a literary analysis of a short story or poem	■ Can write a discursive essay that discusses people's expectations about major life events in detail	contrary AWL emerge AWL ensure AWL intense AWL outcome AWL persist AWL rave (about) thereby AWL

AWL = Academic Word List item

	UNIT	GRAMMAR	READING
PART **6** **Adjective Clauses**	**14** **Adjective Clauses: Introduction** Page 228 THEME Personality	■ Can use *who*, *which*, *that*, *whose*, *where*, and *when* with adjective clauses to modify nouns ■ Can use adjective clauses as subjects or objects of sentences ■ Can distinguish between identifying and nonidentifying adjective clauses, using commas with nonidentifying adjective clauses PRONUNCIATION Identifying and Nonidentifying Adjective Clauses	Psychology Article: *What Type Are You?* ■ Can extract information and ideas from a linguistically complex text about an academic subject
	15 **Adjective Clauses and Phrases** Page 247 THEME Culture Shock	■ Can use adjective clauses with prepositions ■ Can use the pattern quantifier + *of* + relative pronoun to refer to people or things, and noun + *of which* to refer to things only ■ Can reduce or change adjective clauses to adjective phrases	Sociology Article: *What Is Culture Shock?* ■ Can recognize organizational patterns within a linguistically complex text
PART **7** **Adverbs**	**16** **Adverbs: Sentence, Focus, and Negative** Page 266 THEME Controversial Issues	■ Can use sentence adverbs to modify the meaning of entire sentences ■ Can use focus adverbs before verbs to emphasize a word or phrase ■ Can use negative adverbs at the beginning of sentences to emphasize negative meaning ■ Can force inversion with *here*, *there*, *neither*, and *so* PRONUNCIATION Stressed Words After Focus Adverbs	Radio Transcript: *Time to Sound Off* ■ Can identify and make judgments about different opinions in a linguistically complex interview or transcript
	17 **Adverb Clauses** Page 282 THEME Sports	■ Can use a variety of adverb clauses to indicate when, where, why, or under what condition something happens ■ Can use adverb clauses of contrast such as *whereas*, *even though*, and *while* to establish contrast with ideas expressed in independent clauses	Sports Editorial: *Are Sports Still Sporting?* ■ Can follow abstract argumentation in an editorial, such as the balancing of alternatives and the drawing of conclusions

PART **7** CONTINUES ▼

LISTENING	SPEAKING	WRITING	VOCABULARY
A conversation about university life ■ Can follow a fast-paced conversation about life in a university setting	■ Can summarize findings appropriately in an oral report about a famous person	■ Can write a linguistically complex essay that supports an opinion with a multitude of ideas, facts, or references	conflict (n) AWL data AWL discount (v) enable AWL gravitate insight AWL moreover secure (adj) AWL
A conversation between a student and a guidance counselor ■ Can follow a fast-paced conversation between native speakers	■ Can use a complex graphic to describe their own cultural experiences, using linguistically complex language	■ Can write a grammatically rich, discursive essay that describes a cultural experience in detail	adjustment AWL attain AWL convert (v) AWL disorientation dwarf (v) flexible AWL maturity AWL whereas AWL
An excerpt from a radio call-in show ■ Can follow a fast-paced conversation about a controversial topic, identifying the speakers' opinions	■ Can contribute fluently and naturally to a group debate about a controversial topic	■ Can write a well-developed, grammatically varied essay that states and explains one's opinion on a controversial topic	compulsory controversial AWL fundamentally AWL inherent interfere (with) promote AWL stereotype (n) voluntary AWL
An interview with an athlete ■ Can follow a fast-paced interview given by a fluent speaker well enough to recall detailed information	■ Can offer, defend, and elicit an opinion that's derived from a quotation	■ Can write a well-developed, grammatically varied essay that discusses the pros and cons of sports	awry derive AWL factor (n) AWL infer AWL lurk parallel AWL prevalence shift (v) AWL

AWL = Academic Word List item

UNIT	GRAMMAR	READING
▼ PART 7 CONTINUED		
18 **Adverb and Adverbial Phrases** Page 298 THEME Compassion	■ Can change adverb clauses of time and reason to adverb and adverbial phrases ■ Can change an adverb clause with the simple past or the past perfect to an adverb phrase by changing the verb to *having* + past participle	Magazine Article: *Compassion* ■ Can identify a sequence of events in a linguistically complex article
19 **Connectors** Page 315 THEME Memory	■ Can use a range of common transition words to sequence events ■ Can use both coordinating and subordinating conjunctions to connect ideas within and between sentences ■ Can use a variety of transitions to connect sentences with independent clauses and blocks of text	Scientific Article: *Try to Remember* ■ Can infer the author's attitude in a linguistically complex academic text

PART 8 **Noun Clauses**

UNIT	GRAMMAR	READING
20 **Noun Clauses: Subjects, Objects, and Complements** Page 334 THEME Birth Order	■ Can form and use noun clauses as subjects, objects, and complements ■ Can form and use embedded questions ■ Can form and use noun clauses with *that*, *the fact that*, *if*, and *whether* ■ Can add *-ever* to the end of *wh-* words to produce words that introduce noun clauses	Psychology Article: *Does It Matter When You Were Born?* ■ Can recognize a connection between different theories in an academically rigorous text
21 **Direct and Indirect Speech** Page 352 THEME Communication and Misunderstanding	■ Can report what someone said using direct and indirect speech in both question and sentence form ■ Can make the necessary changes to verb tenses, modals, possessive adjectives, and pronouns when using reported speech	Interview Transcript: *Understanding Misunderstandings* ■ Can extract information, ideas, and opinions from a respected expert in her field

LISTENING	SPEAKING	WRITING	VOCABULARY
A news broadcast about world affairs ■ Can infer opinions in a linguistically complex news broadcast	■ Can contribute to a fast-paced group discussion about experiences that were witnessed in the past	■ Can write a complex discursive essay about a situation that was witnessed or experienced in the past	civility confrontation dawn (on) decrepit elude media ooze (v) status AWL
An excerpt from a workshop ■ Can identify a speaker's point of view in a linguistically complex presentation	■ Can give one's opinion in response to a literary quote and comment on the opinions of others	■ Can write a detailed discursive essay about a memorable experience from the past	core AWL deteriorate enhance AWL highlight AWL induce AWL mitigate recollect vivid
A conversation about a child's problems ■ Can follow a fast-paced conversation between a family therapist and the parents of a troubled child	■ Can elicit and participate in a conversation that is based on data from a survey or questionnaire	■ Can apply an academic theory to one's personal life in a well-developed, grammatically varied essay	compelling (adj) configuration conscientious enterprise innovator AWL niche (n) sole (adj) AWL temperament
An interview about communication techniques ■ Can identify the main ideas and opinions in a fast-paced interview with an expert in her field	■ Can discuss communication techniques in a group setting, using linguistically complex language	■ Can write a complex essay that uses direct and indirect speech to provide a detailed account of an event witnessed in the past	address (v) arbitrary AWL distressed (adj) duration AWL inhibit AWL rancor rigid AWL self-righteous

AWL = Academic Word List item

PART 9
Conditionals and the Subjunctive

UNIT	GRAMMAR	READING
22 **Conditionals; Other Ways to Express Unreality** Page 374 THEME Achievements and Inventions	■ Can use real conditionals to refer to general truths, facts, habits, and repeated events ■ Can use present and past unreal conditionals to refer to hypothetical (counterfactual) past results of a previous action or situation ■ Can use *wish* and *if only* to express sadness or a desire for a different situation	Scientific Article: *How Would Our World Be Different?* ■ Can extract information, ideas, and opinions from a linguistically complex text
23 **More Conditions; The Subjunctive** Page 392 THEME Advice	■ Can use implied and inverted conditions ■ Can use the subjunctive as a verb form to express unreal conditions, wishes, and possibilities ■ Can use the subjunctive with the base form of the verb in noun clauses following verbs and adjectives of advice, necessity, and urgency	Advice Column: *Ask Rosa* ■ Can extract information, ideas, and opinions from a complex text that offers advice or suggestions

LISTENING	SPEAKING	WRITING	VOCABULARY
A classroom discussion ■ Can follow a fast-paced classroom discussion about a technological concept	■ Can use real and unreal conditionals to discuss actual and hypothetical situations	■ Can write a linguistically complex, highly detailed essay about the impact of a technological development or invention	attribute (to) AWL e.g. evolve AWL formulate AWL i.e. mutually AWL ubiquitous utilize AWL
A conversation about advice ■ Can follow a fast-paced conversation held by fluent speakers	■ Can give a formal presentation to a group of peers, advising them to choose specific actions or outcomes	■ Can write a linguistically complex discursive essay that uses the subjunctive to describe past experiences related to following advice	capable AWL manipulate AWL mediate AWL overbearing semblance slob resistant violate AWL

AWL = Academic Word List item

About the Author

Jay Maurer has taught English in binational centers, colleges, and universities in Spain, Portugal, Mexico, the Somali Republic, and the United States; and intensive English at Columbia University's American Language Program. In addition, he has been a teacher of college composition, literature, technical writing, speech, and drama at Santa Fe Community College and Northern New Mexico Community College. Since 1997, he has conducted his own business as an individual English-language coach. He is the co-author with Penny LaPorte of the three-level *Structure Practice in Context* series; co-author with Irene Schoenberg of the five-level *True Colors* series and the *True Voices* video series; co-author with Irene Schoenberg of *Focus on Grammar 1*; and author of *Focus on Grammar 5*, editions 1 through 5. Mr. Maurer holds an M.A. and an M.Ed. in applied linguistics and a Ph.D. in the teaching of English, all from Columbia University. Currently he lives and writes in Arizona and Washington State. *Focus on Grammar 5*, Fifth Edition, has grown out of the author's experiences as a practicing teacher of both ESL and college writing.

Acknowledgments

Writing the fifth edition of *Focus on Grammar 5* has been just as interesting, challenging, and rewarding as writing the first four editions. I'm indebted to many people who helped me in different ways. Specifically, though, I want to express my appreciation to:

- My students over the years.
- **Marjorie Fuchs** and **Irene Schoenberg**—the other members of the FOG author team—for their support and encouragement.
- **Gosia Jaros-White**, the Publisher for *Focus on Grammar*, 5th edition. Gosia has been a perceptive, strong, and effective leader of the project.
- **Don Williams**, the series designer and compositor. Don has an excellent eye for the appearance of text and art on the page.
- **Bernard Seal**, for his vision, dedication, and careful attention to the task. Bernard has been an excellent editorial manager. Thank you greatly.

Above all, I am grateful to:

- **Julie Schmidt**, my editor, for her dedication, her excellent eye for detail and logic, and her focus on quality. Julie has been instrumental in making this a better book. Many thanks.
- My wife, **Priscilla**, for her love, wonderful support, and assistance with the manuscript.
- My best friend.

Reviewers

We are grateful to the following reviewers for their many helpful comments.

Susanna Aramyan, Glendale Community College, Glendale, CA; **Homeretta Ayala**, Baltimore Co. Schools, Baltimore, MD; **Barbara Barrett**, University of Miami, Miami, FL; **Rebecca Beck**, Irvine Valley College, Irvine, CA; **Crystal Bock Thiessen**, University of Nebraska-PIESL, Lincoln, NE; **Janna Brink**, Mt. San Antonio College, Walnut, CA; **Erin Butler**, University of California, Riverside, CA; **Joice Cain**, Fullerton College, Fullerton, CA; **Shannonine M. Caruana**, Hudson County Community College, Jersey City, NJ; **Tonya Cobb**, Cypress College, Cypress, CA; **David Cooke**, Mt. San Antonio College, Walnut, CA; **Lindsay Donigan**, Fullerton College, Fullerton, CA; **Mila Dragushanskya**, ASA College, New York, NY; **Jill Fox**, University of Nebraska, Lincoln, NE; **Katalin Gyurindak**, Mt. San Antonio College, Walnut, CA; **Karen Hamilton**, Glendale Community College, Glendale, CA; **Electra Jablons**, International English Language Institute, Hunter College, New York, NY; **Eva Kozlenko**, Hudson County Community College, Jersey City, NJ; **Esther Lee**, American Language Program, California State University, Fullerton, CA; **Yenlan Li**, American Language Program, California State University, Fullerton, CA; **Shirley Lundblade**, Mt. San Antonio College, Walnut, CA; **Thi Thi Ma**, Los Angeles City College, Los Angeles, CA; **Marilyn Martin**, Mt. San Antonio College, Walnut, CA; **Eve Mazereeuw**, University of Guelph English Language Programs, Guelph, Ontario, Canada; **Robert Mott**, Glendale Community College, Glendale, CA; **Wanda Murtha**, Glendale Community College, Glendale, CA; **Susan Niemeyer**, Los Angeles City College, Los Angeles, CA; **Wayne Pate**, Tarrant County College, Fort Worth, TX; **Genevieve Patthey-Chavez**, Los Angeles City College, Los Angeles, CA; **Robin Persiani**, Sierra College, Rocklin, CA; **Denise Phillips**, Hudson County Community College, Jersey City, NJ; **Anna Powell**, American Language Program, California State University, Fullerton, CA; **JoAnna Prado**, Sacramento City Community College, Sacramento, CA; **Mark Rau**, American River College, Sacramento, CA; **Madeleine Schamehorn**, University of California, Riverside, CA; **Richard Skinner**, Hudson County Community College, Jersey City, NJ; **Heather Snavely**, American Language Program, California State University, Fullerton, CA; **Gordana Sokic**, Douglas College, Westminster, British Columbia, Canada; **Lee Spencer**, International English Language Institute, Hunter College, New York, NY; **Heather Stern**, Irvine Valley College, Irvine, CA; **Susan Stern**, Irvine Valley College, Irvine, CA; **Andrea Sunnaa**, Mt. San Antonio College, Walnut, CA; **Margaret Teske**, Mt. San Antonio College, Walnut, CA; **Johanna Van Gendt**, Hudson County Community College, Jersey City, NJ; **Daniela C. Wagner-Loera**, University of Maryland, College Park, MD; **Tamara Williams**, University of Guelph, English Language Programs, Guelph, Ontario, Canada; **Saliha Yagoubi**, Hudson County Community College, Jersey City, NJ; **Pat Zayas**, Glendale Community College, Glendale, CA

Credits

PHOTO CREDITS

2–3: Potowizard/Fotolia; **4:** Imtmphoto/Fotolia; **12:** (left) Corund/Fotolia, (right) Tang Yan Song/Shutterstock; **15:** (background) Flas100/Fotolia, (top right) Chuchi25/Fotolia; **18:** Andy Dean/Fotolia; **24:** Kiko Calderón/Fotolia; **25:** Jolopes/Fotolia; **27:** (background) Tolgatezcan/Fotolia, (top) Stephen Coburn/Shutterstock; **29:** Dasha Petrenko/Fotolia; **32:** Design Pics Inc/ Alamy Stock Photo; **35:** Darya Petrenko/123RF; **35–36:** Arigato/Shutterstock; **36:** (bottom) Paul Prescott/Shutterstock, (bottom center) Artzenter/Fotolia, (top) Funkyfrogstock/Shutterstock, (top center) Ammit/123RF; **40:** Farang/123RF; **41:** Pxl.store/Fotolia; **42:** Igor Rivilis/Shutterstock; **45:** Andrea Crisante/ Shutterstock; **47:** (bottom) Zozulinskyi/Fotolia, (top left) Ivcandy/DigitalVision/ Getty Images, (top right) Windsor & Wiehahn/The Image Bank/Getty Images; **50–51:** Matthew Jacques/Shutterstock; **52:** (bottom) Robtek/Fotolia, (top) Mtkang/Fotolia; **52–53:** MSPhotographic/Fotolia; **53:** (bottom) Africa Studio/ Fotolia, (top) Kungverylucky/Shutterstock; **61:** (bottom) Patrick/Fotolia, (background) Oly5/Fotolia; **62–63:** Photosvac/Fotolia; **64:** Nattanan726/ Fotolia; **69:** Max8xam/Fotolia; **75:** Imtmphoto/Fotolia; **76:** Kravka/Shutterstock; **76–77:** Tanawatpontchour/Fotolia; **77:** Jkraft5/Fotolia; **81:** (bottom left) David Parker/Alamy Stock Photo, (bottom right) Norbel/Fotolia, (top left) Bryan Busovicki/Fotolia, (top right) Yü Lan/Fotolia; **84–85:** Fer Gregory/ Shutterstock; **87:** CSU Archives/Everett Collection Historical/Alamy Stock Photo; **95:** (background) Ruslan Ivantsov/Fotolia, (top) Pablo Hidalgo/123RF; **96:** (background) Rangizzz/123RF, (top) Mary Evans Picture Library/Alamy Stock Photo; **97:** Africa Studio/Fotolia; **98:** (bottom) Storm/Fotolia, (background) Katusha161107/Fotolia; **99:** Everett Collection Historical/Alamy Stock Photo; **101:** S–F/Shutterstock; **102:** Epa european pressphoto agency b.v./ Alamy Stock Photo; **114:** Jakkarin/Fotolia; **115:** Aloysius Patrimonio/123RF; 119 (bottom) Auipuistock/Fotolia, (background) THPStock/Fotolia, (top) M. Cornelius/Shutterstock; **122–123:** Liseykina/Shutterstock; **124–125:** LZ Image/ Shutterstock; **125:** Syda Productions/Fotolia; **130:** Akhenatonimages/Fotolia; **132:** Lightpoet/Fotolia; **134:** Wavebreakmedia/Shutterstock; **135:** (background) Roman Samokhin/Fotolia, (top) Vitanovski/Fotolia; **141:** (background) Olhakostiuk/ Fotolia, (center) Sergey Nivens/Fotolia; **149:** Narstudio/Fotolia; **151:** Gang/ Fotolia; **152:** VTT Studio/Fotolia; **155:** (bottom) Jacob Lund/Shutterstock, (top) Nyul/Fotolia; **158–159:** Creative Soul/Fotolia; **161:** IxMaster/Shutterstock; **171:** F11photo/Fotolia; **173:** Samsonovs/Fotolia; **174:** Pixelrobot/Fotolia; **178–179:** Flas100/Fotolia; **179:** (center) Bbsferrari/Fotolia, (left) Michaklootwijk/ Fotolia, (right) Chris Hill/Fotolia; **185:** Maxoidos/Fotolia; **186–187:** Tiero/Fotolia; **188:** (bottom) Ron Hilton/Shutterstock, (top) IPK Photography/Shutterstock; **189:** Roman Samokhin/Fotolia; **191:** Take Photo/Shutterstock; **194:** VIP Design/ Fotolia; **195:** Picsfive/Fotolia; **202:** Somartin/Fotolia; **206:** Kamira/Shutterstock; **211:** Kai Pfaffenbach/Reuters; **212:** Warner Bros. Pictures/Everett Collection; **218:** Studio 8/Pearson Education, Inc.; **220:** Stillfx/Fotolia; **221:** Flavio Beltran/ Shutterstock; **222:** Flas100/Fotolia; **223:** Everett Historical/Shutterstock; **226–227:** Lee Snider/Alamy Stock Photo; **228:** (bottom) Vilor/Fotolia, (left) lava777/Fotolia; **228–229:** Weedezign/Fotolia; **229:** (bottom) Doppelganger4/ Shutterstock, (center) Doppelganger4/Shutterstock, (top) Doppelganger4/ Shutterstock; **230:** Doppelganger4/Shutterstock; **239:** Roman Samokhin/Fotolia; **240:** Shutterstock; **243:** (bottom) Doppelganger4/Shutterstock, (center bottom) Doppelganger4/Shutterstock, (center top) Doppelganger4/Shutterstock, (top) Doppelganger4/Shutterstock; **244:** UPPA/Photoshot/Newscom; **247:** Blend Images/Alamy Stock Photo; **248:** Blend Images/Alamy Stock Photo; **255:** Jenner/ Fotolia; **257:** Nikkytok/Shutterstock; **258:** Shutterstock; **259:** Alexzaitsev/ Fotolia; **264–265:** Agsandrew/Fotolia; **267:** Richard Ellis/Alamy Stock Photo; **272:** Alekseykh/Fotolia; **278:** Oksanazahray/Fotolia; **282:** Lefteris Papaulakis/ Fotolia; **282–283:** Paladin1212/Fotolia; **283:** Charlie Ans/Splash News/ Newscom; **289:** (bottom center left) Igor Sokolov/Fotolia, (bottom center right) Michael Flippo/Fotolia, (bottom left): Stillfx/Fotolia, (bottom right) Mtsaride/ Fotolia, (top center left) Zimmytws/Fotolia, (top center right) Neyro/Fotolia, (top left): Denyshutter/Fotolia, (top right): Alekss/Fotolia; **291:** Dkidpix/Fotolia; **292:** Yossarian6/Fotolia; **294:** Picsfive/Fotolia; **295:** (center left) Dusan Kostic/ Fotolia, (center right) Gennadiy Poznyakov/Fotolia, (left) Mike Langish/Cal Sport Media/Newscom, (right) Ben Keith/Fotolia; **298:** (bottom) Picture frame/Fotolia, (background) AP Images; **306:** (bottom) Alta Oosthuizen/Fotolia, (background) Nata777_7/Fotolia; **309:** Banprik/Fotolia; **311:** Sgar80/Fotolia; **312:** Maridav/ Fotolia; **315:** M. Dykstra/Fotolia; **316:** (center) 9nong/Fotolia, (left) Sripfoto/ Fotolia, (right) LuckyImages/Fotolia; **326:** Roman Samokhin/Fotolia; **329:** J. Paul Getty Museum; **332–333:** Olly/Fotolia; **335:** (background) Dasha Petrenko/Fotolia, (top) Casanowe/Fotolia; **343:** Verkoka/Fotolia; **346:** (background) Weedezign/ Fotolia, (top) Kanate/Fotolia; **347:** Piotr Marcinski/Fotolia; **348:** Goir/Fotolia; **353:** Fuse/Corbis/Getty Images; **354:** Pikselstock/Fotolia; **362:** (bottom center left) Picsfive/Fotolia, (bottom right) Picsfive/Fotolia, (top center left) Picsfive/ Fotolia, (top left) Picsfive/Fotolia, (top right) Picsfive/Fotolia; **365:** Shutterstock; **372–373:** Apinan/Fotolia; **374:** Juulijs/Fotolia; **374–375:** Tackgalichstudio/123RF; **384:** (bottom left) Georgejmclittle/Fotolia, (bottom right) Georgejmclittle/ Fotolia, (center left) Minerva Studio/Fotolia, (center right) Korta/Fotolia, (top left) Alexandra Gl/Fotolia, (top right) Dade72/Fotolia; **386:** Alen D/Fotolia; **387:** (left) Alexey Protasov/Fotolia, (right) Andy Lauwers/REX/Newscom; **389:** Locotearts/ Fotolia; **392:** (bottom)Yanush/Fotolia, (top) Locotearts/Fotolia; **393:** Locotearts/ Fotolia; **401:** Hank Frentz/Shutterstock; **405:** ASK Fotografie/Fotolia; **406:** (left) Scaliger/Fotolia, (right) SeanPavonePhoto/Fotolia; **407:** (left) Windowseat/Fotolia, (right) Mihai Simonia/Fotolia; **439:** S–F/Shutterstock; **440:** Roman Samokhin/ Fotolia; **442:** Locotearts/Fotolia

ILLUSTRATION CREDITS

Steve Attoe – pages 35, 106, 402, 403
Burmar Technical Corporation – page 112
A. J. Garces – page 86
Chris Gash – page 79
Jock MacRae – page 291
Andy Meyer – page 325
Tom Newsom – page 368
Dusan Petricic – pages 30, 66, 307, 308
Susan Scott – pages 242, 327

Adjective Clauses

UNIT **14**

Adjective Clauses: Introduction

PERSONALITY

UNIT **15**

Adjective Clauses and Phrases

CULTURE SHOCK

PART 6

OUTCOMES

- Modify subjects and objects of sentences with adjective clauses
- Identify key details in a psychology article
- Identify and comment on key details from a conversation about university life
- Discuss personality traits of various people
- Conduct research about a famous person and present findings to the class
- Write an essay about the personality type that fits you

OUTCOMES

- Form and use adjective clauses with prepositions, quantifiers, and nouns
- Form and use adjective phrases
- Identify key details in an sociology article
- Identify key details of a conversation in an academic setting
- Discuss culture and culture shock
- Write an essay describing a cultural experience

UNIT 14

Adjective Clauses: Introduction

PERSONALITY

OUTCOMES

- Modify subjects and objects of sentences with adjective clauses
- Identify key details in a psychology article
- Identify and comment on key details from a conversation about university life
- Discuss personality traits of various people
- Conduct research about a famous person and present findings to the class
- Write an essay about the personality type that fits you

STEP 1 GRAMMAR IN CONTEXT

BEFORE YOU READ

Discuss the questions.

1. Complete the sentence with an adjective that describes your personality well: "I am a person who is ________________."
2. Is it helpful to classify people into personality types or to place yourself in a personality category? Why or why not?

READ

14|01 **Read this article about personality.**

What Type Are You?

IMAGINE YOU'RE AT A PARTY where you know several people well. The hosts have a new party game that involves comparing each person to a flower. Which flower would you choose for each person and which flower for yourself? Are you the kind of person who resembles a daisy, open to the world most of the time? Or are you more like a morning glory, which opens up only at special moments?

Why do we enjoy party games like these that reveal our personality traits and help us to classify people's personalities? Classifying personalities can enable us to understand both ourselves and others better. Moreover, it can assist us in working together effectively and minimizing conflict. For these reasons, over the last century, many personality types have been recognized, and tests have been devised that help us to identify these types. Personality identification has become a science.

Carl Jung, a Swiss psychiatrist who is regarded as one of the fathers of modern psychiatry, published a famous work on personality in 1921. Isabel Briggs Myers, an American author who studied and admired Jung's theories, felt that Jung's ideas were important and should be made understandable to the general public. Briggs Myers was very disturbed by the global conflict of World War II and had a strong desire to help people to understand each other better. Along with her mother, Katharine Briggs, Briggs Myers created the Myers-Briggs Type Indicator, or MBTI. The MBTI, which is constantly being revised and improved, has become the world's most popular test of personality identification. The MBTI is now used for a variety of purposes, such as marital counseling, training of executives, and career decisions.

In the 1950s, cardiologists Meyer Friedman and Ray Roseman proposed two new personality categories, Type A and Type B, based on the idea that some people (Type As) were more likely to suffer from heart disease than others (Type Bs). This idea has now been discounted, but the basic outlines of these personality types have become popular, and Type C and D categories have followed them into common use.

What type of personality do you have? What about your co-workers, friends, and family? Try to place yourself and people you know into the following categories. Bear in mind, though, that most people don't fit perfectly into a single category.

TYPE A
Self-driven, competitive

Type As are "drivers," competitive individuals who have a no-nonsense approach to life. They're the kind of people who tell you exactly what they think without mincing words.[1] They embrace risk and change and often turn out to be entrepreneurs.[2] Nancy, who started her own greeting card business three years ago, is the perfect example. However, Nancy is impatient with detail and routine, which is why she has hired Paul and Mandy to manage her business.

TYPE B
Charismatic, easy-going

Type Bs are socializers. They're extroverts, the kind of people who love the spotlight. They love to entertain people. They often gravitate toward jobs in sales or marketing or as performers on radio and TV. Nancy's husband, Jack, whom most people consider a charismatic[3] person, is a good example. He's the host of a two-hour talk radio show.

TYPE C
Introverted, stress-prone

Type Cs are lovers of detail and data. They tend to be individuals who become accountants, programmers, or engineers. Paul, an accountant, is an example. He's the type of person who loves the details that Nancy hates. Type Cs are sensitive, which can cause them to have trouble communicating with others.

1 *without mincing words:* speaking of something negative with plain, direct language
2 *entrepreneurs:* people who own and run a business
3 *charismatic:* having personal qualities that attract and hold people

TYPE D

Loves routine, follows orders

Type D people are those who like routine and tend not to enjoy adventure. Not surprisingly, they usually resist change. They feel secure when they're told what to do. They're often compassionate. Mandy, who loves her office job, is Type D. She wouldn't be happy as the boss. Nor would Paul. But they both appreciate working for Nancy.

What did you learn by classifying personalities in this way? Did it give you any insight into yourself and others?

AFTER YOU READ

A VOCABULARY **Complete the sentences with the words in the box.**

conflict	data	discount	enable	gravitate	insight	moreover	secure

1. Myers was disturbed by the global ______________ in the 1940s.
2. That idea has been proven wrong, and people now ______________ it.
3. Type Ds feel ______________ when they're told what to do.
4. Type Bs often ______________ towards sales jobs.
5. Type Cs enjoy working with ______________.
6. Did your research give you any ______________ into the problem?
7. Understanding personality types can ______________ us to understand others better.
8. Linda is very confident. ______________, she is aggressive and extroverted.

B COMPREHENSION **Read the statements. Check (✓) *True* or *False*.**

	True	False
1. Carl Jung was important in the development of modern psychiatry.	☐	☐
2. Isabel Briggs Myers wanted to help people understand each other better.	☐	☐
3. The Myers-Briggs inventory has not been changed since it was devised.	☐	☐
4. Most people belong to only one personality category.	☐	☐
5. A Type A person likes change.	☐	☐
6. A Type B person generally doesn't like to be the center of attention.	☐	☐
7. A Type C person sometimes has trouble communicating with others.	☐	☐
8. A Type D person does not like to be told what to do.	☐	☐

C DISCUSSION **Work with a partner. Compare your answers in B. Give reasons for your answers. Then describe a person you know who fits closely into one of the personality categories.**

STEP 2 GRAMMAR PRESENTATION

ADJECTIVE CLAUSES

Adjective Clauses: Placement

Main Clause		Adjective Clause	
	Noun/Pronoun	Relative Pronoun	
They met a	woman	**who**	**teaches psychology**.
This is the	personality test	**that**	**I took**.

Main Clause	Adjective Clause		Main Clause Continued
Noun/Pronoun	Relative Pronoun		
The woman	**who**	**teaches psychology**	is also a writer.
The personality test	**that**	**I took**	was very revealing.

Relative Pronouns as Subjects: *Who*, *Which*, *That*

People		
I have friends	**who**	love to talk.
I have a friend	**that**	loves to talk.

Things		
This is a book	**which**	is useful.
These are books	**that**	are useful.

Relative Pronouns as Objects: *Who(m)*, *Which*, *That*, *Ø**

People		
This is the doctor	**who(m)** **that** **Ø**	we consulted.

Things		
This is the test	**which** **that** **Ø**	he gave us.

*Ø = no pronoun

Whose + Noun to Indicate Possession

People
She is the woman **whose son** is so famous.
She is the woman **whose son** I am tutoring.

Things
It's the book **whose reviews** were so good.
It's the book **whose reviews** I have just read.

Where and *When* in Adjective Clauses

Where		
Place		
I remember the café	**where**	we met.

When		
Time		
I remember the day	**(when)** **(that)** **Ø**	we parted.

Adjective Clauses: Identifying or Nonidentifying

Adjective Clauses That Identify
No Commas
The woman **who created the test** studied psychology. The test (**that**) **she created** describes personality types.

Adjective Clauses That Do Not Identify
Commas
Sara Gomez, **who created the test**, studied psychology. The Gomez test, **which she created**, describes personality types.

GRAMMAR NOTES

1 Definition of Adjective Clauses

A **clause** is a group of words that contains at least one **subject** and a **verb** showing past, present, or future time.

Clauses are either independent or dependent.	
Independent clauses can stand alone as **complete sentences**.	The house is in the suburbs. *(independent)*
Dependent clauses **cannot stand alone**. They need to be linked with another clause to be fully understood.	that we bought *(dependent)* The house **that we bought** is in the suburbs. *(dependent clause linked to independent clause)*
An **adjective clause** is a **dependent** clause that **modifies a noun or a pronoun** in a main (independent) clause.	The elderly lady **who lives down the street** is a very interesting personality. *(The dependent clause modifies "elderly lady.")*
A sentence with an adjective clause can be seen as a combination of two sentences. An adjective clause can occur **after** or **inside** a main clause.	John is a man. + He works hard. John is a man **who works hard**. Mary is interesting. + I like her a lot. Mary, **whom I like a lot**, is interesting.
An adjective clause commonly begins with a relative pronoun: ***who***, ***whom***, ***which***, ***whose***, or ***that***. It can also begin with ***when*** or ***where***. For a list of pronouns that can introduce adjective clauses, see Appendix 22 on page 420.	Frank, ***who* is quite shy**, spends a lot of time alone. Let's do something ***that* is fun**. I can remember a time ***when* I was carefree**.
The word that begins an adjective clause usually comes **directly after the noun** or **pronoun** that the clause modifies.	**Toronto**, ***which*** is the largest city in Canada, is a beautiful place.

2 Subjects in Adjective Clauses

The **subjects** in adjective clauses can refer to **people or things**.

To refer to **people**, use ***who*** and ***that*** as the subjects of verbs in adjective clauses. *That* is less formal than *who*.	The Ings are the **people *who*** bought the house. Sam is the **man *that*** lives next door to me.
To refer to **things**, use ***which*** and ***that*** as the subjects of verbs in adjective clauses.	Math is the **subject *which*** is the hardest for me. This is the **car *that*** is the nicest.
The **verb** in an adjective clause **agrees** with the **noun** or pronoun that the clause modifies.	There are many ***people*** who **have taken** this personality test. Myers-Briggs is the ***test*** that **is** the best known.
BE CAREFUL! Do not use a **double subject** in an adjective clause.	Type C individuals are **people who** love detail and data. NOT Type C individuals are people who ~~they~~ love detail and data.
BE CAREFUL! Do not use *which* to refer to **people**. Use ***who*** or ***that***.	Ann is a **person *who*** spends a lot of time alone. NOT Ann is a person ~~which~~ spends a lot of time alone.

3 Objects in Adjective Clauses

The **objects** in adjective clauses can refer to **people** or **things**.

To refer to **people**, use ***whom***, ***who***, or ***that*** as the **objects** of verbs in adjective clauses. *Whom* is quite formal and is more common in writing than in speech. *Who* and *that* are used in both formal and informal situations. When it refers to people, *that* is less formal than *who* and is commonly used in conversation and informal writing.	Mr. Pitkin, ***whom* I mentioned yesterday**, is my boss. Mr. Pitkin was the person ***who* I mentioned.** Mr. Pitkin was the person ***that* I mentioned.**
To refer to **things**, use ***which*** and ***that*** as the **objects** of verbs in adjective clauses. *Which* is a bit more formal than *that*.	The test ***which* I took** was difficult. The test ***that* James took** was easy.
USAGE NOTE In conversation and informal writing, you can **omit** the **relative pronoun** if it is an **object**. This is the most common spoken form for sentences containing adjective clauses. (See Note 7 for more information on omitting relative pronouns.)	Mrs. Gomez is the woman **I met.** The car **we bought** was cheap.
BE CAREFUL! Make sure that the **verb agrees** with the **subject**, not the object of the clause.	The Wangs are the people that ***Sally* knows.** NOT The Wangs are the people that Sally ~~know~~.

4 *Whose* in Adjective Clauses

Use ***whose*** to introduce an adjective clause that indicates **possession**.

Use ***whose*** to replace ***his/her/its/their*** + a **noun**. An adjective clause with *whose* can modify people or things:	
• **people**	Ken is the man. + We met his wife. = Ken is the man ***whose* wife we met.**
• **things**	It's a theory. + Its origins go back many years. = It's a theory ***whose* origins go back many years.**
BE CAREFUL! The relative pronoun *whose* **cannot be omitted**.	Harvey, ***whose* house we're renting**, is a lawyer. NOT Harvey, ~~house we're renting~~, is a lawyer.

5 *Where* in Adjective Clauses

Use ***where*** to introduce an adjective clause that modifies a noun of **place**.

Use ***where*** to replace the adverb ***there***.	This is the restaurant. + We ate there. This is the restaurant ***where* we ate.**
You can replace *where* with ***which* or *that* + a preposition**, such as *in, at,* or *for*. In this type of adjective clause, *which/that* can be omitted.	
• ***which***	This is the building ***where* she works.** This is the building (***which***) she works **in**.
• ***that***	This is the hotel ***where* we stayed.** This is the hotel (***that***) we stayed **at**.
BE CAREFUL! Use an adjective clause with ***where*** only if you can restate the location with the word ***there***. Do not use an adjective clause with *where* if the location cannot be stated in this way.	Chihuahua is the town ***where* I was born.** = Chihuahua is the town. I was born ***there***. Stockholm is a city ***that* has beautiful scenery.** NOT Stockholm is a city ~~where has beautiful scenery~~.

6 *When* and *That* in Adjective Clauses

Use ***when*** and ***that*** to introduce an adjective clause that modifies a noun of **time**.	I can't think of a **time *when*** I wasn't happy. She told us about a **time *that*** she was carefree.
USAGE NOTE In conversation and informal writing, you can **omit *when*** and ***that*** in this type of adjective clause.	I can't think of a **time I wasn't happy**. She told us about a **time she was carefree.**

7 Identifying and Nonidentifying Adjective Clauses

Two types of adjective clauses are **identifying** and **nonidentifying**.

An **identifying adjective clause** (also called **essential**) is **necessary to identify** the **noun** that it refers to.

Identifying adjective clauses **are not enclosed in commas**.

People **who embrace risk and change** are classified as Type A people.
(shows which kind of people are called Type A people)

People **who love the spotlight** are classified as Type B people.
(shows which kind of people are called Type B people)

A **nonidentifying adjective clause** (also called **nonessential**) **gives additional information** that is not necessary to identify the noun or pronoun to which it refers.

Nonidentifying adjective clauses **are enclosed in commas**.

Maryam**, who is undoubtedly a Type A person,** is the student body president.
(does not distinguish Maryam from any other person but gives extra information about her)

BE CAREFUL! You can **omit** relative pronouns only in **identifying** adjective clauses. You **cannot omit** the relative pronoun in **nonidentifying** adjective clauses.

The man **you met on Friday** is Tarik.
Tarik, ***who* just took the personality inventory**, is originally from Lebanon.
NOT Tarik, ~~just took the personality inventory~~, is originally from Lebanon.

BE CAREFUL! You can use **that** as a relative pronoun only in an **identifying** clause. Don't use *that* as a relative pronoun in a **nonidentifying** clause. Use ***which*** in this type of clause.

The Myers-Briggs test, ***which* I took a long time ago**, has proved to be accurate.
NOT The Myers-Briggs test, ~~that~~ I took a long time ago, has proved to be accurate.

8 Special Use of *Which* in Adjective Clauses

In conversation and informal writing, you can use the relative pronoun ***which*** to refer to an **entire previous idea**.

Jamal is a socializer. + That quality impresses me =
Jama is a socializer, ***which*** impresses me.

Paris is beautiful and exciting. + Those qualities are why I like going there =
Paris is beautiful and exciting, ***which*** is why I like going there.

IN WRITING In more formal speaking and in writing, use a **noun** at the **beginning** of a *which* or *that* clause.

Jamal is a socializer, **a quality *which*** impresses me.
Paris is beautiful and exciting, **qualities *that*** make me like going there.

PRONUNCIATION NOTE

14|02 **Pausing in Identifying and Nonidentifying Clauses**

Sentences with identifying adjective clauses and nonidentifying adjective clauses are not pronounced in the same way.

Identifying clauses have **no pauses** before and after them.	The woman **who is wearing a red skirt and a green blouse** is my friend's mother. The tie **which has a stain on it** needs to be dry-cleaned.
Nonidentifying clauses have **pauses** before and after them. The pauses correspond to **commas** in written sentences.	The woman, **who is wearing a red skirt and a green blouse**, is my friend's mother. The tie, **which has a stain on it**, needs to be dry-cleaned.

STEP 3 FOCUSED PRACTICE

EXERCISE 1 DISCOVER THE GRAMMAR

A GRAMMAR NOTES 1–8 **Read these sentences based on the reading. Could the underlined words be replaced by the words in parentheses without creating a different meaning or making an incorrect sentence? Write *Y* (*Yes*) or *N* (*No*).**

__Y__ **1.** Are you the kind of person who resembles a daisy? (that)

____ **2.** Or are you more like a morning glory, which opens up only at special moments? (that)

____ **3.** Try to place yourself and people whom you know in these categories. (Ø)

____ **4.** Type As are competitive individuals who take a no-nonsense approach to life. (that)

____ **5.** They're the kind of people who tell you exactly what they think. (Ø)

____ **6.** Nancy is impatient with detail and routine, which is why she has hired Paul and Mandy to manage her business. (that)

____ **7.** Type Bs are the kind of people who love the spotlight. (whom)

____ **8.** Mandy, who loves her office job, wouldn't be happy as the boss. (that)

B GRAMMAR NOTE 7 **Read the sentences based on the reading. Underline the adjective clause in each sentence. Then identify the clause as *identifying* (*I*) or *nonidentifying* (*NI*).**

__I__ **1.** Imagine you're at a party where you know several people well.

____ **2.** Try to place yourself and people you know into one or more categories.

____ **3.** Nancy, who started her own business several years ago, is the perfect example.

_____ **4.** Type Cs tend to be the kind of people who become accountants, programmers, or engineers.

_____ **5.** He's the type of person who loves details.

_____ **6.** Nancy is impatient with detail and routine, which is why she has hired Paul and Mandy to manage her business.

_____ **7.** Nancy's husband, Jack, whom most people consider a charismatic person, is a good example.

_____ **8.** Type Cs are sensitive, which can translate into trouble communicating with others.

_____ **9.** Type D people are those who like routine and tend not to enjoy adventure.

EXERCISE 2 RELATIVE PRONOUNS

GRAMMAR NOTES 2–4, 8 **Complete the paragraph. Circle the correct answers.**

I come from a family (which) / whom (1.) has eight members. I have three sisters and two brothers, who / which (2.) made a lot of noise in the house when we were growing up. Our house, which / that (3.) is four stories high, has eight bedrooms. The members of my family, who / whom (4.) are all interesting, fit nicely into the Type A to D categories of personality types. My mother and father, who / whom (5.) both like to be with people a great deal, are extroverts. My favorite brother, with who / whom (6.) I still spend a lot of time, is an introvert. My other brother, who / which (7.) is a Type A, is a great guy, but always has to be right. My favorite sister, who / whose (8.) fiancé is the same age as I am, is a Type A. Of my other two sisters, the one Ø / which (9.) I am closer to is a Type C. I'm less close to the sister who / Ø (10.) is much older than I am. She's a Type D.

EXERCISE 3 IDENTIFYING AND NONIDENTIFYING CLAUSES

GRAMMAR NOTES 2–7 **Combine each pair of sentences into one sentence with an adjective clause, using the word in parentheses. Use the first sentence in each pair as the main clause. Add commas where necessary. The sentences are connected as a story.**

1. The company makes computers. I work for the company. (that)
   The company that I work for makes computers.
2. The company has existed for fifteen years. It is named Excelsior Computer. (which)
   ____
3. The building is located downtown. We do most of our work in the building. (where)
   ____

4. The office has been remodeled. I work in the office. (that)

____

5. Darren Corgatelli is the perfect Type A boss. His wife is my aunt. (whose)

____

6. Darren is an excellent manager. I've known him since I was a child. (whom)

____

7. Darren's wife, Sarah, keeps the company running smoothly. She is a perfect Type C. (who)

____

8. I joined the company in 1995. I graduated from college then. (when)

____

9. I really admire the personalities of my colleagues. Their advice has been invaluable. (whose)

____

10. I have to do some telemarketing. I don't like telemarketing. (which)

____

EXERCISE 4 FORMAL AND INFORMAL ADJECTIVE CLAUSES

GRAMMAR NOTES 2–3, 7–8 Read two reports by an attorney. Using the words in parentheses, complete the spoken report with informal adjective clauses. Omit relative pronouns if possible and use contractions. Then complete the written report with formal adjective clauses. Do not omit relative pronouns and do not use contractions. Put all verbs in the correct forms.

Spoken Report

Our client is a guy ___*who's been in trouble*___ (1. have / be / in trouble) for minor offenses in the past, but I don't think he's a murderer, ______________ (2. be / why) I feel comfortable defending him. He did time in the penitentiary from 2008 to 2010, and according to all the reports he was a really social Type B person ______________ (3. the other prisoners / respect). Since he got out of jail in 2010, he's had a good employment record with Textrix, an electronics company ______________ (4. he / have / be working for). The psychological reports on him show that when he was in prison he was a person ______________ (5. the psychiatrists / consider) well-balanced and even-tempered, ______________ (6. be / why) I don't think he's guilty.

Written Report

EAGER, BARNES, AND KIRBY
ATTORNEYS-AT-LAW
555 NORTH LIBERTY • BOSTON MA 02110

Our client is a man ___who has been in trouble___ (7. who / be / in trouble) for minor offenses in the past, but I do not believe that he is a murderer, ______________________ (8. an opinion / make / me) comfortable defending him. He served time in the penitentiary from 2008 to 2010, and according to all the reports he was a highly social Type B person ______________________ (9. the other prisoners / respect). Since he was released from prison in 2010, he has had a good employment record with Textrix, an electronics company ______________________ (10. have / employ / him). His psychological profile suggests that when he was in prison he was a person ______________________ (11. the psychiatrists / consider) well balanced and even-tempered, ______________________ (12. evidence / make / me) believe that he is not guilty.

EXERCISE 5 PAUSING IN IDENTIFYING AND NONIDENTIFYING CLAUSES

14|03 **A** PRONUNCIATION NOTE Listen for the pauses in the sentences. Place commas around the adjective clauses if necessary. Then identify each clause as *identifying* (*I*) or *nonidentifying* (*NI*).

__NI__ 1. The man, who lives down the street from me, is a friend of my father.

____ 2. The man who lives down the street from me is a friend of my father.

____ 3. The teacher who handed out the awards is really a well-known scientist.

____ 4. The teacher who handed out the awards is really a well-known scientist.

____ 5. The student who lives close to the campus has low gasoline bills.

____ 6. The student who lives close to the campus has low gasoline bills.

____ 7. The garden which Mary planted is the most beautiful one of all.

____ 8. The garden which Mary planted is the most beautiful one of all.

B Work with a partner. Read the sentences in A aloud in a different order. Your partner guesses which type of adjective clause is in each sentence—identifying or nonidentifying.

EXERCISE 6 EDITING

GRAMMAR NOTES 1–8 Read the message from a college student to her parents. There are eleven mistakes in the use of adjective clauses. The first mistake is already corrected. Find and correct ten more.

TO: grants36@yoohoo.com
FR: AliceG@yoohoo.com
RE: My first week at college

Dear Mom and Dad,

Well, the first week of college has been kind of tough, but it's turned out OK. My advisor, who ~~he~~ is also from Winnipeg, told me about growing up there, so we had something who we could talk about.

Since I'm still thinking about what my major is going to be, my advisor had me take one of those tests show you what you're most interested in. It was called the Strong Interest Test. I found out that I'm most interested in things involve being on the stage and performing in some way, that doesn't surprise me a bit. I always liked being in school plays. Remember? So I signed up for two drama courses seem like they're going to be really interesting.

My advisor also had me do one of those personality inventories that they tell you what kind of person you are. This is something that is all new to me, but I found out some things whose are really interesting. According to the test I took, I'm a person whom is classified as a Type B person. I had no idea what that meant, but I've learned that a Type B person is someone which likes people a lot and likes to socialize. That fits me pretty well, I think.

Classes start on Wednesday, and I'm getting to know the other people in the dormitory which I live. It's pretty exciting being here. That's it for now. I'll call in a week or so.

Love,
Alice

STEP 4 COMMUNICATION PRACTICE

EXERCISE 7 LISTENING

14|04 **A** Listen to a telephone conversation that Al had with his parents. What is Al doing these days?

____

14|04 **B** Read the pairs of sentences. Then listen again to the conversation. Circle the answer that correctly describes what you heard.

1. (**a.**) Al likes his dormitory.
   b. Al doesn't like his dormitory.
2. **a.** The dormitory has one supervisor.
   b. The dormitory has more than one supervisor.
3. **a.** Both of Al's roommates are from Minnesota.
   b. One of Al's roommates is from Minnesota.
4. **a.** There is one group of girls living in the dormitory.
   b. There is more than one group of girls living in the dormitory.
5. **a.** The girls live on the same side of the building as Al.
   b. The girls live on the other side of the building from Al.
6. **a.** Al has one English class.
   b. Al has more than one English class.
7. **a.** Al has one history class.
   b. Al has more than one history class.
8. **a.** Al's writing class is going to be easy.
   b. Al's math class is going to be easy.
9. **a.** Al has one advisor.
   b. Al has more than one advisor.

C Work with a partner. Discuss these questions.

1. What is the best place that you've lived since you became a student? The worst?
2. What are benefits that you have gained in living with others?
3. What is the easiest course you have taken? The hardest?
4. Have you had advisors who have been helpful? How did they help you?

EXERCISE 8 A NIGHT AT THE MOVIES

A PICTURE DISCUSSION Work in a group. Carefully examine the picture. Describe the people in the picture. What are they doing? What kinds of personalities do you think they have? Write sentences with adjective clauses.

EXAMPLE: The man who is talking on his cell phone is annoying some of the people near him. He seems to be a person that is loud and inconsiderate.

B Share your results with the rest of the class. Which group has created the most sentences?

EXERCISE 9 WHAT TYPE ARE YOU?

A SURVEY Walk around the classroom and find four people who believe they fit into one of these personality types: Type A, Type B, Type C, or Type D. Find out why they think they have one of these personality types. Write the name of the student in the chart and the reasons that they gave you.

Personality Type	Name	Reasons
Type A Self-driven, competitive 		
Type B Charismatic, easy-going 		
Type C Introverted, stress-prone 		
Type D Loves routine, follows orders 		

B Read your sentences about each person aloud. Add other facts you may know about the person. Don't say the person's name. The class attempts to guess the name of the student you are describing.

EXAMPLE: A: This is a person who considers himself or herself a Type A person. This person, who is very competitive, has been studying English for five years.
B: Is it Carlos?
A: Yes!

EXERCISE 10
HE WAS A GREAT SCIENTIST WHO . . .

A PRESENTATION You are going to give a presentation about the personality of a famous person in the world, either in the present or the past. Choose a person from the box, or choose another person who interests you. Do research on the Internet to find information about the personality of the individual you have chosen. Then complete the chart.

Albert Einstein	Lionel Messi
Lady Gaga	Marilyn Monroe
Nelson Mandela	Mother Teresa
Angela Merkel	Kanye West

Name	
Occupation	
Nationality	
Life Dates	
Accomplishments	
Personal Characteristics	

B Write a presentation about the person you researched in A. Use adjective clauses in your sentences.

Albert Einstein, who was a theoretical physicist and one of the greatest scientists of all time, was born in Ulm, Germany in 1879. He died in Princeton, New Jersey in the United States in 1955. Einstein, whose theory of relativity is considered a major contribution to scientific knowledge, left Germany when Adolf Hitler came to power. He was a peace-loving individual who . . .

C Make your presentation to the class.

FROM GRAMMAR TO WRITING

A BEFORE YOU WRITE Consider the personality categories that have been mentioned in this unit and choose the one that fits you best. Write a few sentences about why you believe you fit into this particular category.

B WRITE Using your ideas in A, write a five-paragraph essay about the personality type that best fits you. Remember to use identifying and nonidentifying adjective clauses. Try to avoid the common mistakes shown in the chart. Use the example below to help you begin your essay.

EXAMPLE: No single personality type applies perfectly to a person, but for me one comes closer than all the others. The personality category that fits me most closely is Type B. First, Type Bs are social people who are basically extroverts. I've always enjoyed my friends, which is why I think this category fits me quite well. . . .

Common Mistakes in Using Adjective Clauses

Use ***who***, not *which*, to refer to **people**.	The neighbor **who** is the nicest is Mrs. Lopez. NOT The neighbor ~~which~~ is the nicest is Mrs. Lopez.
Don't use a **double subject** in an adjective clause.	I'm impressed by people **who** are kind and helpful. NOT I'm impressed by people who ~~they~~ are kind and helpful.
Don't enclose identifying adjective clauses with **commas**.	People who put others before themselves are admirable. NOT People, who put others before themselves, are admirable.
Don't use *that* to introduce a **nonidentifying** adjective clause. Use ***who***, ***whom***, or ***which***.	Hussein, **who** is my best friend, was born in Tanzania. NOT Hussein, ~~that~~ is my best friend, was born in Tanzania.

C CHECK YOUR WORK Look at your essay. Underline adjective clauses. Use the Editing Checklist to check your work.

Editing Checklist

Did you . . . ?

- ☐ use *who* or *whom* to refer to people and *which* to refer to things
- ☐ avoid using a double subject in adjective clauses
- ☐ enclose nonidentifying clauses with commas
- ☐ avoid using *that* to introduce a nonidentifying adjective clause

D REVISE YOUR WORK Read your essay again. Can you improve your writing? Make changes if necessary.

UNIT 14 REVIEW

Test yourself on the grammar of the unit.

A **Complete the sentences. Circle the correct answers.**

1. The lady who / which is my teacher is the third from the right.
2. Hong Kong is the city that / where I was born.
3. Elena, that / whom I met at the conference, has a Type A personality.
4. The man whose / which car we borrowed is my father's boss.
5. Boris Popov is very detail-oriented, that / which is why we should hire him.
6. I can't remember a time where / when he wasn't helpful.
7. Lions are the animals that Lea like / likes the best.
8. Chuy is a person who / who he prefers to be alone.

B **If necessary, place commas in the correct places in the sentences.**

1. The man who lives next door is very talkative.
2. The book Sara bought was written by Junot Díaz.
3. Mrs. Ching whose dog is always barking is very wealthy.
4. The people I work with all have Type D personalities.
5. Yaoundé is the city in which I was born.
6. Ms. Voicu who is a student is from Romania.
7. Tumba whose children are very energetic is always exhausted.

C **Find and correct five mistakes.**

Last week in my psychology class, we took a personality test who is designed to determine what kind of person you are. The test, that I found interesting, took a couple of hours to complete. Today I got my results, whose were pretty much what I expected. I have many friends whom mean a lot to me, so it's not surprising that I'm classified as an extrovert. I would recommend that everyone wants to find out more about himself or herself should take a test like this.

Now check your answers on page 430.

UNIT 15

Adjective Clauses and Phrases

CULTURE SHOCK

OUTCOMES
- Form and use adjective clauses with prepositions, quantifiers, and nouns
- Form and use adjective phrases
- Identify key details in an sociology article
- Identify key details of a conversation in an academic setting
- Discuss culture and culture shock
- Write an essay describing a cultural experience

STEP 1 GRAMMAR IN CONTEXT

BEFORE YOU READ

Discuss the questions.

1. What problems do you think that someone who moves to a new country might face?
2. Have you ever lived in a different culture from the one you grew up in? If so, what was your experience like?

READ

15|01 Read this article about culture shock.

What Is Culture Shock?

Jamal is a young man who has been in New York City for five months and is studying at an American university. When he first got to the United States, everything seemed exciting and wonderful. He met a lot of new students that he immediately became friends with. He got acquainted with a number of Americans, most of whom were kind and helpful to him. He fell in love with many aspects of New York, including its towering downtown skyscrapers and its amazing subway system. That was five months ago. Now things have changed considerably. The Americans he has met don't seem as kind or helpful as they did at the beginning. His friends, some of whom he continues to see regularly, are still here, but many of them don't have time to get together anymore. The subway, which he was initially so impressed with, now just seems dirty, noisy, and much too crowded. The skyscrapers which had previously seemed so magnificent now make him feel dwarfed. New York simply just isn't as wonderful as it was at the beginning.

What has happened? Jamal is suffering from culture shock, a type of disorientation often resulting from a change to a new locale, a new social setting, or a new country. We can identify four stages of culture shock: honeymoon, negotiation, adjustment, and mastery.

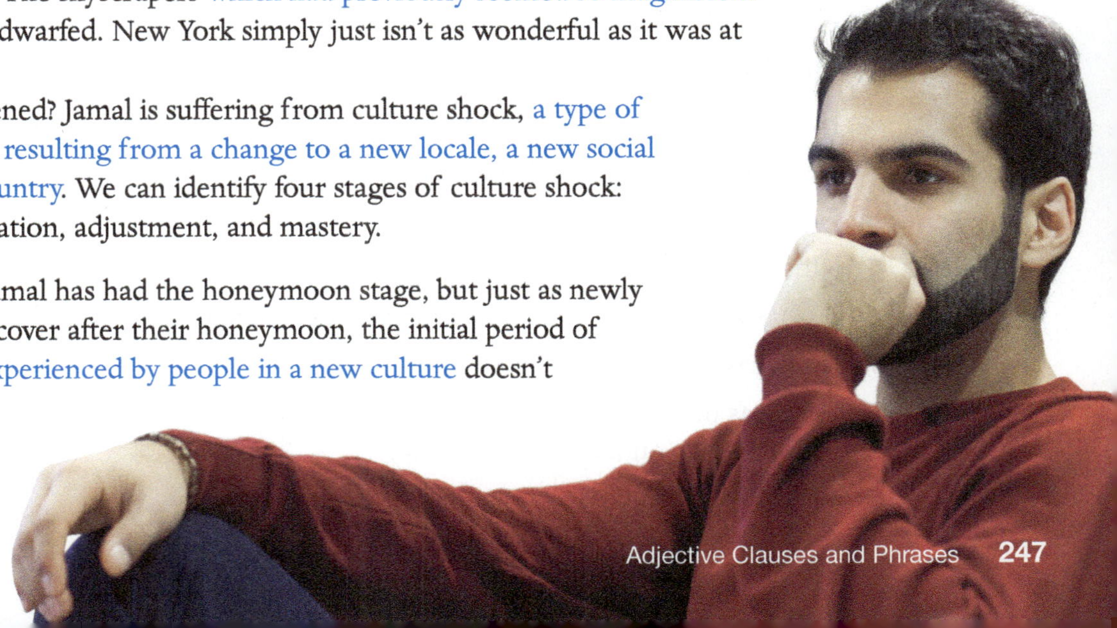

HONEYMOON: Jamal has had the honeymoon stage, but just as newly married couples discover after their honeymoon, the initial period of joyful excitement experienced by people in a new culture doesn't last. The delight they felt with the new and perhaps exotic food, the new language, and their new surroundings is replaced by the feelings of frustration that will characterize the next stage.

NEGOTIATION: Three months or more after one has made an entry into a new culture, the honeymoon stage is generally replaced by the negotiation stage. This stage is normally characterized by negative feelings, examples of which include anxiety, loneliness, and homesickness. Jamal is lacking the support of his parents, his extended family, and his friends. Even worse, he has been having trouble communicating with others. Whereas Americans were previously impressed with his mastery of English, suddenly people don't seem to understand him very well. He can't find the kinds of food he wants to eat. He longs for the friends, family, and the customs he has been accustomed to in his native land. Jamal's stage of negotiation is probably the most difficult of the four stages for anyone experiencing culture shock to get through.

ADJUSTMENT: Somewhere between six and twelve months, there usually begins a period of adjustment characterized by a gradual acceptance of the new culture. Jamal, tiring of his months of negativity, has come around to the idea that New York City might be worth living in after all. His several months of discontent have gradually given way to a kind of maturity involving acceptance of the culture and adopting a more normal lifestyle.

MASTERY: Sometime in his second year of living in New York, Jamal reaches the stage of mastery, in which he feels comfortable with the culture and is again content to be here. In this period, often called the bicultural stage, Jamal has attained the ability to participate completely in the New York culture and regard it favorably. This does not mean that he has been converted into an American. It does mean that he is flexible enough to keep many aspects of his native culture while adopting those parts of his new culture that appeal to him. Jamal wasn't able to avoid culture shock, but he was able to master it.

AFTER YOU READ

A VOCABULARY Match the words in **bold** with their meanings.

_____ 1. The skyscrapers cause him to feel **dwarfed**.
_____ 2. Jamal is experiencing **disorientation**.
_____ 3. He is **flexible** enough to keep his native culture.
_____ 4. Negotiation is followed by a time of **adjustment**.
_____ 5. Jamal has now gained a kind of **maturity**.
_____ 6. He has **attained** the ability to participate completely.
_____ 7. Jamal has not been **converted** into an American.
_____ 8. **Whereas** people used to be impressed with his English, now they don't understand him well.

a. changed
b. although
c. full development
d. adaptation to a new situation
e. made to appear small
f. able to change easily
g. confusion
h. succeeded in getting

B COMPREHENSION **Complete the sentences based on the reading.**

1. Jamal quickly became friends with other ________________.
2. He fell in love with the New York City ________________ system.
3. The New York City skyscrapers seemed ________________ at first.
4. The first stage of culture shock is the ________________ stage.
5. In culture shock, initial feelings of delight are replaced by feelings of ________________.
6. The ________________ stage is probably the most difficult stage to get through.
7. The period of adjustment involves a gradual ________________ of the new culture.
8. The bicultural stage is also called the ________________ stage.

C DISCUSSION **Work with a partner. Compare your answers in B. Give reasons for your answers. Then discuss this question: Do you agree that people who experience culture shock go through the four stages described in the article?**

STEP 2 GRAMMAR PRESENTATION

ADJECTIVE CLAUSES AND PHRASES

Adjective Causes with Prepositions

<table>
<tr><th>Main Clause</th><th colspan="4">Adjective Clause with Preposition</th></tr>
<tr><th>People/Things</th><th>Preposition</th><th>Relative Pronoun</th><th></th><th>Preposition</th></tr>
<tr><td rowspan="2">He's the man</td><td>to</td><td>whom</td><td>she was talking.</td><td></td></tr>
<tr><td></td><td>who(m)
that
Ø*</td><td>she was talking</td><td>to.</td></tr>
<tr><td rowspan="2">It's the company</td><td>for</td><td>which</td><td>he works.</td><td></td></tr>
<tr><td></td><td>which
that
Ø</td><td>he works</td><td>for.</td></tr>
<tr><td>That's the professor</td><td rowspan="2"></td><td rowspan="2">whose</td><td>classes I told you</td><td>about.</td></tr>
<tr><td>That's the teacher</td><td>class I spoke</td><td>of.</td></tr>
</table>

*Ø = no pronoun

Adjective Clauses with Quantifiers

<table>
<tr><th>Main Clause</th><th colspan="4">Adjective Clause with Quantifier</th></tr>
<tr><td>People/Things</td><td>Quantifier</td><td>Of</td><td>Relative Pronoun</td><td></td></tr>
<tr><td>I have many friends,</td><td rowspan="3">all
most
many
a number
some
a few
several
a couple
both
two</td><td rowspan="3">of</td><td>whom</td><td>are colleagues.</td></tr>
<tr><td>I played in a lot of games,</td><td>which</td><td>were victories.</td></tr>
<tr><td>I've met new colleagues,</td><td>whose</td><td>relatives live nearby.</td></tr>
</table>

Adjective Clauses with Nouns

<table>
<tr><th>Main Clause</th><th colspan="3">Adjective Clause with Noun</th></tr>
<tr><td>Things</td><td>Noun</td><td>Of which</td><td></td></tr>
<tr><td>Professor Brown writes mysteries,</td><td>an example</td><td rowspan="2">of which</td><td>is The Ghosts in the Tower.</td></tr>
<tr><td>I love her books,</td><td>a chapter</td><td>I just read.</td></tr>
</table>

Reducing Adjective Clauses to Adjective Phrases

	Adjective Clause
She's the student	**who's from Nigeria**.
I saw the film	**which is about culture shock**.
That's the man	**who was in charge of personnel**.
That's the gym	**that's near my house**.

	Adjective Phrase
She's the student	**from Nigeria**.
I saw the film	**about culture shock**.
That's the man	**in charge of personnel**.
That's the gym	**near my house**.

Changing Adjective Clauses to Adjective Phrases

	Adjective Clause
Bob's the colleague	**who lives** downtown.
I read a book	**which describes** World War II.
We saw a movie	**that takes** place in Pakistan.

	Adjective Phrase
Bob's the colleague	**living** downtown.
I read a book	**describing** World War II.
We saw a movie	**taking** place in Pakistan.

GRAMMAR NOTES

1 Adjective Clauses with Prepositions

An **adjective clause** is a dependent clause that modifies a noun or pronoun in a main (independent) clause. (See Unit 14.) The relative pronouns ***who(m)***, ***that***, ***which***, and ***whose*** can be used after a noun as **objects of prepositions** in adjective clauses.

The **preposition** can appear at the beginning or end of the adjective clause.	
Sentences with the preposition at the **beginning** of the clause are **formal**.	Bill is the man ***to* whom** I spoke. That's the book ***to* which** he referred.
Sentences with the preposition at the **end** of the clause are **informal**.	Dr. Gomez is the professor **who(m)** I spoke ***to***. New York City is the place **which** he referred ***to***.
A preposition can come at the **beginning** of a clause with ***whom*** or ***which***. It cannot come at the beginning of a clause with *that*.	It's the firm ***for* which** he works. NOT It's the firm ~~for that~~ he works.
Identifying (essential) and **nonidentifying** (nonessential) clauses can also occur with prepositions.	The company **for which I work** is Excelsior. *(identifying)* Excelsior, **which I work for**, is an excellent firm. *(nonidentifying)*
We can **omit** the relative pronouns *who(m)*, *that*, and *which* **after** a preposition. When we do this, the preposition moves to the **end** of the clause.	She is the friend ***to* whom I was referring**. She's the friend **I was referring *to***. That is the film ***about* which he was lecturing**. That's the film **he was lecturing *about***.
BE CAREFUL! The relative pronoun ***whose*** cannot be omitted.	She's the friend ***whose* car I ran into**. NOT She's the friend ~~car I ran into~~.

2 Adjective Clauses with Quantifiers

Some adjective clauses have the pattern **quantifier** + ***of*** + **relative pronoun**.

IN WRITING **Quantifiers** occur only in clauses with ***whom***, ***which***, and ***whose***. These clauses may refer to **people** or **things**. They are formal and are found mostly in writing and in careful speech.	He has made many friends at the university, ***all* of whom** he likes. His university has many beautiful buildings, ***most* of which** are old. My degree requires four science courses, ***none* of which** I've taken yet.
If a clause with a quantifier occurs **within** the main clause, it is enclosed in **commas**. If it occurs **after** the main clause, a comma **precedes** it.	Her novels**, most of which I've read,** are popular. I like her novels**, most of which I've read.** My Swahili professor has written two books**, neither of which is available yet in this country**.

3 Adjective Clauses with Noun + *of which*

Some adjective clauses have the pattern **noun +** ***of which***. Adjective clauses with this pattern refer to **things**.	New York City has many impressive tourist attractions, **an example of which** is the Empire State Building.
If a clause with a noun + *of which* occurs **within** the main clause, it is **enclosed in commas**. If it occurs **after** the main clause, a **comma precedes** it.	International celebrations**, occurrences of which are common at my university,** are a welcome change to the usual routine. Our faculty has won numerous awards**, examples of which include the Nobel and Pulitzer Prizes.**
BE CAREFUL! Adjective clauses with the pattern noun + *of which* refer **only** to **things**. They do not refer to people.	There are many students living in my dormitory, **a few of whom** are from other countries. NOT There are many students living in my dormitory, ~~a few of which~~ are from other countries.

4 Reducing Adjective Clauses to Adjective Phrases

Unlike a clause, a **phrase** is a group of words that **does not have both a subject and a verb showing time**. Adjective **clauses** with a ***be*** verb can be **reduced** to adjective phrases.

To reduce an adjective clause with a *be* verb, **delete** the **relative pronoun** and the ***be*** **verb**.	Any student **who is studying abroad** must learn the language of the country. *(adjective clause)* Any student **studying abroad** must learn the language of the country. *(adjective phrase)*
If an adjective clause needs **commas**, the corresponding adjective phrase also needs commas.	The Guggenheim Museum**, which was founded in 1939,** is very popular. The Guggenheim Museum**, founded in 1939,** is very popular.
BE CAREFUL! **Don't reduce** adjective clauses with a ***be*** verb when ***whose*** is the subject pronoun.	We met Professor Mandel, **whose classes are very popular**. NOT We met Professor Mandel, ~~classes are very popular~~.

5 Changing Adjective Clauses without a *Be* Verb

If there is **no** ***be*** **verb** in an adjective clause, it is often possible to **change** the adjective clause to an adjective phrase. To do this, **delete** the **relative pronoun** and **change** the **verb** to its ***-ing*** **form**. You can do this only when ***who***, ***which***, or ***that*** is the **subject pronoun** of the clause.	Frank Okawilo, **who currently studies at Harvard University**, is going to graduate this year. Frank Okawilo, **currently *studying* at Harvard University**, is going to graduate this year. The tenants **who currently live in that apartment building** will have to move soon. The tenants **currently *living* in that apartment building** will have to move soon.

STEP 3 FOCUSED PRACTICE

EXERCISE 1 DISCOVER THE GRAMMAR

A GRAMMAR NOTES 1–5 **Look at the sentences based on the reading. Underline the adjective clauses containing prepositions. Circle the noun referred to in each adjective clause and draw an arrow between the noun and the clause.**

1. He met a lot of students that he immediately became friends with.
2. He also met many Americans, most of whom were kind and helpful to him.
3. This stage is normally characterized by negative feelings, examples of which include anxiety, loneliness, and homesickness.
4. Jamal reaches the stage of mastery, in which he again feels comfortable with the culture.
5. The subway, which he was initially so impressed with, now seems dirty and noisy.
6. He longs for the things he has been accustomed to in his native land.

B GRAMMAR NOTES 4–5 **Look at the underlined adjective phrases based on the reading. Change each phrase to a clause by adding a relative pronoun and the correct form of a verb.**

1. He fell in love with many aspects of New York, including its skyscrapers and its subway system.
   which included its skyscrapers and its subway system
2. Culture shock is a kind of disorientation resulting from a change to a new locale.
   ______ from a change to a new locale
3. The initial period of excitement experienced by people in a new culture doesn't last.
   ______ by people in a new culture
4. The negotiation stage is probably the most difficult of the four stages for anyone experiencing culture shock to get through.
   ______ culture shock
5. He is experiencing a number of negative feelings, including depression and frustration.
   ______ depression and frustration
6. There is a period of adjustment characterized by acceptance of the new culture.
   ______ by acceptance of the new culture
7. Jamal, tiring of his negativity, has come around to the idea that New York might be worth living in.
   ______ of his negativity
8. He has developed a kind of maturity involving acceptance of the culture.
   ______ acceptance of the culture

EXERCISE 2 PREPOSITIONS AT THE END OF CLAUSES

GRAMMAR NOTE 1 **Change the following formal sentences to more informal sentences by moving the preposition to the end of the clause and deleting the relative pronoun.**

1. Asha is happy in the new country to which she moved.
   Asha is happy in the new country she moved to.
2. She got a job at a company about which she had heard good things.
   ____
3. She appreciates the kindness of the supervisor to whom she reports.
   ____
4. She is fond of the other employees with whom she works.
   ____
5. She is amazed at the variety of countries from which they come.
   ____
6. However, the long commute is the one thing of which she is tired.
   ____
7. Nonetheless, Asha is happy with the company at which she works.
   ____

EXERCISE 3 ADJECTIVE CLAUSES WITH QUANTIFIERS

GRAMMAR NOTE 2 **Complete the statements with the correct form of the words in parentheses. Use adjective clauses with the pattern quantifier + preposition + relative pronoun.**

1. People from other countries, *some of whom have never lived abroad before* (some / have never / live / abroad before), often experience culture shock in the United States.
2. These people, ______________________________ (most / become homesick for their native country), eventually get through their difficulties.
3. Most problems of culture shock, ______________________________ (all / seem serious at the time), fade away after the negotiation stage.
4. People from other countries often have to take jobs in the United States, ______________________________ (many / do not pay well).
5. Newcomers to the United States, ______________________________ (most / their families / are not with them), often suffer loneliness as well as homesickness.
6. Newcomers to the United States, ______________________________ (few / lose / their native languages and accents), generally become comfortable with the culture in the mastery stage.

EXERCISE 4 ADJECTIVE PHRASES

GRAMMAR NOTES 4–5 **Combine each pair of sentences into one sentence with an adjective phrase and a main clause. Use the underlined sentence to write the adjective phrase. Use the correct forms of verbs and punctuate correctly.**

1. Bi-Yun was born in a small town in South Korea. He has overcome his struggle with culture shock in the United States.

   Bi-Yun, born in a small town in South Korea, has overcome his struggle with culture shock in the United States.

2. Los Angeles is often a difficult place to adjust to. It has become Bi-Yun's new home.

   ______

3. Bi-Yun has had several jobs in the United States. These include driving a taxi and washing dishes.

   ______

4. At the university, he has participated in extracurricular activities. They involve music and sports.

   ______

5. Bi-Yun is currently dating a fellow student. She is in his history class.

   ______

6. Bi-Yun shares an apartment with four other students. He is a very social person.

   ______

7. Bi-Yun is currently on the university track team. He was a star athlete in South Korea.

   ______

EXERCISE 5 CLAUSES TO SENTENCES

GRAMMAR NOTES 2–5 **Each of the following sentences was formed from an original pair of sentences. Write the original pairs. Include the words in parentheses in each answer.**

1. People who live in foreign countries face many problems in their new culture, examples of which are language difficulties and homesickness. (these problems)

   People who live in foreign countries face many problems in their new culture. Examples of these problems are language difficulties and homesickness.

2. Sundar has made friends from many different countries, including South Africa and Japan. (these countries)

   ____

   ____

3. After he arrived in Seattle, Sundar faced a number of challenges, including finding an affordable place to live and making friends with his neighbors. (these challenges)

   ____

   ____

4. Sundar's favorite tourist attractions are the Seattle Art Museum and the Space Needle, both of which he has been to several times. (these attractions)

   ____

   ____

5. He got to know his landlord and his next-door neighbor, both of whom he greatly respects, very well. (these people)

   ____

   ____

EXERCISE 6 ADJECTIVE CLAUSES AND PHRASES

GRAMMAR NOTES 2–5 **Read the example sentences. Then think about experiences relating to culture shock that you have had or know about. Write sentences about these experiences using the phrases in the box.**

born and raised in	including	(quantifier) + *of which*
examples of which	involving	(quantifier) + *of whom*

My cousin Lin, born and raised in China, did not experience serious culture shock after he moved to the United States.

I met a lot of interesting people, most of whom were very helpful, when I lived in Canada.

EXERCISE 7 EDITING

GRAMMAR NOTES 1–5 Read the email from Elena Gutierrez to her sister Rosa in Colombia. There are eight mistakes in the use of adjective clauses and phrases. The first mistake is already corrected. Find and correct seven more. Delete verbs, change pronouns, or add words where necessary. Do not change punctuation.

TO: Rosa111@yoohoo.com
FROM: ElenaGut@gomail.com
RE: Life in L.A.

Hi Rosa,

I'm writing this in English because I think we both need the practice. How are you doing? Please say "hi" to everyone back there, ~~included~~ *including* all our friends in the neighborhood.

I'm still having a hard time here in Los Angeles, but things are a little better than they were. I'm not quite as lonely as before because I've met some people in my neighborhood, many of which are friendly, but so far I don't know anyone really well. I do have some friends who from my classes at the university, most whom are very interesting. I'm looking forward to getting to know them better as time goes on. The hardest thing is the food, most of it I just don't like very much. It's difficult to find quality food that's not too expensive.

I did do one really fun thing recently. One of my friends from school and I went to Universal Studios. We took a tram tour around the park and saw several actors working, some of that I recognized. I felt like jumping off the tram and shouting, "Would everyone is famous please give me your autograph?" Universal is where the last Indiana Jones movie was filmed—you know, those movies starred Harrison Ford?

I've got to get back to studying. I can hardly wait to see you and the family in the summer. Email me.

Love,
Elena

STEP 4 COMMUNICATION PRACTICE

EXERCISE 8 LISTENING

15|02 **A** Listen to the conversation between a student and a guidance counselor. What is Miryam's major problem?

____

____

____

15|02 **B** Read each statement. Then listen to the conversation again. Check (✓) *True* or *False*.

		True	False
1.	Miryam is doing well in all of her classes.	☑	☐
2.	Her personal life is something with which Miryam is not satisfied.	☐	☐
3.	Miryam has met several girls, few of whom seem nice.	☐	☐
4.	Miryam has something in common with most of the people she's met.	☐	☐
5.	Miryam is upset about people laughing at her.	☐	☐
6.	Miryam's problem is something experienced by few foreign students.	☐	☐
7.	The counselor thinks that Miryam should spend more time with people who are from Tanzania.	☐	☐
8.	The counselor gives Miryam tips, one of which is to learn more about American culture.	☐	☐
9.	Another thing Miryam should do is to laugh at her American friends.	☐	☐
10.	The counselor thinks that the feelings which Miryam has been experiencing will go away eventually.	☐	☐

C Work with a partner. Discuss the questions.

1. Have you ever been in a situation like Miryam's in which things that used to be interesting now seem boring? If so, describe it.
2. Have you ever been in a situation in which you met people with whom you had nothing in common? Describe the situation.

EXERCISE 9 REVERSE CULTURE SHOCK

A DISCUSSION **You are going to discuss the topic of reverse culture shock. First, read this article.**

Reverse Culture Shock

Did you know that there is such a thing as reverse culture shock? There is indeed. This kind of culture shock has basically the same stages as people experience when they are first living in a foreign country. Here's how these stages go:

1. **The Honeymoon:** When you return to your native land, you may have built up in your mind a vision of your home country that is not completely accurate. No doubt you've missed your family and friends, all of whom are excited and glad to see you back. You've missed the food, the city or town, the neighborhoods of your native country—all of which are delightful at first. At this point, everything seems interesting and fulfilling.
2. **Reverse Shock:** After a while back home, you start to feel annoyed and sad and begin to be critical of your home country. You may feel "reverse homesickness," missing the country you've returned from. You've idealized your home country in your mind, but it's not measuring up to your expectations. You start comparing it negatively to the country left behind.
3. **Recovery:** This is similar to the adjustment stage experienced when you left your native land. It takes a while, but eventually you come to terms with the characteristics of your original culture.
4. **Reintegration:** This is similar to the mastery stage when you went abroad the first time.

If this type of situation applies to you, a few suggestions may be in order: One is to expect reverse culture shock. This will make it easier to get through. Don't expect it to be easy to return to your original culture. Thomas Wolfe, the author of *Look Homeward, Angel*, is famous for this saying: "You can't go home again." You can of course go home, but you shouldn't expect things to be the same as they were when you left. Your country has changed. More significantly, you have changed.

B **Work in a group. Discuss the questions. Then share your conclusions with the class.**

1. How do people returning to their native country usually feel when they first arrive?
2. In the reverse shock stage, how do returning people compare their native country to the country they recently left?
3. How is the recovery stage similar to the adjustment stage experienced when people have left their native land?
4. Do you think Thomas Wolfe's statement that "you can't go home again" is true? Why or why not?

EXERCISE 10 ANOTHER CULTURE

A CROSS-CULTURAL COMPARISON You are going to discuss a foreign culture. Think about the United States and its culture, or another foreign culture that you have spent time in or are familiar with. Complete the chart below.

Positive Things About the Culture	Negative Things About the Culture

B Work in a group with other students who have completed charts about the foreign culture you chose. Compare your charts. Do you agree on what is positive and what is negative? Then answer the questions.

1. How much time has each person in your group spent in the foreign culture?
2. Do you see a connection between the amount of time each person has spent in the culture and his or her opinions about the culture? Do people who have been in the culture for a short time have more positive feelings about the culture, or more negative ones?

C Share your conclusions with the class.

EXAMPLE: A: One positive thing about American culture experienced by most of the members of our group is that American people are usually friendly.

B: In our group, people who have been in the United States for a long time think that Americans are friendly, but people who have been here a short time think they are unfriendly.

A: The people who think they are unfriendly may be experiencing culture shock. . . .

EXERCISE 11 WHAT'S BEEN YOUR EXPERIENCE?

A DISCUSSION **You are going to discuss your personal experiences with culture shock. First, study the diagram. Compare your experiences with the ones shown here. Write sentences based on your own experiences that correspond to each stage of the process of adjustment. Try to include adjective clauses and phrases in your sentences.**

1. *I left South Africa, the country which is my home.*
2. *I arrived in Canada, the new country that I moved to.*
3. *After my honeymoon period, I began to feel somewhat unhappy. I'd met a lot of Canadians, many of whom were friendly and kind, but few of whom became long-term friends . . .*

The Stages of Culture Shock and Reverse Culture Shock

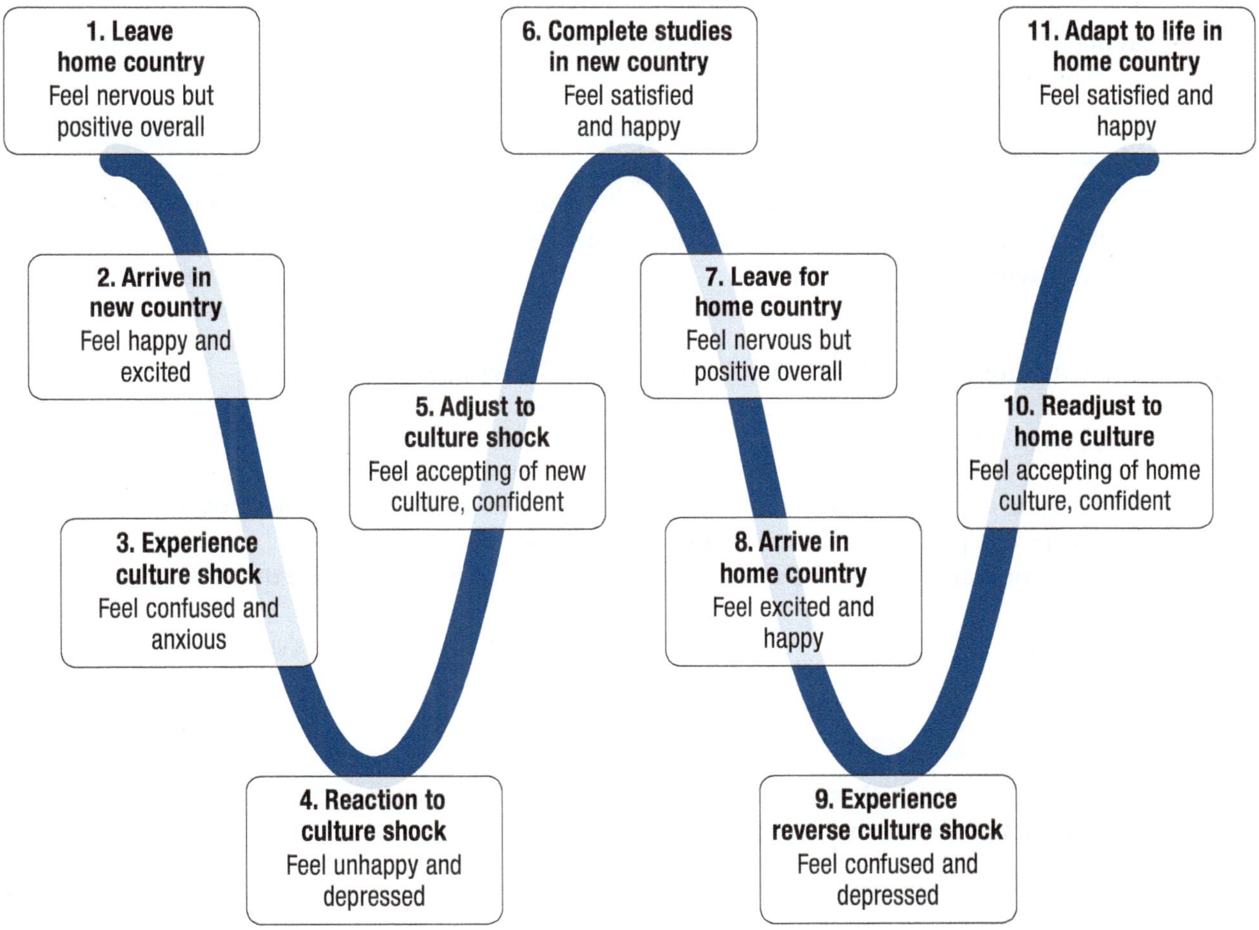

B **Work in a group. Compare your experiences with the processes of culture shock and reverse culture shock.**

EXAMPLE: A: I think I've experienced all the stages of culture shock and reverse culture shock described in this chart.

B: I haven't. I guess I had a few problems related to culture shock when I first moved to the United States, but . . .

FROM GRAMMAR TO WRITING

A BEFORE YOU WRITE You are going to write an essay about the problems that foreign students might experience when moving to a different country and then returning home again. Write a few sentences about the problems students might expect to face.

B WRITE Using your ideas in A, write a five-paragraph essay about problems foreign students might expect to find when they move to another country. Remember to use adjective clauses and phrases. Try to avoid the common mistakes shown in the chart. Use the example below to help you begin your essay.

EXAMPLE: There are a few problems foreign students should be prepared for when they move to another country and then return to their home country.

The first problem they should expect to encounter involves the food in the new country. Foreign students may have difficulty finding food they're used to eating back home. They may eat a lot of fast food instead, including such things as hamburgers, french fries, and hot dogs. Fast food is usually easy to find and cheap, but it's not healthy.

The second problem . . .

Common Mistakes in Using Adjective Clauses and Phrases

Don't confuse *who/whom* with *which*. ***Which*** is used to refer only to **things**, and ***who*** and ***whom*** are used only to refer to **people**.	I've met a lot of interesting people, **some of whom** have become long-term friends. NOT I've met a lot of interesting people, some of ~~which~~ have become long-term friends.
Move the **preposition** to the **end** of an **adjective clause** if you are **deleting** the **relative pronoun** (*who, whom, that, which*).	It's the store **at which he works**. It's the store **he works at**. NOT It's the store ~~he works~~.
If you are changing an adjective clause without a *be* verb to an adjective phrase, be sure to **delete the relative pronoun** and change the verb to its *-ing* form.	Helene was the woman **who lived down the street from me**. Helene was the woman **living down the street from me**. NOT Helene was the woman ~~lived~~ down the street from me.

C CHECK YOUR WORK Look at your essay. Underline adjective clauses and phrases. Use the Editing Checklist to check your work.

Editing Checklist

Did you . . . ?

- ☐ use *which* to refer only to things and *who/whom* to refer only to people
- ☐ move prepositions to the end of their clauses if you have deleted the relative pronoun
- ☐ delete the relative pronoun and change the verb to its *-ing* form to form adjective phrases

D REVISE YOUR WORK Read your essay again. Can you improve your writing? Make changes if necessary.

UNIT 15 REVIEW

Test yourself on the grammar of the unit.

A **Complete the sentences. Circle the correct answers.**

1. Dr. Brand and Dr. Wang, neither of whom / which I've met yet, are well-known professors.
2. Professor Meemook, which / whose classes I enjoy, is originally from Thailand.
3. My two roommates, both of who / whom are from Nigeria, are experiencing culture shock.
4. Hamburgers and hot dogs, neither of them / which I like, are not popular in my country.
5. Rashid and Hussein, who / whom are both newcomers to this country, work in a grocery store.
6. Anyone interested / interesting in culture shock should attend the lecture.
7. Pelé, born / was born in Brazil, used to be a great soccer player.
8. You can do several things to get over culture shock, includes / including befriending local people and learning more about their culture.

B **Complete the sentences with words from the box. You will use some words more than once.**

that	which	who	whom	whose

1. I've met five new colleagues, all of ________________ I like.
2. I'm taking three new courses, none of ________________ are very interesting.
3. I made two friends, both of ________________ are teachers, this week.
4. I've lived in several countries, examples of ________________ are Chile and Mexico.
5. Two famous authors, both of ________________ books I've read, are here today.
6. I read a novel about a young man ________________ is caught in a dead-end job.
7. The country ________________ Emiko moved to is very different from Japan.

C **Find and correct five mistakes.**

Newcomers to a country begin to suffer from culture shock often develop communication problems. They may be acquainted with many people, most of which they were previously able to talk with easily. Now they find it difficult to talk to these people. Moreover, aspects of the new culture, most of whom used to seem interesting and exciting, now begin to seem boring and unappealing. These newcomers may begin to experience negative emotions, included anger, hostility, and depression. Fortunately, this is only a temporary attitude is soon replaced by gradual acceptance.

Now check your answers on page 431.

Adverbs

PART 7

OUTCOMES

- Use adverbs to modify sentences and to bring focus to words or phrases in sentences
- Identify key details in conversations on controversial topics
- Discuss controversial topics, expressing opinions, agreeing and disagreeing
- Participate in a debate about a controversial topic
- Write an essay on a controversial topic

OUTCOMES

- Use adverb clauses to indicate when, where, why, or under what condition something happens
- Identify key arguments in a newspaper editorial
- Identify key details in an interview
- Discuss the topic of sports, expressing opinions, agreeing and disagreeing
- Write an essay about benefits and drawbacks of sports

OUTCOMES

- Form and use adverb and adverbial phrases
- Identify a sequence of events in a news story
- Comment on key details from a news broadcast
- Discuss the topic of compassion, expressing and supporting opinions with examples
- Write an essay about a compassionate act

OUTCOMES

- Use a range of connectors and transition words to connect ideas
- Identify key details in a scientific article
- Identify key points in a training workshop
- Discuss the topic of memory, expressing opinions, agreeing and disagreeing
- Write an essay about a memorable experience

UNIT 16

Adverbs: Sentence, Focus, and Negative

CONTROVERSIAL ISSUES

OUTCOMES

- Use adverbs to modify sentences and to bring focus to words or phrases in sentences
- Identify key details in conversations on controversial topics
- Discuss controversial topics, expressing opinions, agreeing and disagreeing
- Participate in a debate about a controversial topic
- Write an essay on a controversial topic

STEP 1 GRAMMAR IN CONTEXT

BEFORE YOU READ

Discuss the questions.

1. What is military service?
2. Have you ever done military service? If not, would you like to? Why or why not?

READ

16|01 Read this transcript of a radio call-in show.

Time to Sound Off

MIKE: Good evening, and welcome to *Sound Off*, the international talk show where you express your uncensored opinions on today's controversial issues. I'm Mike McGaffey. Tonight's topics: Should military service be required or voluntary? Should women join the military, and if they do, should they fight in combat? Let's see if we can shed some light[1] on these issues. Here's our first caller, Jerry Burns, from Kingston, Jamaica. Where do you stand, Jerry?

JERRY: Hi, Mike. Basically, I think military service should be voluntary. And I'm definitely against women being in combat.

MIKE: OK. Why should it be voluntary? Why shouldn't it be required of everyone?

JERRY: Because, overall, young people are not all the same. Some people have a military orientation. For them, military service is fine. Others aren't oriented that way. Compulsory military service interferes with their freedom, essentially.

MIKE: But many argue that we all owe our country something. It protects us and gives us benefits. Shouldn't we give something in return?

JERRY: We should if we're motivated to. But it shouldn't be an obligation. And I'd go further: Military forces have done a lot of evil. Maybe we shouldn't even have them.

MIKE: Hmm. I don't know, Jerry—I'm a pretty accepting guy, but even I find that suggestion extreme. But let's go to your second point. Why shouldn't women be in combat?

JERRY: We need to maintain the difference between the sexes. Men and women have inherent differences. If we put women in combat, we're saying that,

1 *shed some light:* provide new information that makes something easier to understand

fundamentally, they're the same as men. But women just aren't as physically strong and tough as men. Therefore, they aren't suited for combat.

MIKE: Are you saying that only men are strong enough? That's clearly an old stereotype.

JERRY: I'm not saying that. I just don't think fighting is feminine.

MIKE: Wow. All right, Jerry, very interesting. I expect we'll hear some pretty spirited responses to what you've said. Our next caller is Sarah Lopez from Toronto, Canada. Sarah, does Jerry have a valid point, or is this just fuzzy[2] thinking?

SARAH: Thanks, Mike. Actually, I couldn't disagree more with Jerry. It's not fuzzy thinking. He was clear in making his point, but I just don't agree with him.

MIKE: OK. So military service shouldn't be voluntary?

SARAH: No. If we're going to have it, it should be required.

MIKE: Why?

SARAH: It's the only way to ensure fair treatment for all. People in the military make major sacrifices—sometimes they risk their lives. That kind of risk should be spread out evenly. Actually, I'd go further: I'd support required national service. It wouldn't have to be only military.

MIKE: Expand a bit on that.

SARAH: There are lots of worthwhile things citizens can do for their country—like working in day care centers, hospitals, or the Peace Corps. National service has been started in a few countries, and hopefully it will be adopted in many more.

MIKE: All right. Now, Jerry opposes women being in combat. What's your position? Should it be allowed?

SARAH: Not only should it be allowed, but it should also be promoted. I should know: I've been in the military for eighteen months. So have several of my friends.

MIKE: You have?

SARAH: Yes. I disagree with the way Jerry characterizes women. No way is combat unfeminine!

MIKE: Have you ever been in combat?

SARAH: No, but if I'm ever called to combat, I'll be willing to go. Jerry also said we need to maintain the difference between the sexes. I don't agree with that, and neither do any of my friends.

MIKE: OK, Sarah. . . . Oops! There goes the buzzer. Time to hear from another caller. Here's Lu Adijojo from Singapore. Lu, what's your view? . . .

2 *fuzzy:* unclear, confused

AFTER YOU READ

A VOCABULARY **Choose the answer that is closest in meaning to the word in bold.**

1. On this show, people express their uncensored opinions on today's **controversial** issues.
   a. interesting b. causing disagreement c. well-known d. extremely important
2. Should military service be required or **voluntary**?
   a. done for money b. done for advancement c. done for enjoyment d. done willingly
3. The first caller doesn't think military service should be **compulsory**.
   a. optional b. required c. difficult d. unpleasant
4. He believes forced military service would **interfere with** people's freedom.
   a. limit b. increase c. have no impact on d. cancel
5. Men and women have **inherent** differences.
   a. natural b. accidental c. extreme d. slight
6. If we put women in combat, we're saying that, **fundamentally**, they're the same as men.
   a. partially b. definitely not c. possibly d. basically
7. That's an old **stereotype**, clearly.
   a. idea b. recording c. rule d. characteristic
8. Not only should it be allowed, but it should also be **promoted**.
   a. considered b. financed c. encouraged d. opposed

B COMPREHENSION **Complete the sentences based on the reading.**

1. Jerry, the first caller, thinks ________________ service should be voluntary.
2. Jerry thinks that only people who have a military ________________ should have to join the military.
3. Jerry is ________________ women being in combat.
4. Jerry doesn't think fighting is ________________.
5. Sarah, the second caller, thinks military service should be ________________.
6. In her opinion, it's the only way to ensure ________________ treatment for everyone.
7. Sarah does not believe combat is ________________.
8. If Sarah were called to combat, she would go ________________.

C DISCUSSION **Work with a partner. Discuss your viewpoints on the questions.**

1. Should military service be required or voluntary?
2. Should women fight in combat?

STEP 2 **GRAMMAR PRESENTATION**

ADVERBS: SENTENCE, FOCUS, AND NEGATIVE

Sentence Adverbs: Placement

Beginning	**Clearly**, these are bitter controversies.
Middle	These are **clearly** bitter controversies.
End	These are bitter controversies, **clearly**.

Focus Adverbs: Placement and Meaning

Placement				Meaning
They	**just** don't	support what	he says.	They think he's wrong.
	don't **just**			They agree with him 100 percent.
Even	he	can do	that.	Almost anyone can do that task.
She	can do	**even**	that.	It's amazing how many things she can do.
Only	men	can	attend.	Women can't.
Men	can	**only**		They can't do anything else.

Negative Adverbs: Placement and Inversion

We	**rarely**	agree	on such things.
Rarely	do we		
I have	**seldom**	heard	that idea.
Seldom	have I		
They	**never**	disagreed	with him.
Never	did they	disagree	

Other Adverbs: Placement and Inversion

Here	comes	**the bus**.
Here	**it**	comes.
There	goes	**the train**.
There	**it**	goes.
Maria	has done	military service.
So	have	**I**.

GRAMMAR NOTES

1 Sentence Adverbs

Adverbs modify verbs, adjectives, and other adverbs.

Simple adverbs modify **single words** or phrases.	Sarah spoke **hopefully** about her future. *(simple adverb modifies the way in which she spoke)*
Sentence adverbs, also called **viewpoint adverbs**, modify entire **sentences**.	**Hopefully**, national service will be adopted in many more countries. *(sentence adverb modifies the entire sentence—It is to be hoped that this will happen.)*
Common sentence adverbs include the following: *absolutely*, *actually*, *basically*, *clearly*, *definitely*, *essentially*, *fortunately*, *generally*, *hopefully*, *obviously*, *overall*, *perhaps*, *possibly*, *surely*	**Fortunately**, the Army paid for Bill's college education. *(It is fortunate that the Army paid for Bill's college education.)*
Some adverbs can function **either** as sentence adverbs or as simple adverbs.	**Clearly**, he is a good speaker. *(It's clear that he is a good speaker.)* He speaks **clearly**. *(simple adverb modifies* speaks*)*
You can use sentence adverbs in various places in a sentence:	
• If the adverb comes **first or last** in a sentence, we usually separate it from the rest of the sentence with a **comma**.	**Basically,** I'm in favor of that. I'm in favor of that**, basically.**
• If the adverb comes elsewhere in the sentence, it usually comes **after** the verb ***be*** and **before other verbs**.	I ***am*** **basically** in favor of that. I **basically *agree*** with the plan.

2 Focus Adverbs

Focus adverbs **focus attention** on a word or phrase.

Focus adverbs usually go **before the word or phrase focused on**. Common focus adverbs are *even*, *just*, *only*, and *almost*.	**Even *I*** believe that. *(focuses on* I*)* I believe **even *that***. *(focuses on* that*)* We **almost *spent* $50** but then didn't buy anything. *(focuses on* spent*)* We spent **almost *$50***. *(focuses on* $50*—We spent between $47 and $49.)*
Changing the position of a focus adverb often **changes the meaning** of the sentence.	**Just *teenagers*** can attend the meetings. *(Teenagers are the only ones allowed to attend.)* Teenagers can **just *attend*** the meetings. *(Teenagers can't do anything else in the meetings.)*

3 Negative Adverbs

Negative adverbs are single words or expressions that are **inherently negative** in meaning.

We often place negative adverbs at the **beginning of a sentence** to emphasize the negative meaning. When a negative adverb begins a sentence, it **forces inversion** of the **subject** and the **verb** or auxiliary. Common negative adverbs include the following: *barely* / *never* *hardly* / *not only* *in no way* (informal *no way*) / *only* *little* / *rarely* *neither* / *seldom*	SUBJECT VERB ADVERB **Women are** drafted **only** in Israel. ADVERB VERB SUBJECT **Only** in Israel **are women** drafted. SUBJECT VERB ADVERB **He is seldom** on time. ADVERB VERB SUBJECT **Seldom is he** on time.
If the **verb** in the sentence (except for *be*) is in the **simple present** or **simple past**, use ***do***, ***does***, or ***did*** after an initial negative adverb.	**Mothers rarely make** a career of the military. **Rarely *do* mothers make** a career of the military.
The negative adverb ***not only*** often combines with ***but . . . also***. There is inversion after *not only* but **no inversion** between *but* and *also*.	***Not only* should we** allow that, ***but* we should *also*** encourage it.
If the verb is in the **perfect** form, place the **auxiliary before** the **subject**.	**I had never** heard such a strange idea. **Never had I** heard such a strange idea.
Sentences beginning with ***neither*** are common in both formal and informal English.	My grandfather didn't join the military. **Neither** did my father.
IN WRITING Sentences beginning with other negative adverbs often sound formal. Use them more in writing.	**Seldom** have women served in combat.

4 Other Adverbs

Here and ***there*** are other adverbs that **force inversion** when they come at the **beginning** of a sentence.	**Here is** your money. **There goes** the bus.
So is another adverb that often **forces inversion** of subject and verb or auxiliary when it occurs at the beginning of a sentence. *So* is used to **connect two positive statements**, while *neither* is used to connect two negative statements.	Sarah is in favor of required military service. **So am I.** My father supports capital punishment. **So does my brother.**
BE CAREFUL! In a sentence beginning with *here* or *there*, invert the subject and verb or auxiliary if the subject is a noun. **Don't invert** them if the subject is a **pronoun**.	**Here comes *the bus*.** **Here *it* comes.** NOT Here ~~the bus comes~~. NOT Here ~~comes it~~.

16|02 **PRONUNCIATION NOTE**

Stressing Words After Focus Adverbs

In sentences with **focus adverbs**, the word following the focus adverb normally has the strongest stress in the sentence.	Even **I** like the cold weather. I even **LIKE** the cold weather. Only **TEENAGERS** can attend. Teenagers can only **ATTEND**.

REFERENCE NOTE

For a list of **sentence adverbs**, see Appendix 21 on page 420.

STEP 3 FOCUSED PRACTICE

EXERCISE 1 DISCOVER THE GRAMMAR

GRAMMAR NOTES 1–3 **Underline the adverb in each sentence. Then identify the adverb as a *sentence adverb* (*S*), *focus adverb* (*F*), or *negative adverb* (*N*).**

__F__ **1.** Sarah doesn't <u>just</u> support the idea of women in combat.

_____ **2.** Basically, I think service should be voluntary.

_____ **3.** Young people aren't all the same, obviously.

_____ **4.** I'm an accepting guy, but even I find that suggestion extreme.

_____ **5.** Men and women are clearly different.

_____ **6.** Little do many people realize how dangerous military service can be.

_____ **7.** I just don't agree with the basic idea.

_____ **8.** In some countries, women are only allowed to perform medical duties in the military.

_____ **9.** Not only should it be allowed, but it should also be promoted.

_____ **10.** In Switzerland, only men are allowed to serve in combat.

EXERCISE 2 SENTENCE ADVERBS

GRAMMAR NOTE 1 **Combine each pair of statements into one statement containing a sentence adverb. Use the adverb form of the word in parentheses. Vary your sentences so that the sentence adverb appears in different positions in the sentences: beginning, middle, and end.**

1. National service is beneficial. (obvious)

   National service is obviously beneficial.

2. Military service can be dangerous. (unfortunate)

   ____

3. I'm against the death penalty because I consider it cruel. (essential)

   ____

4. There's a lot more violence in movies than in the past. (certain)

   ____

5. Nuclear weapons can be eliminated. (hopeful)

   ____

6. A vaccine against AIDS can be developed. (possible)

   ____

7. The prime minister's position is wrong. (clear)

   ____

EXERCISE 3 FOCUS ADVERBS

GRAMMAR NOTE 2 **Complete the sentences. Circle the correct answers.**

1. Bill believes that women should not fight. He feels _____ in noncombat roles.
   (a.) they should only serve **b.** only they should serve
2. Carrie thinks women can do most jobs men can do, but she feels _____ in combat.
   a. men should serve only **b.** only men should serve
3. Samantha is against gambling, but _____ the benefits of lotteries.
   a. even she can recognize **b.** she can even recognize
4. I'm in favor of higher taxes. _____ taxing food and medicine.
   a. Even I'm in favor of **b.** I'm even in favor of
5. My husband has some good reasons for supporting nuclear power. However, I _____.
   a. don't just agree **b.** just don't agree
6. My father _____ the military draft; he's a military recruiter.
   a. doesn't just support **b.** just doesn't support
7. My friend and I _____ $100 for the tickets, but the concert was worth the money.
   a. almost paid **b.** paid almost

EXERCISE 4 NEGATIVE ADVERBS

GRAMMAR NOTE 3 **Rewrite the sentences using the negative adverb in parentheses.**

1. I didn't support the government's decision to invade that country last year. My friends didn't support the government's decision. (neither)

   I didn't support the government's decision to invade that country last year. Neither did my friends.

2. There are many women in the military worldwide. Women fight alongside men in combat. (rarely)

   ____

   ____

3. Some uninformed people oppose the military. Military service is useless. (in no way)

   ____

   ____

4. Violence won't ever be completely eliminated. Poverty won't be completely eliminated. (neither)

   ____

   ____

5. Climate change has become a popular topic. We heard about it in the past. (seldom)

   ____

   ____

6. I bought an SUV. It had occurred to me that SUVs could harm the environment, but I learned they can. (never)

   ____

   ____

7. We should support access to health care for everyone. We should take action to make it happen. (not only/but . . . also)

   ____

   ____

8. The political candidate gave a wonderful speech. I knew that he was being insincere. (little)

   ____

   ____

EXERCISE 5 NEGATIVE AND FOCUS ADVERBS

GRAMMAR NOTES 2–3 Study the chart. Then complete each sentence with the adverb *even*, *just*, *only in*, or *not only/but . . . also* and the correct form of the verb in parentheses.

Country	Has a military	Has required military service	Allows women to serve in the military	Drafts women to serve in the military	Allows women to serve in combat
Brazil	X		X		X
Canada	X		X		X
China	X	X	X	X	
Costa Rica					
Israel	X	X	X	X	
Switzerland	X	X			
The United States	X		X		X
Venezuela	X		X		X

Facts about military service in eight countries:

1. (there / be)

   ___Only in___ Costa Rica ___is there___ no military.

2. (have)

   Though officially neutral, ______ Switzerland ______ a military.

3. (there / be)

   ______ three countries ______ required military service.

4. (they / allow)

   ______ do Brazil, Canada, the United States, and Venezuela allow women to serve in the military, ______ them to serve in combat.

5. (men / be required)

   ______ to serve in combat in Brazil, Canada, the United States, and Venezuela.

6. (women / be required)

   ______ Israel and China ______ to do military service.

EXERCISE 6 *HERE, THERE,* AND *SO*

GRAMMAR NOTE 4 **Complete the conversation with the correct forms of the words in parentheses.**

ILHAN: How long have we been waiting for our stupid bus? *Here comes another 44* (1. come / here / another 44). That's two 44s in the last half hour. I'm really getting tired of waiting.

PAVLINA: ______________ (2. I / so), but complaining about it won't make it get here any faster.

ILHAN: Yeah, you're probably right. But these buses! They're always late, and they're way too expensive. I think bus service should be free in the downtown area.

PAVLINA: ______________ (3. I / so), but the chance of that happening is pretty slim.

ILHAN: Hey, look—______________ (4. come / here / it) now. Finally!

(One minute passes.)

PAVLINA: Oh, no! It's not stopping. . . . ______________ (5. go / there / it). It says "NOT IN SERVICE."

ILHAN: Hey, ______________ (6. come / here / a taxi). Let's take that instead.

EXERCISE 7 STRESSING WORDS AFTER FOCUS ADVERBS

16|03 **A** PRONUNCIATION NOTE **Listen to the sentences. Underline the word that each adverb focuses on.**

1. Bill can even understand this math.
2. Even Bill can understand this math.
3. I don't just agree with Nancy.
4. I just don't agree with Nancy.
5. We don't even like this food.
6. Even we don't like this food.
7. Only women can visit this club.
8. Women can only visit this club.

16|03 **B** **Listen again and repeat the sentences.**

EXERCISE 8 EDITING

GRAMMAR NOTES 1–4 **Read the email. There are nine mistakes in the use of adverbs. The first mistake is already corrected. Find and correct eight more.**

TO: dave111@yoohoo.com
FR: ken0@yoohoo.com
RE: waiting for the train

Hi, Dad,

I'm waiting for the 5:25 train, so *I just* ~~just I~~ thought I'd drop you an email. I've been at the global warming conference. Actually, I almost didn't get to the conference because almost we didn't get our taxes done on time. Vicky and I stayed up late last night, though, and I mailed the forms this morning.

I hate income taxes! Only once in the last ten years we have gotten a refund, and this time the form was so complicated that Vicky got even upset, and you know how calm she is. Maybe we should move to Antarctica or something. No taxes there.

Besides that, we've been having problems with Donna. It's probably nothing more serious than teenage rebellion, but whenever we try to lay down the law, she gets defensive. Rarely if ever she takes criticism well. When we try to correct her, she usually says, "Why can't you just leave me alone?" Fortunately, Sam has been behaving like an angel, and Toby so has. But they're not teenagers!

Meanwhile, Donna's school has started a new open-campus policy. Students can leave the campus whenever they don't have a class. Even they don't have to tell the school office where they're going or when they'll be back. No way Vicky and I approve of that policy! School time, in our view, is for studying and learning, not for socializing. Little do those school officials realize how much trouble unsupervised teenagers can get into.

Well, Dad, here the train comes. I'll sign off now. Email or text me soon.

Love,
Ken

STEP 4 COMMUNICATION PRACTICE

EXERCISE 9 LISTENING

16|04 **A** Listen to the radio call-in show. Overall, what does the caller think about human nature?

____

____

____

16|04 **B** Read each statement. Then listen to the talk show again. Check (✓) *True* or *False*.

	True	False
1. Capital punishment is used in every state in the United States.	☐	☑
2. The host of the radio show says that there clearly seems to be a worldwide movement to abolish capital punishment.	☐	☐
3. The caller is in favor of capital punishment, overall.	☐	☐
4. Capital punishment is apparently used in China.	☐	☐
5. Generally, the caller feels that people have gotten more civilized.	☐	☐
6. The caller believes that robbery is clearly a capital crime.	☐	☐
7. According to the caller, rehabilitation is clearly impossible for all criminals.	☐	☐
8. The caller hopes that the death penalty will not be abolished worldwide.	☐	☐

C Work with a partner. Discuss the questions. Give reasons for your answers.

1. Do you basically agree or disagree with the viewpoint of the caller in the Listening?
2. Do you believe that, overall, people have become more or less civilized than they were in ancient times?
3. Do you believe that, generally, criminals are capable of rehabilitation?

EXERCISE 10 HOW DO YOU FEEL ABOUT . . . ?

A SURVEY Work in a group. Ask your classmates for their opinions on the controversial issues in the chart on page 279. Then add up your group's responses, noting the number of students supporting and opposing each viewpoint.

EXAMPLE: A: How do you feel about making all schools coeducational?
B: I'm absolutely in favor of it. Boys and girls should go to school together.
C: I'm against it, overall. Coeducational schools are fine, generally, but some students do better in single-sex schools.

Topic	Absolutely in Favor	In Favor, Overall	Against, Overall	Absolutely Against
Making all schools coeducational				
Adopting children from foreign countries				
Requiring military service				
Cloning				
Government providing health care				

B **Analyze the responses and draw conclusions from the data you collected. Report your conclusions to the class.**

EXAMPLE: The people in our group are against making all schools coeducational, overall. Three people were completely in favor of this, but seven were against it, overall. Many of my classmates clearly believe that single-sex schools have some benefits.

EXERCISE 11 LET'S HAVE A DEBATE

A DEBATE **You are going to have a debate. Work in a group. Choose a controversial topic that might be discussed on a TV or radio call-in show. Select a topic from the box or choose one of your own. Brainstorm points supporting both sides of the issue. Make a list of pros and cons.**

Electric cars	Making voting compulsory	Using standardized tests in school
Gun control	Providing free education	

PROS:

- *Gun control is clearly necessary.*
- *Apparently, people don't really know how to use guns safely, and they often shoot people accidentally.*
- *Not only are guns dangerous, but they are also . . .*

CONS:

- *Basically, everyone needs to have access to guns for protection.*
- *Clearly, strong enough guns laws already exist, but many times they're not even enforced. . . .*

B **Divide into two smaller groups. One group is for the topic (pro), and the other is against it (con). Further develop arguments for your list of points from A. Do research on the Internet if necessary.**

EXAMPLE: Gun control is clearly necessary because, in the United States, more than 100,000 people are hurt or killed by guns every year. If we didn't have gun control, everyone would have guns, and many more people would obviously get injured. . . .

C **Work in your original group from A again. Conduct the debate, using your arguments from B.**

FROM GRAMMAR TO WRITING

A BEFORE YOU WRITE You are going to write an essay on a controversial topic. Choose one of the topics in Exercise 11 or another topic. Write a few sentences on both sides of the issue. Then choose one viewpoint to focus on in your essay.

B WRITE Using your ideas from A, write a five-paragraph essay about the controversy you have chosen. Remember to use sentence, focus, and negative adverbs. Try to avoid the common mistakes shown in the chart. Use the example below to help you begin your essay.

EXAMPLE: Should we have national service in our country? Our government provides a lot of benefits to us, and we should certainly give something in return. Therefore, I think national service should be established in our nation. Not only should national service be available, but it should also be required of every citizen.

Here are the reasons why I believe this. . . .

Common Mistakes in Using Adverbs

Don't omit necessary **commas** next to **sentence adverbs**.	Gun control is a controversial **issue, clearly**. NOT Gun control is a controversial ~~issue clearly~~.
Invert the **subject** and the **verb** after **negative** adverbs at the **beginning** of a sentence.	***Rarely* have I** heard such a bad idea. NOT Rarely ~~I have~~ heard such a bad idea.
Don't misplace the focus adverbs ***almost***, ***even***, ***just***, and ***only***. Place a **focus adverb** immediately **before** the word it focuses on.	She doesn't ***even* listen** to me. NOT She ~~even doesn't~~ listen to me. I don't ***just* like** that idea; I love it. NOT I ~~just don't~~ like that idea; I love it. **Only** students are eligible; adults are not. NOT ~~Students are only~~ eligible; adults are not.
Invert the **subject** and **verb** if the words *here*, *there*, or *so* begin a sentence and a noun follows.	Here **is *the book*** I borrowed from you. NOT Here ~~the book is~~ I borrowed from you.

C CHECK YOUR WORK Look at your essay. Underline sentence, focus, and negative adverbs. Use the Editing Checklist to check your work.

Editing Checklist

Did you . . . ?

- ☐ punctuate sentence adverbs correctly
- ☐ invert the subject and the verb after negative adverbs
- ☐ use correct word order with focus adverbs
- ☐ use correct word order after the words *here*, *there*, and *so*

D REVISE YOUR WORK Read your essay again. Can you improve your writing? Make changes if necessary.

UNIT 16 REVIEW

Test yourself on the grammar of the unit.

A Complete the sentences. Circle the correct answers.

1. Mom tries to get me to eat oatmeal, but I don't just / just don't like it.
2. Never had we / we had seen such a fine performance.
3. Bill is pro-military; he even thinks / even he thinks the draft should be renewed.
4. In our club, members can only / only members can attend meetings.
5. I just don't / don't just love him; I want to marry him.
6. Pau is a terrible cook, but even he can / he can even boil eggs.
7. Rarely does Eva / Eva does arrive late at the office.
8. Here the train comes / comes the train.

B Complete the sentences with the correct forms of the words in parentheses.

1. Only in Australia ______________________________ .
(kangaroos / found)
2. ______________________________ .
(something / clear / have to / change)
3. ______________________________ ,
(not only / education / should / be / available to everyone)
but it should also be free.
4. ______________________________ .
(seldom / our team / lose)
5. ______________________________ ; non-citizens cannot.
(citizens / only / can / vote)
6. ______________________________ that I owe you.
(here / the money / be)
7. ______________________________ .
(there / the plane / go)

C Find and correct five errors.

Ben is my partner on our debate team, and he's one of my best friends, but sometimes he irritates me. Not only he is often late for debates, but I never know if he's going to be prepared. Rarely he will accept criticism, and at times even he won't listen. I never just know what kind of mood he's going to be in. He's an excellent debater fortunately. So, if his heart is in the debate, we usually win it.

Check your answers on page 431.

UNIT

17 Adverb Clauses

SPORTS

OUTCOMES

- Use adverb clauses to indicate when, where, why, or under what condition something happens
- Identify key arguments in a newspaper editorial
- Identify key details in an interview
- Discuss the topic of sports, expressing opinions, agreeing and disagreeing
- Write an essay about benefits and drawbacks of sports

STEP 1 GRAMMAR IN CONTEXT

BEFORE YOU READ

Discuss the questions.

1. What are some benefits of sports?
2. What are some negative aspects of sports?

READ

17|01 Read this editorial about sports.

EDITORIAL

Are Sports Still Sporting?

AS I WRITE THIS EDITORIAL, preparations for the 2016 Summer Olympics are in full swing in Rio de Janeiro, Brazil. This international competition seems likely to be a big success, with 206 countries expected to participate in the first games ever to be played in South America. The 2012 Summer Games in London, England, and the 2014 Winter Olympics in Sochi, Russia, were artistic triumphs. The popularity of sports worldwide continues to rise. But while sports may look good on the surface, problems lurk underneath. For one thing, there's a vast overemphasis on fame and the worshipping of famous athletes. Then there's the increasingly large role money is playing in sports today, since there are ever-increasing possibilities for product endorsement by athletes. Finally, sports violence has certainly not diminished. In April of 2013, for example, a coach in an amateur soccer game in Salt Lake City was punched in the face by a player because he had penalized that player. The coach later died from the injury. What is wrong? I've concluded that the whole sports scene is in need of repair and have identified three major excesses:

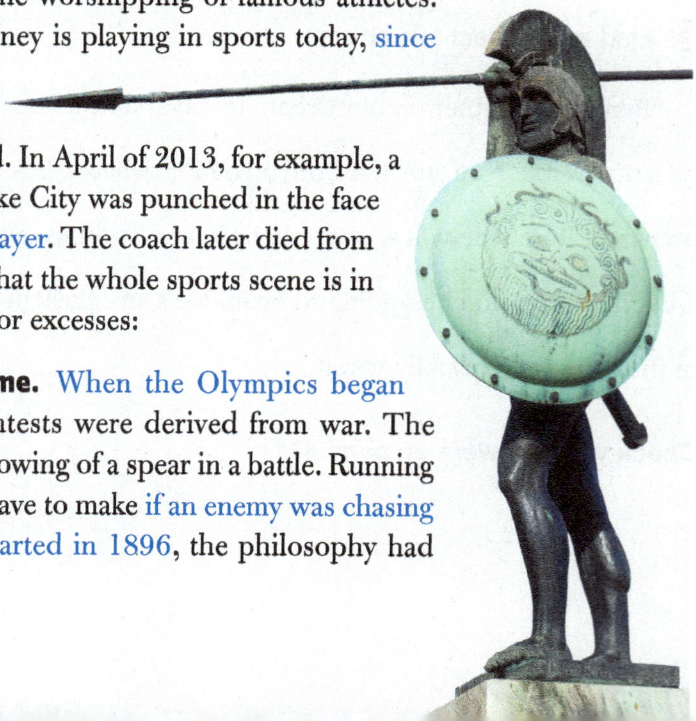

FIRST EXCESS: Misplaced focus on fame. When the Olympics began about 2,700 years ago in Greece, the contests were derived from war. The javelin throw, for example, paralleled the throwing of a spear in a battle. Running paralleled the physical exertion you might have to make if an enemy was chasing you. When the modern Olympic games started in 1896, the philosophy had shifted to the promotion of peace. However, emphasis was still placed on demonstrating physical stamina[1] and excellence in challenging contests. How things have changed! Although athletes still try to achieve their personal best, the focus has shifted to the breaking of records and the achievement of fame. Can we really say that someone who finishes the 400-meter freestyle swim one-tenth of a second ahead of his or her nearest rival is a champion, while that rival is an also-ran[2]?

SECOND EXCESS: Money. Consider the cost of attending a major athletic competition. In the United States, the average cost of a ticket to a National Football League game in 2015 was about $84. If you add up the cost of taking a family of four to a game, the total was over $440. A ticket to an NBA basketball game is about $52. Baseball is cheaper, though it's not really a bargain at an average ticket cost of about $30. I wondered why tickets are so expensive until I remembered the key factor: players' salaries. NBA basketball star LeBron James earns about $23 million a year. Baseball player Alex Rodriguez made about $22 million in 2015. Is anyone worth that much money? Meanwhile, the president of the United States earns $400,000 a year, and U.S. public schoolteachers make a median yearly salary of about $53,000. We can infer a lot about what we value by looking at what we pay people. When we compensate professional athletes so highly, are we rewarding the people who are truly valuable to society?

LeBron James

THIRD EXCESS: Prevalence of violence. We see it wherever we look, and it's certainly not decreasing. Fights occur frequently in professional sports, with ice hockey one of the worst offenders. In one of the best-known cases, for instance, NHL player Steve Moore had to be hospitalized because another player hit him in the head with his hockey stick. Unfortunately, there seems to be increasing acceptance of violence as "just part of the game." But once we assume violence is inevitable, it will be almost impossible to stop. This sort of thing doesn't just happen in North America. We've all heard about the well-publicized violence surrounding soccer games in Europe. In another example that occurred in December of 2012, a Dutch amateur linesman was beaten to death after a youth match concluded.

Sports have enormous potential to benefit society, but somehow, in becoming big business entertainment, they have gone awry. What to do? Well, we can pay more attention to local athletics and events such as the Special Olympics. We can refuse to pay ridiculously high ticket prices. We can demand an end to violence. Above all, we need to get back to this idea: It's not whether you win or lose; it's how you play the game.

1 *stamina:* strength of body or mind to fight tiredness, illness, etc.
2 *also-ran:* a loser in a competition

AFTER YOU READ

A VOCABULARY **Complete the definitions with words from the box.**

awry	derive	factor	infer	lurk	parallel	prevalence	shift

1. When you take something from an original source, you ________________ it from that source.
2. When something changes in practice or position, it is said to ________________.
3. To wait somewhere secretly is to ________________.
4. Something that matches another situation is said to ________________ it.
5. The common, general, or wide existence of something is termed ________________.
6. An element, part, or ingredient of something is termed a(n) ________________.
7. To ________________ something is to deduce or draw a conclusion.
8. Something that has not happened the way it was planned is said to have gone ________________.

B COMPREHENSION **Complete the sentences. Circle the correct answers.**

1. When the Olympics began in ancient Greece, athletic contests were related to ____.
   a. politics b. money c. war
2. The modern Olympic Games were designed to promote ____.
   a. political harmony b. peace c. economics
3. According to the author, the emphasis in today's Olympic Games has shifted to ____.
   a. the pursuit of excellence b. the achievement of fame c. training for war
4. Tickets for ____ games are currently the least expensive of the three major U.S. sports.
   a. baseball b. basketball c. football
5. The author says that the high cost of tickets today is most directly related to the need to ____.
   a. pay taxes to the government b. provide help for team owners c. pay players' salaries
6. In the United States today, the average annual salary of ____ is about $50,000.
   a. the president b. a public schoolteacher c. a professional athlete
7. According to the author, sports violence is ____.
   a. decreasing b. staying about the same c. increasing
8. To improve the sports scene, the author recommends ____.
   a. supporting local athletics b. making sports events more expensive c. ignoring violence

C DISCUSSION **Work with a partner. Discuss: Do you agree or disagree with the author of the editorial about the excesses of sports? Give reasons for your answer.**

STEP 2 GRAMMAR PRESENTATION

ADVERB CLAUSES

Placement and Punctuation

Main Clause	Adverb Clause
We watched TV a lot	**when the Olympics were on.**
Tickets cost more	**because athletes earn so much.**

Adverb Clause	Main Clause
When the Olympics were on,	we watched TV a lot.
Because athletes earn so much,	tickets cost more.

Types

Adverb Clauses of Time	
Before I played basketball,	I was a soccer player.
The coach met with her players	**after the game was over.**
While the team was on the field,	the fans cheered continuously.

Adverb Clauses of Place	
I've seen children playing soccer	**everywhere I've been.**
Anywhere you go,	sports stars are national heroes.
I work out at a gym	**wherever I travel.**

Adverb Clauses of Reason	
Since she plays well,	I want her on our team.
He was unable to play in the final game	**as he had hurt his ankle.**
Now that TV covers the Games,	billions of people can see the Olympics.

Adverb Clauses of Condition	
Unless the tickets cost too much,	we'll go to the game next Saturday.
You'll be comfortable inside the dome	**even if it's cold and raining outside.**
Only if she wins the gold medal	will she get a professional contract.

Adverb Clauses of Contrast	
They won the game,	**though they didn't really deserve the victory.**
Although their team is talented,	they didn't win.
Swimmers are rarely injured,	**whereas hockey players are often hurt.**

GRAMMAR NOTES

1 Definition of Adverb Clauses

Remember that a **clause** is a group of words that contains at least one **subject** and a **verb** showing past, present, or future time. Clauses can be **independent** or **dependent**. (See Unit 14.)	
Adverb clauses are **dependent** clauses that indicate **how**, **when**, **where**, **why**, or **under what conditions** things happen.	I went home **when the game was over.** *(when)* She dropped out of the race **because she was injured**. *(why)*
Adverb clauses can also introduce a **contrast**.	They won the game, **although the score was very close**. *(contrast)*
Adverb clauses begin with **subordinating conjunctions** (also called subordinating adverbs), which can be either single words or phrases.	It began to rain ***while* we were playing**. I have to practice ***now that* I'm on the team**.
Sentences containing both an independent clause and a dependent clause are called **complex sentences**. In a complex sentence, the **main idea** is normally in the **independent clause**.	DEPENDENT CLAUSE: **If we can get tickets**, INDEPENDENT CLAUSE (MAIN IDEA): we'll go to the game.
Adverb clauses sometimes occur **inside independent** clauses.	The weather **when the game started** was terrible.
In a complex sentence, the clauses can come in either order. If the **dependent** clause comes **first**, we place a **comma** after it.	**Whenever I exercise,** I feel good. I feel good **whenever I exercise**.
BE CAREFUL! In complex sentences, do not use *will* or *be going to* in the dependent clause to show future time.	We'll leave when they **get** here. NOT We'll leave when they ~~will~~ get here.

2 Adverb Clauses of Time

Adverb clauses of time indicate **when** something happens.

To introduce an adverb clause of time, use ***after***, ***as***, ***as soon as***, ***before***, ***by the time***, ***once***, ***since***, ***until/till***, ***when***, ***whenever***, ***while***, etc.	The race will start ***as soon as* everyone is in place.** We always drink water ***before* we start a game.** ***As* we were walking**, we heard shouts from the stadium.
The subordinating conjunction ***once*** means *starting from the moment something happens*.	She'll earn a good salary ***once* she starts playing regularly**.
The subordinating conjunctions ***until*** and ***till*** have the same meaning. *Till* is more informal and used more in conversation.	I will wait here ***until* they arrive.** They won't be here ***till* after the plane lands.**

3 Adverb Clauses of Place

Adverb clauses of place indicate **where** something happens.

To introduce an adverb clause of place, use *anywhere*, *everywhere*, *where*, *wherever*, etc.	Professional sports are played ***where* there are big stadiums.** Star athletes are popular ***wherever* they go.**

4 Adverb Clauses of Reason

Adverb clauses of reason indicate **why** something happens.

To introduce an adverb clause of reason, use *as*, *because*, *now that* (= because now), *since*, etc.	She won ***because* she'd practiced tirelessly.** ***Since* he didn't register in time**, he can't play.
You can use *since* both in adverb clauses of reason and of time.	***Since* Anna doesn't like sports**, she refused to go to the game. *(reason:* since = because*)* Barry has played sports ***since* he entered high school**. *(time:* since = starting from that point*)*
You can use *as* both in adverb clauses of reason and of time.	***As* he was badly hurt**, he had to drop out of the game. *(reason:* as = because*)* He set a world record ***as* we were watching the Summer Olympics**. *(time:* as = while*)*

5 Adverb Clauses of Condition

Adverb clauses of condition indicate **under what conditions** something happens.

To introduce an adverb clause of condition, use *even if*, *if*, *only if*, *in case*, *unless*, etc.	You'll improve ***if* you practice daily.**
Even if means that the condition does not matter; the result will be the same.	***Even if* he practices constantly**, he won't make the team.
Only if means that only one condition will produce the result.	Bi-Yun will make the team ***only if* another athlete drops out.**
Unless means that something will happen or be true if another thing does not happen or is not true.	***Unless* you train a great deal**, you won't be a champion.
In case means that something should be done to prepare for a possible future happening.	We'd better take along some extra money ***in case* the tickets are more expensive than we thought.**
If the sentence begins with *only if*, invert the subject and verb of the main clause, and don't use a comma.	**Only if** another athlete drops out ***will* Bi-Yun** make the team.
BE CAREFUL! Don't confuse *even if* (or *even though*) with *even*.	**Even** my mother knows the rules of baseball. **Even if** they win, they won't be the champions. NOT ~~Even~~ they win, they won't be the champions.

6 Adverb Clauses of Contrast

Adverb clauses of contrast make a contrast with the idea expressed in the independent clause.

To introduce an adverb clause of contrast, use ***although***, ***even though***, ***though***, ***whereas***, ***while***, etc.	He lost the race, ***although* he was favored.** ***Even though* she is tall**, she doesn't score much.
We often use ***although***, ***even though***, and ***though*** when we want to show an **unexpected result**.	***Although* he is young**, he was selected for the team. ***Though* he didn't start playing basketball until his senior year**, he quickly became a star.
We often place a **comma before and after** a dependent clause of contrast.	We attended the Olympics**, even though it cost a lot.** **Even though it cost a lot,** we attended the Olympics.
To make a direct contrast, use ***while*** or ***whereas***. *Whereas* is a bit more formal than *while*.	***While* snowboarding is pricey**, skating is cheap. ***Whereas* my sister loves athletics**, my brother couldn't care less about them.
Use ***while*** to introduce both a clause of contrast and a clause of time.	***While* they lost the game**, they played their best. *(contrast)* We ate ***while* we were watching the game.** *(time)*

REFERENCE NOTES

For a list of **subordinating conjunctions**, see Appendix 22 on page 420.
For more information on **future time clauses**, see Unit 3 on page 38.

STEP 3 FOCUSED PRACTICE

EXERCISE 1 DISCOVER THE GRAMMAR

GRAMMAR NOTES 1–6 **Read the sentences based on the reading. Underline the adverb clause in each sentence. Then identify the adverb clause as a clause of *contrast*, *place*, *time*, *reason*, or *condition*.**

time 1. As I write this editorial, preparations are in full swing for the 2016 Olympics.

______ 2. While sports may look good on the surface, problems lurk underneath.

______ 3. Because he penalized a player, a British referee received death threats.

______ 4. When the Olympic Games started about 2,700 years ago in Greece, the contests held were basically those derived from war.

______ 5. Running paralleled the physical exertion you might have to make if an enemy was chasing you.

______ 6. Although athletes still try to achieve their personal best, the emphasis has shifted away from the individual pursuit of excellence.

______ 7. I wondered why tickets are so expensive until I remembered the key factor: players' salaries.

______ 8. Baseball is cheaper, though it's not really a bargain at an average ticket cost of $30.

______ 9. We see violence wherever we look.

______ 10. Once we assume violence is inevitable, it will be almost impossible to stop.

EXERCISE 2 SUBORDINATING CONJUNCTIONS IN ADVERB CLAUSES

GRAMMAR NOTES 2, 4–6 **Read the sentences about various sports. Circle the correct subordinating conjunction in each sentence.**

1. Before / Because you can ski, you need a lift ticket.

2. If / Although the overall score is forty love, one player's score is zero.

3. You can't play this game if / unless you have ice skates.

4. You go to the free-throw line before / after you've been fouled.

5. Though / Since you can use your head, you can't use your hands.

6. While / When you've finished the course, you've run 26.2 miles.

7. Your team can't bat until / in case the other team makes three outs.

8. Although / If your team scores a touchdown, it earns six points.

EXERCISE 3 MAIN CLAUSES AND ADVERB CLAUSES

GRAMMAR NOTES 2, 4–6 **Combine each pair of sentences into one sentence containing an adverb clause and a main clause. Keep the clauses in the same order. Choose subordinating conjunctions from the box, using a different one in each sentence. Add necessary punctuation.**

after	although	because	before	if	since	when	~~while~~

1. There are similarities between the ancient Olympics and modern Olympics. There are also differences.

   While there are similarities between the ancient Olympics and modern Olympics, there are also differences.

2. Greek city-states were often at war with one another. Olympic contestants stopped fighting during the games.

   ____

3. They had been held for over 1,000 years. The ancient Olympic Games were outlawed by the Roman Emperor Theodosius I.

   ____

4. Romans thought the Greeks wore too few clothes. Theodosius outlawed the games in 393.

   ____

5. French educator Pierre de Coubertin revived the Olympics. He thought they would promote international peace.

   ____

6. Tug-of-war was dropped from the Olympics in 1920. American and British athletes disagreed about how it should be played.

   ____

7. New Olympic sports often appear as demonstration events. They are adopted as medal sports.

   ____

8. Any sport can potentially become a medal event. It can be scored and fulfills certain criteria.

   ____

EXERCISE 4 CONDITION, CONTRAST, REASON, TIME

GRAMMAR NOTES 2, 4–6 Look at the pictures. Use the type of adverb clause given to complete the sentences describing each picture. Use a different subordinating conjunction in each clause.

1. **CONDITION**

   The Sharks will win the game *if the player makes the basket.* ________________

2. **CONDITION**

   The other team can't win ________________________________

3. **CONTRAST**

   ________________________________, their fans still love them.

4. **CONTRAST**

   The players are doing their best ________________________________

5. **REASON**

   ________________________________, the competition was postponed.

6. **TIME**

   The competition won't be held ________________________________ improves.

EXERCISE 5 EDITING

GRAMMAR NOTES 1–6 **Read the student essay. There are ten mistakes in the use of adverb clauses. The first mistake is already corrected. Find and correct nine more.**

Why Sports?

People are criticizing school athletics these days. Supposedly, there's too much emphasis on sports, ~~if~~ *while* there's not enough emphasis on education. People say that sports are too dangerous and encourage violence. I disagree. In my opinion, school sports are a positive force.

Sports are positive although they get students involved in something. We constantly hear that violence is increasing. But I think a lot of people get involved in crime when they don't have enough to do. After you'll play any kind of sport for two or three hours, it's hard to commit a violent act even you want to.

Second, sports teach people a lot of worthwhile things. If students play on a team, they learn to get along and work with others. Wherever their team wins, they learn how to be good winners. When their team loses they find out that they have to struggle to improve. They discover that winning a few and losing a few are part of the normal ups and downs of life. Also, students improve their physical condition unless they participate in sports.

Finally, sports are positive though they allow students who don't have enough money for college to earn sports scholarships and improve their chances for a successful life. Unless a young soccer player from a small village in Africa can get a scholarship, he will have a chance to get an education and probably make his life better. If a young woman with little money earns a scholarship to join a college swim team, she'll have the chance to earn a college degree and go on to a worthwhile job. Because school sports programs have some problems that need to be fixed, their benefits outweigh their disadvantages. I should know because I got a sports scholarship myself. School sports must stay.

STEP 4 COMMUNICATION PRACTICE

EXERCISE 6 LISTENING

17|02 **A** Listen to the interview with Lillian Swanson, a sports star. Why does Lillian think she became successful?

____

17|02 **B** Read the questions. Then listen again and answer each question with a complete sentence.

1. When did Lillian learn to swim?
   She learned to swim when she was four.
2. Why did Lillian and her family spend a lot of time at the beach?
   ____
3. What did Lillian decide when she was twelve?
   ____
4. Under what conditions did Lillian's parents agree to pay for lessons?
   ____
5. Although people know that sports make people physically stronger, what positive benefits of sports are they less aware of?
   ____
6. According to Lillian, what happens to kids whenever they play sports?
   ____
7. When did Lillian get discouraged?
   ____
8. Why can't Lillian imagine herself doing anything else?
   ____

C Work with a partner. Discuss the questions.

1. Because Lillian loves swimming, she can't imagine doing anything else. Do you enjoy doing sports? If you do, why? Describe experiences you've had with sports.
2. In your opinion, should parents pressure their children to participate in sports?
3. Once Lillian had made the decision to try to get to the Olympics, her parents promised to support her if she stuck to her plan. Do you think that parents should require their children to stick to plans they've promised to carry out?

EXERCISE 7 FAMOUS SPORTS QUOTATIONS

CRITICAL THINKING **Work in a group. Read the quotations about sports. Choose five quotations and discuss them. What do they mean? Do you agree with them? Why or why not? Then report your conclusions to the class.**

1. Champions keep playing until they get it right. —*Billie Jean King, tennis player*

   EXAMPLE: A: I think it's true that champions keep playing until they get it right. If you give up before you learn to do something well, you can never become a champion.
   B: That's true. But I think people shouldn't try to get something right unless they are good at it already. Not everyone can be a champion. . . .

2. The Six Ws: Work will win when wishing won't. —*Todd Blackledge, football player*
3. A good hockey player plays where the puck is. A great hockey player plays where the puck is going to be. —*Wayne Gretzky, hockey player*
4. You are never really playing an opponent. You are playing yourself, your own highest standards, and when you reach your limits, that is real joy. —*Arthur Ashe, tennis player*
5. Most people give up just when they're about to achieve success. They quit on the one yard line. They give up at the last minute of the game, one foot from a winning touchdown. —*Ross Perot, businessman and U.S. presidential candidate*
6. Good, better, best. Never let it rest—until your good is better and your better is best. —*Tim Duncan, basketball player*
7. When you lose a couple of times, it makes you realize how difficult it is to win. —*Steffi Graf, tennis player*
8. If it is a cliché to say athletics build character as well as muscle, then I subscribe to the cliché. —*Gerald Ford, U.S. president*

EXERCISE 8 SPORTS AND VIOLENCE

A DISCUSSION **Work in a group. Read the quotation from novelist George Orwell. Do you agree or disagree with his statements? Discuss the questions.**

1. When athletes play sports seriously, are they concerned with fair play?
2. Although hatred, jealousy, and boastfulness can be found in the sports scene, do most athletes show these emotions when they compete?
3. Do a significant number of spectators take pleasure in witnessing violence whenever they watch sporting competitions?
4. Do you agree or disagree with Orwell's statement that sport is like war without the shooting? Why?

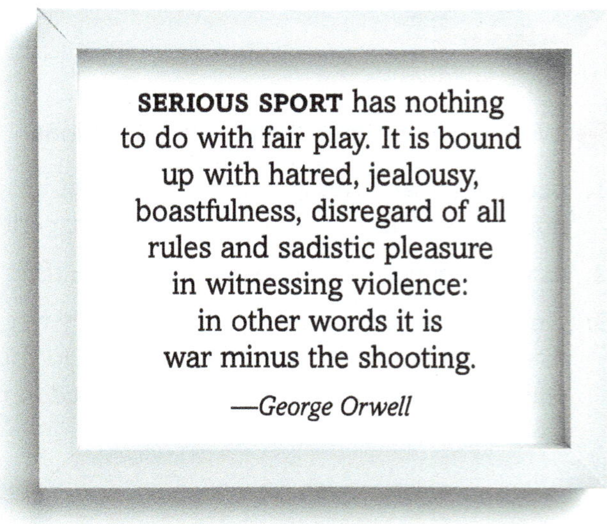

B Share your group's conclusions with the class.

EXAMPLE: Our group felt that even though some athletes aren't concerned with fair play, the majority are concerned with it. They have to be because . . .

EXERCISE 9 THE SPORTS SCENE

A PICTURE DISCUSSION **You are going to discuss different aspects of sports. First, study the photos. Then write *A* (*agree*) or *D* (*disagree*) for the statements below.**

_____ **1.** Since too many athletes and fans are getting hurt, we need to solve the problem of sports violence as soon as possible.

_____ **2.** We should encourage young people to play sports. When young people play sports, they grow physically, mentally, and psychologically.

_____ **3.** Sports are worthwhile because they entertain people and provide enjoyment.

_____ **4.** Sports are beneficial for everyone. Even though some people have different abilities, they can still participate in them.

B **Work in a group. Compare your answers to the questions in A. Give reasons for your answers.**

EXAMPLE: A: I agree with Statement 1. I think that we should try to stop sports violence because too many athletes and fans are getting hurt.

B: I agree. We think that the police should always be at athletic events in case violence occurs. They should arrest people immediately if they start to act violently.

C: Well, although sports violence does happen sometimes, I don't think it's such a serious problem. I think that sports are positive overall because . . .

C **Report your conclusions to the class. Then discuss: What do sports mean to you personally?**

EXAMPLE: A: Sports mean very little to me personally. If I had the choice of going to a sporting event or staying home and reading a book, I'd stay home and read.

B: I have a different viewpoint. Sports mean a lot to me because . . .

FROM GRAMMAR TO WRITING

A BEFORE YOU WRITE **You are going to write an essay about the benefits and drawbacks of sports. Choose one of these topics and write a few sentences about it.**

- Sports are valuable to society because they provide entertainment.
- Sports have become too violent.
- Sports stars earn ridiculously large salaries.
- Sports provide opportunities to people who have few other opportunities.
- Sports provide psychological and physical benefits for those who participate in them.

B WRITE **Using your ideas from A, write a five-paragraph essay about the topic you have chosen. Remember to use adverb clauses. Try to avoid the common mistakes shown in the chart. Use the example below to help you begin your essay.**

EXAMPLE: Though many people say that sports are too important in our culture, my view is that the advantages of sports outweigh their disadvantages. I strongly believe this because sports provide opportunities to people who don't have many other opportunities. Consider a boy from a poor family, for example. His parents can't afford to send him to college, even though he's a good student. He's very good at basketball. . . .

Common Mistakes in Using Adverb Clauses

Don't use *will* or *be going to* in **adverb clauses** expressing future **time**. Use the **simple present**.	As soon as Jomo **calls**, I'll get the tickets. NOT As soon as Jomo ~~will call~~, I'll get the tickets.
Don't use normal word order if an adverb clause begins with ***only if***. **Invert** the subject and verb or auxiliary.	**Only if** she works hard ***will*** **she** succeed. NOT Only if she works hard ~~she will~~ succeed.
Don't confuse ***even if*** with ***even***.	**Even if** Omar comes soon, we'll be late. NOT ~~Even~~ Omar comes soon, we'll be late.
Be sure to place a **comma** after an introductory adverb clause.	**If Jane makes the team,** I'll be happy. NOT If Jane makes the ~~team I'll~~ be happy.

C CHECK YOUR WORK **Look at your essay. Underline the adverb clauses. Use the Editing Checklist to check your work.**

Editing Checklist

Did you . . . ?

- ☐ use the simple present in adverb clauses expressing future time
- ☐ invert the subject and the verb in adverb clauses beginning with *only if*
- ☐ avoid confusing *even if* and *even*
- ☐ place a comma after an introductory adverb clause

D REVISE YOUR WORK **Read your essay again. Can you improve your writing? Make changes if necessary.**

UNIT 17 REVIEW

Test yourself on the grammar of the unit.

A Complete the sentences. Circle the correct answers.

1. You won't be a champion if / unless you practice regularly.
2. Since / Even though the team is in the playoffs, I doubt they'll win the title.
3. We're taking along our racquets in case / although there's time to play.
4. Whenever / As Hai was running toward the goal line, he sprained his ankle.
5. Once / Because Bahdoon gets used to his new position, he'll start playing well.
6. Nelson and Elena don't go dancing once / now that they have children.
7. Famous athletes are in demand wherever / whereas they go.
8. We'll be leaving when / since she arrives.

B Complete the sentences with the words from the box.

although	as soon as	because	only if	unless	whenever	while

1. I visit my cousin ____________ I'm in town.
2. ____________ she arrives, we'll be leaving.
3. ____________ I study for the next two weeks, I probably won't pass the exam.
4. ____________ she's seldom at home, I don't often stop to see her.
5. ____________ he exercises will he lose weight.
6. ____________ they played with great skill, they lost the game.
7. ____________ flying costs a lot, bus travel is inexpensive.

C Find and correct five mistakes.

A: As soon as Mom will get here, we can leave for the game.

B: You mean Mom is coming with us to the game? She won't understand what's going on even we give her a long explanation.

A: Unless we explain it slowly and carefully, she'll get the basic idea.

B: I'm not so sure. Only if we can take an hour or so to explain it she'll get the overall picture.

A: Even though she might not understand everything she'll enjoy being with us.

Check your answers on page 431.

UNIT 18

Adverb and Adverbial Phrases

COMPASSION

OUTCOMES
- Form and use adverb and adverbial phrases
- Identify a sequence of events in a news story
- Comment on key details from a news broadcast
- Discuss the topic of compassion, expressing and supporting opinions with examples
- Write an essay about a compassionate act

STEP 1 GRAMMAR IN CONTEXT

BEFORE YOU READ

Discuss the questions.

1. What is your definition of compassion?
2. How important a value is compassion in society?

READ

18|01 Read this article about compassion.

Compassion

It was the evening of September 29, 1994. Having spent a wonderful day exploring the ruins at Paestum in southern Italy, Reg and Maggie Green were driving south in the region of Italy known as the boot, their children Nicholas and Eleanor sleeping peacefully in the back seat. Suddenly an old, decrepit car pulled up alongside them. An Italian with a bandanna over his face yelled at them while motioning for them to stop. Not knowing what to do, Reg quickly considered the options. If they stopped, they risked a potentially deadly confrontation with criminals; if they sped away, they might escape. Guessing that their newer-model car could probably elude the old car the criminals were driving, Reg stepped on the gas. Shots rang out, shattering both windows on the driver's side of the car. The Greens' car took off, easily outdistancing the bandits' car. On checking the children, Reg and Maggie found them still sleeping peacefully in the back seat.

Nicholas Green

A bit farther down the road, Reg saw a police car parked on the shoulder and pulled over to alert the authorities. Upon opening the door, he saw blood oozing from the back of Nicholas's head. After being rushed to a hospital, Nicholas remained in a coma for two days, his status not changing. Then doctors declared him brain-dead. This was not the end of the story, however. As Nicholas lay on his deathbed, Reg and Maggie decided that something good should come out of the situation. Realizing that it would be far better to return good for evil than to seek revenge, they offered Nicholas's organs for transplant. "Someone should have the future he lost," Reg said. Profoundly moved by the gesture, Italians poured out their emotions. Maurizio Costanzo, the host of a talk show, summed up the common feeling by saying, "You have given us a lesson in civility . . . shown us how to react in the face of pain and sorrow."

The great irony of this tragedy was that it was a mistake. According to investigators' later determinations, Nicholas was killed by two petty[1] criminals who thought the Greens were jewelers carrying precious gems. The criminals were placed on trial after being turned over to the police.

People all over Europe and North America reacted in sorrow. Headlines in the Italian media spoke of *La Nostra Vergogna* ("Our Shame"). Wherever the Greens went, they met Italians who asked for their forgiveness. The Greens were given a medal, Italy's highest honor, by the prime minister.

Some good has indeed come out of Nicholas's death. Seven Italians received Nicholas's heart, liver, kidneys, islet cells, and corneas.[2] Perhaps more importantly, a blow was struck[3] for organ donation. Having heard Reg and Maggie speak on TV, 40,000 French people pledged to donate their organs when they died. On returning to the United States, the Greens began to receive requests to tell their son's story and speak about organ donation. "It gradually dawned on us," said Reg, "that we'd been given a life's work."

Nicholas Green is gone, but others live on because of his parents' compassionate act. How many of us would do the same thing, given the opportunity?

1 *petty:* small, unimportant
2 *corneas:* protective coverings on the outer surface of eyes
3 *a blow was struck:* progress was made

AFTER YOU READ

A VOCABULARY **Match the words in bold with their meanings.**

_____ 1. Suddenly an old, **decrepit** car pulled up.
_____ 2. They risked a deadly **confrontation** with criminals.
_____ 3. Reg's vehicle could probably **elude** the criminals' car.
_____ 4. He saw blood **oozing** from Nicholas's head.
_____ 5. Nicholas lay in a coma, his **status** not changing.
_____ 6. You have given us a lesson in **civility**.
_____ 7. Headlines in the **media** spoke of "Our Shame."
_____ 8. It **dawned on** us that we'd been given a life's work.

a. flowing slowly
b. became apparent to
c. news sources
d. in bad condition
e. politeness, courtesy
f. condition, position
g. angry or tense encounter
h. escape from

B COMPREHENSION Complete the sentences based on the reading.

1. The Greens were traveling in the region of Italy known as the ______________.
2. The Greens' car was newer than the ______________ car.
3. The shots ______________ the windows on the driver's side of the car.
4. After the shooting, Nicholas lay in a ______________ for two days.
5. The Greens thought it was better to return good for evil than to seek ______________.
6. Italians were profoundly ______________ by the Greens' donation of Nicholas's organs.
7. The ironic aspect of the Greens' tragedy was that it was a ______________.
8. The criminals were placed on ______________ after being turned over to the police.

C DISCUSSION Work with a partner. Compare and justify your answers in B. Then discuss this question: Do you feel it was the right thing for the Greens to offer Nicholas's organs for transplant? Give reasons for your answer.

STEP 2 GRAMMAR PRESENTATION

ADVERB AND ADVERBIAL PHRASES

Reducing Adverb Clauses of Time to Adverb Phrases

Adverb Clause

While they were in Italy,	they had trouble.
While I was in Italy,	
When I am traveling,	I call her a lot.
When Sue is traveling,	

Adverb Phrase

While in Italy,	they had trouble.
Ø*	
When traveling,	I call her a lot.
Ø	

*Ø = no change possible

Changing Adverb Clauses of Time to Adverb Phrases

Adverb Clause	
Before we left,	we visited Rome.
Before Ann left,	
After they (had) investigated,	the police identified the killers.
When they heard Reg speak,	many Italians were moved.

Adverb Phrase	
Before leaving,	we visited Rome.
Ø	
After investigating,	the police identified the killers.
After having investigated,	
On hearing Reg speak,	many Italians were moved.
Upon hearing Reg speak,	

Changing Adverb Clauses of Time to Adverbial Phrases

Adverb Clause	
While they waited at the hospital,	they were deeply troubled.
When they heard the news,	they decided what to do.

Adverbial Phrase	
Waiting at the hospital,	they were deeply troubled.
Having heard the news,	they decided what to do.

Changing Adverb Clauses of Reason to Adverbial Phrases

Adverb Clause	
As he saw the guns,	he chose to flee.
Because they were unable to catch him,	the pursuers fired several shots.
Because I've been to Bari,	I hope to return.
Because I'd been to Bari,	I hoped to return.
Since they were accused by the police,	they had to appear in court.

Adverbial Phrase	
Seeing the guns,	he chose to flee.
Being unable to catch him,	the pursuers fired several shots.
Having been to Bari,	I hope to return.
	I hoped to return.
Accused by the police,	they had to appear in court.

GRAMMAR NOTES

1 Definition of Adverb Phrases

A **phrase** is a group of words that does not have both a subject and verb showing time.
An **adverb phrase** is a group of words that often **modifies a main clause** in a sentence.

Adverb phrases commonly include:
- **present participles**
- **past participles**

Before *traveling* abroad, I had seldom seen poverty.

People will often help others **when *given* the chance.**

Negative adverb phrases contain the words ***not*** or ***never*** before the participle.

After ***not* eating** all day, we were very hungry.

2 Reducing Adverb Clauses with *Be*

Adverb clauses can be **reduced** to adverb phrases when the clause has a form of ***be***.

To **reduce** an adverb clause to an **adverb phrase**, **omit** the **subject pronoun** and the form of ***be***. If the original sentence has commas, keep the commas in the reduced sentence.	ADVERB CLAUSE **While they were driving,** they were attacked by bandits. ADVERB PHRASE **While driving,** they were attacked by bandits.
An adverb phrase can come **first** or **second** in the sentence. When it comes first, we usually place a **comma** after it.	**While driving,** they were attacked by bandits. They were attacked by bandits **while driving**.
BE CAREFUL! You can reduce an adverb clause to an adverb phrase *only if* the **subjects in both clauses** of the sentence refer to the **same person or thing**.	**Reg and Maggie** drove while **the children** were sleeping. NOT Reg and Maggie drove ~~while sleeping~~.

3 Changing Adverb Clauses of Time

Adverb clauses of time beginning with *after*, *before*, *since*, and *while* can be **changed to adverb phrases** when the clause has **no form of *be***.

To change an adverb clause to an **adverb phrase**, **omit** the **subject pronoun** and change the verb to its **-*ing* form**. Keep the subordinating conjunction and original punctuation.	ADVERB CLAUSE **After they visited** Paestum, the Greens drove south. ADVERB PHRASE **After *visiting*** Paestum, the Greens drove south.
BE CAREFUL! You can change an adverb clause of time to an adverb phrase *only if* the subjects in the two clauses of the sentence refer to the same person or thing.	After **the bandits** saw the Greens' car, **the Greens** sped away. NOT ~~After seeing the Greens' car~~, the Greens sped away.

4 Changing Adverb Clauses with Past-Time Verbs

To change an adverb clause with a **simple past** or **past perfect verb** to an adverb phrase, change the verb to ***having*** **+ past participle**. Keep the original punctuation.	**After they (had) opened** the door, they saw the blood. ***Having* opened** the door, they saw the blood.
In a sentence with a simple past or past perfect verb, you can also change the clause to a phrase by changing the verb to its -*ing* form and keeping the subordinating conjunction and the original punctuation.	After **opening** the door, they saw the blood.

5 Replacing *When* with *On* or *Upon* in Adverb Phrases

We don't use *when* in adverb phrases if the meaning is "at the time something occurred." If *when* has this meaning in an adverb clause, replace it with ***on*** or ***upon*** **+ *-ing*** when you reduce the clause to an adverb phrase.

ADVERB CLAUSE
When they realized what had happened, they pulled to the side of the road.

ADVERB PHRASE
Upon *realizing* what had happened, they pulled to the side of the road.
On *realizing* what had happened, they pulled to the side of the road.

6 Definition of Adverbial Phrases

An adverb phrase **without a subordinating conjunction** is called an **adverbial phrase**.

We sometimes **omit** the **subordinating conjunction** in a phrase. When we do this, the adverb phrase changes to an **adverbial phrase**.

ADVERB PHRASE
While sitting on the porch, I thought about my future.

ADVERBIAL PHRASE
Sitting on the porch, I thought about my future.

7 Changing Adverb Clauses of Reason

Adverb **clauses of reason** can be changed to adverbial **phrases**.

To change an adverb clause of reason to an adverbial phrase, **omit** the subordinating conjunctions ***because***, ***since***, or ***as*** at the beginning of a clause. These conjunctions **must be omitted**.

ADVERB CLAUSE
Because the children were sleeping in the car, they were not aware of what was happening.

ADVERBIAL PHRASE
Sleeping in the car, the children were not aware of what was happening.
NOT ~~Because~~ sleeping in the car, the children were not aware of what was happening.

You can change ***because/since/as*** + a form of ***be*** to ***being*** in an adverbial phrase.

Since they were angry, they decided to do something about the problem.
Being angry, they decided to do something about the problem.

You can change a **present perfect** or **past perfect verb** in an adverb clause to ***having* + past participle** in an adverbial phrase. We generally use *having* + past participle to suggest that the action in the adverbial phrase occurred at an earlier time than the action in the independent clause.

Because they had been moved by the situation, people became organ donors.
***Having* been moved** by the situation, people became organ donors.

8 Changing Passive Clauses

You can change a clause containing a **passive** verb to an adverbial phrase with a **past participle only**.

If you can omit the subordinating **conjunction** in an adverbial phrase **without changing the meaning** of the sentence, **delete the subject** and any auxiliaries in a passive sentence.

Since I was given two options, I chose the harder of the two.
Given two options, I chose the harder of the two.

BE CAREFUL! Sometimes the subordinating conjunction **cannot be omitted without changing the meaning** of the sentence. In these cases, to form an **adverb phrase**, delete the subject and change the form of *be* to ***being***.

Before I was told the nature of the problem, I had no idea what to do.
Before *being* told the nature of the problem, I had no idea what to do.
NOT ~~Told the nature of the problem~~, I had no idea what to do.

REFERENCE NOTE

For information on **shortening adjective clauses to adjective phrases**, see Unit 15 on page 249.

STEP 3 FOCUSED PRACTICE

EXERCISE 1 DISCOVER THE GRAMMAR

A GRAMMAR NOTES 1–5 **Look at the sentences based on the reading. Underline the adverb phrase in each sentence. Circle the subordinating conjunction.**

1. An Italian screamed at them while signaling them to stop.
2. On checking the children, Reg and Maggie found them in the back seat.
3. Before speeding away, Reg quickly weighed his options.
4. Upon realizing the danger they were in, Reg floored the gas pedal.
5. The criminals were placed on trial after being turned over to the police.
6. On returning to the United States, Nicholas's parents received requests to tell their son's story.

B GRAMMAR NOTES 1–8 **Read each pair of sentences based on the reading. Is the second sentence a correct rewriting of the first? Check *Yes* or *No*.**

	Yes	No
1. Having spent the day exploring ruins, Reg and Maggie were driving south. Spending the day exploring ruins, Reg and Maggie were driving south.	☐	☑
2. Not knowing what to do, Reg carefully weighed the options. Because he didn't know what to do, Reg carefully weighed the options.	☐	☐

	Yes	No
3. Shots rang out, shattering both windows on the driver's side of the car. Having shattered both windows on the driver's side of the car, shots rang out.	☐	☐
4. The Greens' car took off, easily outdistancing the bandits' car. Having outdistanced the bandits' car, the Greens' car took off.	☐	☐
5. Upon opening the door, Reg saw blood oozing from Nicholas's head. When he opened the door, Reg saw blood oozing from Nicholas's head.	☐	☐
6. After being rushed to a hospital, Nicholas lay in a coma for two days. After he was rushed to a hospital, Nicholas lay in a coma for two days.	☐	☐
7. Nicholas lay in a coma for two days, his status not changing. Nicholas lay in a coma for two days because his status didn't change.	☐	☐
8. How many of us would do the same thing, given the opportunity? How many of us would do the same thing if we were given the opportunity?	☐	☐

EXERCISE 2 ADVERB CLAUSES TO PHRASES

GRAMMAR NOTES 1–5 **Read the sentences. Circle the subjects in both clauses. If the subjects refer to the same person or thing, shorten the sentence by reducing or changing the adverb clause to a phrase. If the subjects are different, write *cannot be shortened*.**

1. When (I) saw some hungry children working, (they) asked me to buy them a meal.
   cannot be shortened
2. While we were traveling in Europe, we had several opportunities to help people.
   ____
3. Because the travelers had a flat tire, we stopped to help them fix it.
   ____
4. When my friend saw an injured person on the roadside, he pulled over to help.
   ____
5. While my roommate was recuperating in the hospital, I called her parents to inform them of the accident.
   ____
6. Because we realized that our friends were running late, we gave them a ride to the airport.
   ____
7. After the boy fell into the river, his friend dived into the water to rescue him.
   ____
8. As she was trying to fix her computer, Anna realized that she needed her brother's help.
   ____

EXERCISE 3 ADVERB CLAUSES; ADVERB AND ADVERBIAL PHRASES

A GRAMMAR NOTES 2–8 Read the article about animal emotion and compassion. There are ten adverb clauses in the article. The first has already been underlined. Find and underline nine more.

Animal Compassion and Emotion

MANY PEOPLE THINK that animals are fundamentally different from us. Since they are not human, animals supposedly cannot express emotions. Is this true? Are animals incapable of compassion and other emotions? Consider these accounts by Marc Bekoff, a professor emeritus of ecology at the University of Colorado and an expert on animal behavior. Bekoff recounts two situations in which elephants demonstrated compassion and other emotions.

In the first account, Bekoff describes a situation that took place at a reserve in Kenya. While Bekoff and a fellow researcher were observing elephants, they saw that a younger elephant named Babyl walked very slowly. She had trouble walking because she had been crippled some years previously. But Babyl was never allowed to fall too far behind while she was searching for food with her herd. The other elephants waited for Babyl because they sensed she needed protection from predators. Interestingly, Babyl's fellow elephants didn't seem to benefit in any material way from her presence. They seemed to change their regular behavior for her sake since they cared for her and wanted her to remain a part of the herd.

The second situation took place at an elephant sanctuary in Tennessee with two elephants, Shirley and Jenny. Compassionate individuals had brought both elephants to the sanctuary to live because they wanted the animals to recover from abuse they had suffered in the entertainment industry. When Shirley, an older female, arrived at the sanctuary, she was put in a stall next to Jenny, a younger female. To the keepers' astonishment, the two elephants reached out and touched each other through the bars separating them, and they roared in the typical elephant greeting. After their keepers checked the sanctuary records, they discovered that the elephants had been together in a circus twenty-two years previously. At that time, Jenny had been a calf and Shirley a twenty-something. It was obvious that the two elephants remembered each other, and they were happy to see each other. After they were reunited, the two elephants quickly became inseparable.

B Complete the sentences by changing each adverb clause that you underlined in A to an adverb or adverbial phrase.

1. *Not being human*, animals supposedly cannot express emotions.
2. ______________________________, Bekoff and a fellow researcher saw that a younger elephant named Babyl walked very slowly.
3. She had trouble walking, ______________________________.
4. But Babyl was never allowed to fall too far behind ______________________________.
5. The other elephants waited for Babyl, ______________________________.
6. They seemed to change their regular behavior for her sake, ______________________________.
7. Compassionate individuals had brought both elephants to the sanctuary to live, ______________________________.
8. ______________________________, Shirley was put in a stall next to Jenny, a younger female.
9. ______________________________, they discovered that the elephants had been together in a circus 22 years previously.
10. ______________________________, the two elephants quickly became inseparable.

EXERCISE 4 ADVERB AND ADVERBIAL PHRASES AND MAIN CLAUSES

GRAMMAR NOTES 1, 3–8 Look at the pictures, which are connected in a story. Write a sentence with a main clause and an adverb or adverbial phrase to describe the situation in each picture. Use the grammatical prompts and include any other necessary words.

1. (present participle)
Coming out of the train station, the tourists saw a boy selling guidebooks.

2. (present participle)
____
____

3. (*not* + present participle)

4. (past participle)

5. (present participle)

6. (*having* + past participle)

7. (*after* + present participle)

8. (*having* + past participle)

EXERCISE 5 EDITING

GRAMMAR NOTES 1–8 **Read the blog. There are ten mistakes in the use of adverb and adverbial phrases. The first mistake is already corrected. Find and correct nine more.**

A Helping Hand

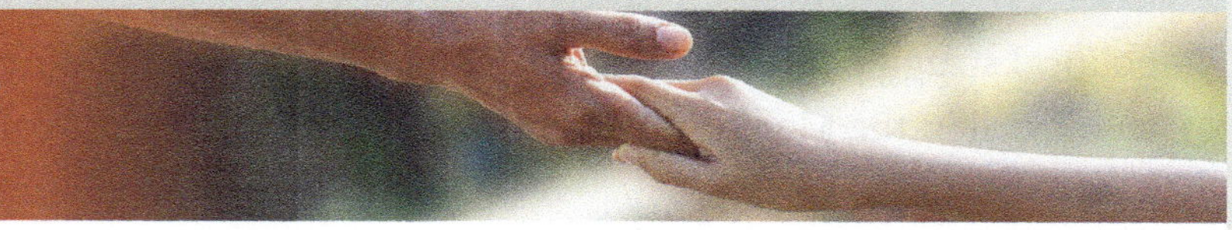

If you're at all like me, you hear a lot of requests to help others. ~~Barraging~~ Barraged by constant appeals for money to support homeless shelters, the Special Olympics, or the like, people tend to tune out. I certainly used to do that. I don't think I was selfish. But subjecting to so many requests, I felt overwhelmed, and my brain was numbed. After listening to yet another TV request asking viewers to sponsor a child overseas, I would say to myself, "I'll bet the money is pocketed by some local politician." Finally, convincing myself that I didn't have enough money to help others in any case, I was able to ignore all the requests. Or at least that was the way I thought before sent by my magazine to South America to do a human interest story on poor children. My opinions changed upon see the reality of the life of a poor child.

While landing in Santa Simona, I took a taxi to my hotel in the center of town, where I met Elena, a girl of ten or eleven. Sat on a dirty blanket on the sidewalk in front of the hotel, she caught my eye. Elena was trying to earn a living by selling mangoes. Smiled at me, she asked, "*Mangos, señor?*—Mangoes, sir?" I bought some mangoes and some other fruit, and we talked together. Elena's life had been difficult. Her parents were both dead, and she lived with an elderly aunt. Having polio at the age of five, she now walked with a limp. She and her aunt often went hungry.

Investigated the question the next day, I talked to several different authorities, and I learned that they were indeed trying to help. Having become convinced that money from sponsors does in fact get to those who need it, I knew my attitude had to change. Learning that I could sponsor Elena for less than a dollar a day, I began to feel ashamed. After all, I spend more than that on my dogs. But what remains most vivid in my mind is my vision of Elena. She didn't beg or feel sorry for herself. Sold her mangoes, she earned a living, and her spirit shone through in the process. So I say to all of you reading this: The next time you hear an ad about sponsoring a child, pay attention.

STEP 4 COMMUNICATION PRACTICE

EXERCISE 6 LISTENING

18|02 **A** **Listen to the news broadcast. Check (✓) the two subjects that are *not* mentioned.**

- ☐ political struggles in the nation of Franconia
- ☐ an oil spill in the Mediterranean
- ☐ a new vaccine for AIDS
- ☐ a new nation comes into existence
- ☐ World Cup news
- ☐ a rescue in a swimming pool

18|02 **B** **Read the questions. Listen again to the news broadcast. Then answer each question in a complete sentence.**

1. How did rebel leader Amalde respond when he was asked if he would go to the peace conference?

   He declined to commit himself to attending the conference.

2. What does the success of the upcoming conference depend on?

   ____

3. How has Mr. Tintor shown that he doesn't really want peace, according to Mr. Amalde?

   ____

4. What did an aide to President Tintor say in an interview about the upcoming peace conference?

   ____

5. What did researchers from the Global Health Foundation acknowledge?

   ____

6. What will the new nation be called?

   ____

7. When did the new government request billions of dollars in foreign aid?

   ____

8. What had Michaels nearly given up hope about?

   ____

9. How had Hutchinson become aware that Michaels was in trouble?

   ____

C **Work with a partner. Discuss the questions.**

1. Listening to the news broadcast in A, do you think the reporter shows compassion for the people he is reporting about? Give reasons for your answer.
2. Do you think journalists should show compassion while reporting the news?
3. When you consider the quality of news reporting today, what is your overall evaluation of it? What changes do you think would make it better?

EXERCISE 7 COMPASSIONATE ACTS

A DISCUSSION You are going to have a discussion about compassionate acts. First, think of a few examples of compassionate acts that you know about or have heard of. Why do these acts illustrate compassion?

B Work in a group. Tell your group members about your examples of compassionate acts. Then report interesting examples to the class.

EXAMPLE: Here's an example that happened to me. Driving through a rough neighborhood late one night with my friend, we saw a car accident. She insisted on stopping to help. I wanted to let the police handle it. We stopped, though, and it's a good thing we did. . . .

EXERCISE 8 GREYFRIARS BOBBY

A CRITICAL THINKING You are going to discuss whether animals can show compassion. First, read this short article about Greyfriars Bobby.

Greyfriars Bobby

A GREAT DEAL OF INFORMATION can be found today about Greyfriars Bobby, his name having been made famous in books and films. Bobby was a Skye terrier who lived in Edinburgh, Scotland. According to the most popular version of the story, Bobby belonged to John Gray, a night watchman for the Edinburgh police force. After having passed away, Gray was buried in Greyfriars Kirkwood, a cemetery in Edinburgh. Bobby is said to have spent fourteen years guarding Gray's grave, greatly mourning the loss of his master. Having become famous for his loyalty, Bobby was buried in the same cemetery upon dying in 1872. Residents of Edinburgh, feeling great admiration for Bobby's love and loyalty, erected a statue of the dog.

This traditional story of Bobby gradually came to be the most generally accepted version. But some people, not believing that the traditional story is accurate, point to different accounts. One such account claims that the real John Gray was a farmer, not a night watchman. Skeptics also claim that there are many documented stories of stray dogs living in European cemeteries. Fed by visitors to the cemeteries, the dogs came to be considered over time the guardians of the graves of their supposed masters.

B Work in a group. Discuss the questions.

1. After reading the article above, which version of the Greyfriars Bobby story do you feel is more accurate? Why?
2. Taking into account your own experiences with animals, do you think they have feelings? Are they capable of showing grief or any other kind of emotion?
3. If possible, give a personal example of an animal showing grief or another emotion.

C Share the main points of your discussion with the class.

EXAMPLE: A: Our group thinks it is obvious that Greyfriars Bobby waited at his master's grave, hoping that he would come back.
B: We disagree. Being animals, dogs can't understand death and loss. . . .

EXERCISE 9 HAVING VISITED ITALY . . .

A GAME **Work in a group. Look at the beginnings of the sentences. For each item, make up at least three sentences that start with these words. Use your imagination.**

EXAMPLE: Having visited Italy before . . .
A: Having visited Italy before, I didn't want to go to Rome again.
B: Having visited Italy before, I decided to go to France instead.
C: Having visited Italy before, I knew the best places to get ice cream!

1. Having visited Italy before . . .
2. While traveling in China . . .
3. Witnessing the accident . . .
4. Having seen the way animals behave . . .
5. Wanting to help people . . .
6. Upon completing my college degree . . .
7. Never having been to Africa . . .
8. After reading the article about refugees . . .
9. Presented with the opportunity to be in a movie . . .
10. Not having any money . . .

B Work with the class. Read some of your sentences aloud. Vote on the most interesting, amusing, or imaginative sentences.

FROM GRAMMAR TO WRITING

A BEFORE YOU WRITE You are going to write an essay about a compassionate act you witnessed. Write a few sentences about it.

B WRITE Using your ideas in A, write a five-paragraph essay about the compassionate act you have chosen. Remember to use adverb and adverbial phrases. Try to avoid the common mistakes shown in the chart. Use the example below to help you begin your essay.

EXAMPLE: The best example of compassion I have witnessed occurred about a year ago. Having been invited to an office party, I stayed at work late, and I finally managed to leave about 10:00 p.m. Driving home on the freeway, I suddenly felt the car slow down and heard a loud noise. Realizing that I probably had a flat tire, I quickly pulled over to the side of the road. I looked for the jack to change the flat but couldn't find it. Just then a group of teenagers slowed down and stopped. I thought to myself, "Uh-oh, I'm in trouble now." That's not what happened, though. . . .

Common Mistakes in Using Adverb and Adverbial Phrases

Don't reduce an adverb clause to an adverb or adverbial phrase unless the **subjects** in the two original clauses are the **same**.	**Running into the room**, Janet announced her engagement. NOT Running into the room, ~~the engagement was announced by Janet~~.
Don't begin an adverb phrase with *when* if the meaning is "at the time something occurred." Use ***on*** or ***upon*** instead.	**On realizing** that a serious accident had happened, we stopped to help. NOT ~~When~~ realizing that a serious accident had happened, we stopped to help.
Don't use a present participle in an adverbial phrase when the time frame of the two original clauses is different. Use ***having*** + **past participle**.	**Having gone** to Spain on our last trip, we went to Portugal on this trip. NOT ~~Going~~ to Spain on our last trip, we went to Portugal on this trip.

C CHECK YOUR WORK Look at your essay. Underline adverb and adverbial phrases. Use the Editing Checklist to check your work.

Editing Checklist

Did you . . . ?

- ☐ make sure the subjects in the original clauses are the same before reducing one of them to an adverb or adverbial phrase
- ☐ use *on* or *upon* + present participle in adverb phrases if the meaning is "at the time something occurred"
- ☐ use *having* + present participle in adverbial phrases when the time frame of the two original clauses is different

D REVISE YOUR WORK Read your essay again. Can you improve your writing? Make changes if necessary.

UNIT 18 REVIEW

Test yourself on the grammar of the unit.

A Complete the sentences. Circle the correct answers.

1. Not knowing / Because not knowing how we could help, we called the volunteer line.
2. Having caught cheating / Caught cheating, she failed the course.
3. Getting the tickets / Having gotten the tickets, we decided to give them to kids who'd never seen a play.
4. Taksim turned off the lights before leaving / before left home.
5. On realizing / When realizing they had no money, we decided to pay their bill.
6. During relaxing / Relaxing at home, I remembered all the people who had helped me.
7. Having visited / Visiting Asia, I knew how beautiful it was.
8. We didn't know where to go before given / being given directions.

B Complete the sentences with the correct forms of the words in parentheses.

1. ______________ (hear) a noise downstairs, Melinda called 911.
2. Juan listens to music ______________ (while / do) his homework.
3. ______________ (eat) too fast, Bill got a bad case of indigestion.
4. ______________ (upon / finish) the project, the crew celebrated.
5. ______________ (be) to Japan previously, we skipped it on our last trip.
6. Sam recovered ______________ (after / take) to the hospital.
7. ______________ (give) the choice, I decided to walk to work.

C Find and correct five mistakes in the paragraph.

When arriving at the Cairo airport, I was certain I had plenty of time to make the connection for my next flight. Not eating on the plane and feel very hungry, I stopped at a restaurant to get some food. Lost track of time, I enjoyed my meal. Then I glanced at my boarding pass and saw I had fifteen minutes to make it to my flight gate. I had a lot of heavy bags, so I grabbed them and started running toward the gate, known I'd never make it on time. Just then, out of the blue, a man I'd never met took a couple of my suitcases and got me to the gate with five minutes to spare. I wish I could have returned the favor.

Now check your answers on page 431.

UNIT 19

Connectors

MEMORY

OUTCOMES
- Use a range of connectors and transition words to connect ideas
- Identify key details in a scientific article
- Identify key points in a training workshop
- Discuss the topic of memory, expressing opinions, agreeing and disagreeing
- Write an essay about a memorable experience

STEP 1 GRAMMAR IN CONTEXT

BEFORE YOU READ

Discuss the questions.

1. What is your earliest memory?
2. Do you ever have trouble remembering things? Are there any strategies that help you to remember?

READ

19|01 Read this article about memory.

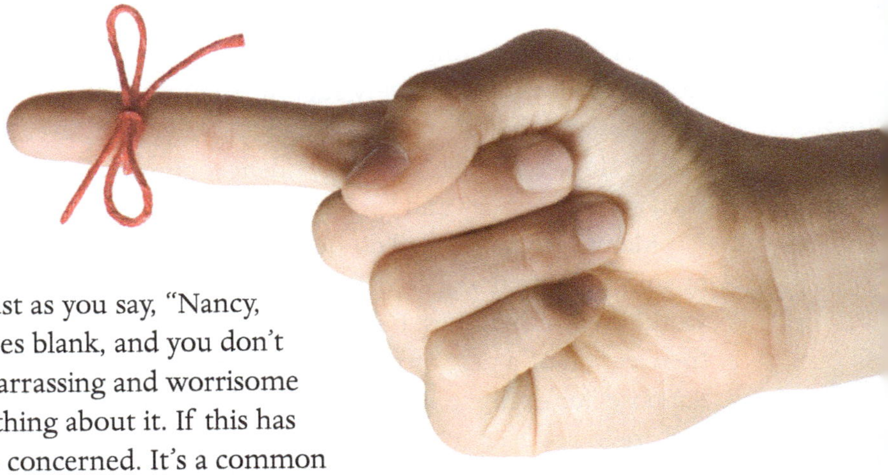

Try to Remember

You're with a friend, and suddenly up walks somebody you've known for a long time. You want to introduce this person to your friend. However, just as you say, "Nancy, I'd like you to meet . . . ," your mind goes blank, and you don't remember the person's name. It's embarrassing and worrisome enough to make you want to do something about it. If this has happened to you, though, don't be too concerned. It's a common problem. As people get older, they tend to become more forgetful. They can't remember everyday details like computer passwords, email addresses, and their friends' names.

I used to worry about memory loss myself. Therefore, I decided to do some research into the problem, and I learned a number of interesting things about memory and how it works. I also discovered that even though memory loss is probably unavoidable, there are things you can do to slow it down.

How does memory work? First of all, there are two types of memory: long-term and short-term. Long-term memory refers to our memories of things that we experienced some time ago and that form the core of our knowledge of ourselves. In contrast, short-term memory can be called "working" memory—the type we use in processing such things as passwords and the names of new people we meet.

As we grow older, our long-term memory holds up remarkably well. Thus, we are able to remember the highlight of the vacation we took to the Everglades at the age of ten and the alligators we saw there. Meanwhile, our short-term memory tends to deteriorate. We

Short-term memory **Long-term memory**

have difficulty remembering things like where we put our house keys because our short-term memory fails us.

Why does short-term memory decline? Short-term memory operations occur in the frontal lobes[1] of the brain. As people age, these lobes tend to lose mass, as much as 5 to 10 percent per decade. Short-term memory operations require space in order to function correctly. Therefore, as the lobes become smaller, short-term memory gets worse.

It is difficult or impossible to completely avoid memory decline. However, it can be slowed. Maintaining a steady supply of glucose[2] can mitigate the problem of shrinking lobes. Consequently, elderly people would do well to eat several small meals each day rather than two or three big ones. There is evidence, moreover, that staying mentally active can help sustain our memory and keep it from deterioration.

Many companies feed on our fears of memory loss, and they attempt to induce us to buy products that will supposedly enhance our ability to remember. Do these products work? Well, sometimes. But it's important to keep in mind that all memory aids depend on the creation of a peg, or mental picture, on which to hang something we want to recollect. Suppose, for example, you have difficulty remembering names. Let's say you're at a party and are introduced to a woman named Sarah Baer. First, look for distinguishing features. You see that Sarah has long, thick hair, rather like a bear's fur. Second, think of words that will help you associate these features with this person. *Baer* = *Bear*. Furthermore, the first syllable of "Sarah" rhymes with "bear." *Sar* and *Baer*. It might work. The point is to create a mental picture you can relate to the person, place, or thing you want to recall. The more vivid the association is, the greater is the chance that you'll remember it.

Most importantly, memory improvement takes work. The real problem in remembering something we learned is often the fact that we weren't paying enough attention when we learned it. Think about the last time you were introduced to someone whose name you immediately forgot. Were you really paying attention to the person's name, or were you focusing on the impression you might be making? Memory courses can work, of course, but they depend on techniques we can create and perform for ourselves. The real trick lies in our willingness to tap[3] and use what's within us.

1 *lobes:* rounded parts of organs
2 *glucose:* a natural form of sugar
3 *tap:* take from an available source

AFTER YOU READ

A VOCABULARY **Match the words in bold with their meanings.**

_____	1. Companies often **induce** us to buy their products.	a.	remember
_____	2. Long-term memory forms the **core** of our self-knowledge.	b.	best aspect
_____	3. We are able to remember the **highlight** of our vacation.	c.	cause, make
_____	4. A steady supply of glucose can **mitigate** the problem.	d.	sharp, clear, colorful
_____	5. Meanwhile, our short-term memory tends to **deteriorate**.	e.	improve
_____	6. Memory aids can **enhance** our ability to remember.	f.	make less harmful
_____	7. We need a peg to help us to **recollect** something important.	g.	become worse
_____	8. The more **vivid** the image is, the better you'll remember.	h.	central part

B COMPREHENSION **Read the statements. Check (✓) *True* or *False*. Correct the false statements.**

	True	False
1. Forgetting things such as another person's name is quite uncommon.	☐	☐
2. Long-term memory refers to things we experienced some time ago.	☐	☐
3. Short-term memory can be termed "working" memory.	☐	☐
4. Our short-term memory holds up better than our long-term memory.	☐	☐
5. Memory problems are generally short-term memory problems.	☐	☐
6. Elderly people should eat several small meals daily.	☐	☐
7. There is no evidence that staying mentally active can slow memory deterioration.	☐	☐
8. A key reason we forget things is that we often weren't paying enough attention when we learned something.	☐	☐

C DISCUSSION **Work with a partner. Compare and justify your answers in B. Do you agree with the statement in the reading that our long-term memory holds up better than our short-term memory? Discuss.**

STEP 2 GRAMMAR PRESENTATION

CONNECTORS

Connectors: Placement and Punctuation

Coordinating Conjunction	I was worried, **so** I did some research.
Subordinating Conjunction	**Because** I was worried, I did some research.
	I did some research **because** I was worried.
Transition	I was worried. **Therefore**, I did some research.
	I was worried. I, **therefore**, did some research.
	I was worried. I did some research, **therefore**.

Connectors: Functions

	Coordinating Conjunctions	Subordinating Conjunctions	Transitions
Addition	and, nor, or		besides, furthermore, indeed, in addition, moreover
Condition	or	if, even if, only if, unless	otherwise
Contrast	but, or, yet	although, though, even though, whereas, while	however, in contrast, meanwhile, nevertheless, nonetheless, on the contrary, on the other hand
Cause/Reason	for	as, because, since	
Effect/Result	so		consequently, otherwise, therefore, thus
Time		after, before, when, while	afterwards, meanwhile, next

Transitions: Connecting Sentences

Addition	She couldn't remember names.	**Furthermore**, she forgot addresses.
	Human brains lose mass.	**Indeed**, they may lose 10 percent a year.
Condition	Older people should eat several small meals a day.	**Otherwise**, their memory might deteriorate.
Contrast	I often have trouble with names.	**However**, I always remember faces.
	We all forget things.	**Nevertheless**, we shouldn't worry.
Effect/Result	I wasn't concentrating when we met.	**Consequently**, I couldn't recall her name.
	He wanted to improve his memory.	**Therefore**, he took a memory course.
Time	He studied for his course.	**Meanwhile**, his wife read a book.
	She completed the book.	**Next**, she bought a memory video.

Transitions: Connecting Blocks of Text	
Listing Ideas in Order of Time/Importance	**First of all**, we need to distinguish between two types of memory.
Giving Examples	**For example**, you need to stay mentally active.
Summarizing	**To summarize**: Memory improvement requires work.
Adding a Conclusion	**In conclusion**, we can prevent the deterioration of memory.

GRAMMAR NOTES

1 Types of Connectors

Connectors (often called **discourse connectors**) are words and phrases that **connect ideas** both within sentences and between sentences and larger blocks of text.

Three types of connectors are:

- **coordinating conjunctions**

  I try hard, **but** I can never remember new people's names.

- **subordinating conjunctions**

  I can't remember her name, **although** I can remember her face.

- **transitions**

  I spent a lot of money on a memory improvement course. **However**, it was a waste of money.

BE CAREFUL! Don't confuse subordinating conjunctions with transitions. They are often similar in their basic meaning but have different sentence patterns. **Subordinating clauses** begin **dependent clauses**. **Transitions** occur in **independent clauses** and often begin them.

Although I've been working on improving my memory, I haven't had much success.
(subordinating conjunction introducing a dependent clause)

I've been working on improving my memory. **However**, I haven't had much success.
(transition between two sentences)

NOT I've been working on improving my memory. ~~Although,~~ I haven't had much success.

2 Coordinating and Subordinating Conjunctions

There are two types of conjunctions: **coordinating conjunctions** and **subordinating conjunctions**.

Coordinating conjunctions join two **independent** clauses. Coordinating conjunctions come between independent clauses and are normally preceded by a comma.

The seven coordinating conjunctions are:

and	*for*	*or*	*yet*
but	*nor*	*so*	

I often forget things, **so** I write everything down.
I heard what you said, **but** what did you mean?

Subordinating conjunctions connect **ideas** within sentences. They come at the **beginning** of subordinate (**dependent**) clauses. If a subordinate clause comes first in a sentence, it is followed by a comma. If a subordinate clause comes second, it is not normally preceded by a comma.

Because I often forget things**,** I write everything down.
I write everything down **because** I often forget things.

BE CAREFUL! The coordinating conjunction ***nor*** is negative. Reverse the subject and verb after it.

Helena doesn't remember names consistently, ***nor* does she** remember passwords.
NOT Helena doesn't remember names consistently, nor ~~she does~~ remember passwords.

3 Definition of Transitions

Transitions are single words or expressions that **connect ideas** between **sentences** or larger sections of text.

Transitions that connect sentences can come at the **beginning** of a sentence, **within** it, or at the **end**. At the beginning of a sentence, a transition is preceded by a period or semicolon and followed by a comma. In the middle of a sentence, it is preceded and followed by a comma. At the end of a sentence, it is preceded by a comma.

Common transitions include:

besides	*in addition*	*otherwise*
consequently	*meanwhile*	*therefore*
however	*nevertheless*	

He said he would support the idea. **However,** I wouldn't count on him.

He said he would support the idea. I wouldn't**, however,** count on him.

He said he would support the idea. I wouldn't count on him**, however**.

BE CAREFUL! If a transition comes at the beginning of an **independent** clause, it must be preceded by a **period** or a **semicolon** and not by a comma.

I can remember people's names **easily; however**, I can't usually remember their phone numbers.
NOT I can remember people's names ~~easily, however,~~ I can't usually remember their phone numbers.

4 Transitions to Connect Sentences and Independent Clauses

There are five principal types of **transitions** that **connect sentences** and independent clauses.

These transitions show **addition**:

additionally	*likewise*	*moreover*
also	*in addition*	*plus*
besides	*in fact*	
furthermore	*indeed*	

I remember her telephone number. **In addition**, I remember what street she lives on.

I live too far away to visit you; **besides**, I can never remember your address.

The transition *otherwise* shows **condition**. This transition indicates that a result **opposite** to what is **expected** will happen if a certain action isn't taken.

I need to write down your email address. **Otherwise**, I'll never remember it.

These transitions show **contrast**:

however	*nevertheless*
in contrast	*nonetheless*
in spite of/despite that	*still*
instead	*though*

Her speech was good; **nevertheless**, I can't support her proposals.

Jim thinks I'm against his ideas. **On the contrary**, I'm one of his biggest supporters.

USAGE NOTE ***Though*** is a **contrast transition** when it occurs at the **end** of an **independent** clause and its meaning is equivalent to that of *however*. In other positions, it is a **subordinating conjunction**.

I carefully wrote down her name on a piece of paper. I lost the piece of paper, **though**. *(transition)*

Though I've told him my name many times, he never remembers it. *(subordinating conjunction)*

These transitions show **effect/result**:

accordingly	*on account of this*
as a result	*otherwise*
because of that	*therefore*
consequently	*thus*

I was not paying close attention when she was introduced. **Consequently**, her name escapes me.

This new memory technique is helpful; **therefore**, I can recommend it to you.

USAGE NOTE ***Otherwise*** shows both **condition** and **effect/result**.

I need to say people's names when I'm introduced to them; **otherwise**, I forget them. *(condition)*

Maryam must take her medications; **otherwise**, she'll get sick. *(result)*

These transitions show **relationships** of actions, events, and ideas **in time**:

after that	*in the meantime*	*next*
afterwards	*meanwhile*	*then*

Bob spent three years in the military. **Meanwhile**, his brother was earning a college degree.

I went to a memory workshop. **Afterwards**, I could remember almost everything I heard.

5 Transitions to Connect Blocks of Text

Some transitions connect **blocks of text**. They usually come at the beginning of a sentence and are commonly followed by a **comma**.

These transitions **list** ideas in **order of time** or **importance**:

finally	*most importantly*	*second*
first (of all)	*next*	*third* (etc.)

First of all, let's consider the question of short-term memory.
Most importantly, let's consider the issue of memory-improvement courses.

These transitions **give examples**:

for example	*to name/mention a few*
for instance	

I can remember lots of things about people. **For example**, I always remember what they're wearing.

I remember many books I've read: *Middlemarch, War and Peace*, and *Things Fall Apart*, **to name a few.**

These transitions **summarize**:

all in all	*in summary*	*to summarize*
in sum	*overall*	

In sum, these are the key points about memory loss.

All in all, the key point is that memory can be improved.

These transitions **add a conclusion**:

in conclusion	*to conclude*

To conclude, let me just say that we can improve our memory if we work at it.

REFERENCE NOTES

For more information on **subordinating conjunctions**, see Unit 17 on page 285 and Appendix 22 on page 420.

For more complete lists of **transitions**, see Appendices 23–24 on page 421.

STEP 3 FOCUSED PRACTICE

EXERCISE 1 DISCOVER THE GRAMMAR

A GRAMMAR NOTES 1–5 **Read the sentences based on the reading. Identify each of the underlined words as a *coordinating conjunction* (C), *subordinating conjunction* (S), or *transition* (T).**

_____ **1.** I decided to do some research into the problem, and I learned a number of interesting things.

_____ **2.** As we grow older, our long-term memory holds up remarkably well. Thus, we are able to remember the highlight of the vacation we took at the age of ten.

_____ **3.** Meanwhile, our short-term memory tends to deteriorate.

_____ **4.** We have difficulty remembering things like names and phone numbers because our short-term memory fails us.

_____ **5.** Suppose, for example, you have difficulty remembering names.

_____ **6.** Were you really paying attention, or were you focusing on the impression you might be making?

B GRAMMAR NOTES 3–5 **Read the sentences based on the reading. Underline the transition in each sentence. Then identify it as a transition of *addition* (*A*), *contrast* (*C*), *effect / result* (*R*), *time* (*T*), or *order of importance or presentation* (*O*).**

_____ **1.** However, just as you start to introduce your friend, your mind goes blank, and you don't remember the person's name.

_____ **2.** The frontal lobes lose mass; therefore, short-term memory gets worse.

_____ **3.** First of all, there are two types of memory, long-term and short-term.

_____ **4.** Consequently, elderly people would do well to eat several small meals each day.

_____ **5.** Meanwhile, things have been happening to our short-term memory.

_____ **6.** It is difficult or impossible to completely avoid memory decline. However, it can be slowed.

_____ **7.** Furthermore, the first syllable of "Sarah" rhymes with "bear."

_____ **8.** Most importantly, memory improvement takes work.

EXERCISE 2 PUNCTUATING SENTENCES WITH CONNECTORS

GRAMMAR NOTES 2–3 **Punctuate the sentences with connectors. Add commas or semicolons as necessary.**

1. Frank has an excellent memory however he doesn't use it to good advantage.
2. Frank has an excellent memory but he doesn't use it to good advantage.
3. Marta was having trouble remembering things so she signed up for a memory course.
4. Marta was having trouble remembering things consequently she signed up for a memory course.
5. You need to start taking better notes otherwise you won't do well on the exam.
6. You need to start taking better notes or you won't do well on the exam.
7. I have difficulty remembering people's names yet I can always remember what they were wearing.
8. I have difficulty remembering people's names on the other hand I can always remember what they were wearing.
9. Amanda forgot to pay her bill so the power company turned off her electricity.
10. Amanda forgot to pay her bill therefore the power company turned off her electricity.

EXERCISE 3 CONNECTORS

GRAMMAR NOTES 2–5 **Read this segment of a radio broadcast. Complete the sentences with the connectors from the box. Use each connector once.**

first	in addition	meanwhile	otherwise	therefore
however	in fact	~~next~~	second	

___Next___ (1.), we focus on the aftermath of the recent earthquake. Investigators have determined that it will cost approximately eight billion dollars to rebuild damaged highways. According to the governor, two actions have to be taken: ______________ (2.), the federal government will have to approve disaster funds to pay for reconstruction; ______________ (3.), insurance investigators will need to determine how much their companies will have to pay in the rebuilding effort. With luck, the governor says, some key highways could be rebuilt within six months. He cautioned, ______________ (4.), that the six-month figure is only an estimate. The process cannot move forward without funds from insurance companies, and certain insurance companies have been slow to approve such funds in the past. The rebuilding effort could, ______________ (5.), drag on for at least a year. ______________ (6.), bad weather could prevent the speedy completion of the project. Listeners may remember that after the last earthquake, repair projects took much longer than government officials had predicted. ______________ (7.), it is taking some people as long as four hours to commute to work, and others haven't been able to get to work at all. Interviewed by our news team, one commuter who works in an office downtown said, "It took me three hours to drive to work last Friday. I knew I'd have to find some other way of getting there; ______________ (8.), I'd never make it. Well, yesterday the train got me there in fifty minutes, and the trip was really pleasant. I even had the chance to read the morning paper. ______________ (9.), I'm going to switch permanently to the train. Hopefully, my memories of traffic jams will be just that: memories."

EXERCISE 4 CONJUNCTIONS AND TRANSITIONS

GRAMMAR NOTES 2–4 Look at the pictures of Hank's stressful morning. Using the words in parentheses, write two sentences describing what happened in each picture. Use commas to join clauses connected by coordinating conjunctions. Use semicolons to join clauses connected by transitions.

1. (and / in addition)
Hank didn't take a shower, and he didn't have any breakfast.
Hank didn't take a shower; in addition, he didn't have any breakfast.

2. (but / however)

3. (so / consequently)

4. (and / moreover)

5. (in the meantime / meanwhile)

6. (or / otherwise)

EXERCISE 5 EDITING

GRAMMAR NOTES 1–5 Read the student composition. There are nine mistakes involving connectors. The first mistake is already corrected. Find and correct eight more. You may add or eliminate words, but do not change word order or punctuation.

My Car Is Moving to the Suburbs

Yesterday, I drove my car to the college. I usually have trouble finding a parking place, ~~however~~ *but* this time it was almost impossible. There were simply no parking places anywhere near the campus, so I had to park in the downtown mall. When I finished class, I walked back to the mall. Therefore, I couldn't remember where I'd parked my car! Believe it or not, it took me forty-five minutes to find it. I've had enough of this, yet I've decided that I'm going to send my car to a new home in the suburbs.

I used to think that a car was the most wonderful thing in the world. I loved the freedom of being able to drive to my job or to the college whenever I wanted. To cut down on costs, I joined a carpool with four other people. The carpool was OK, nevertheless I didn't like having to wait around when my carpool members weren't ready to leave. Consequently, I started driving alone, and that worked really well for a while.

Although, I've recently changed my mind about owning a car. Now it's clear to me that there are just too many disadvantages to having a car in town. For example, sitting stalled in your car in a traffic jam is stressful, besides it's a phenomenal waste of time. Whereas, there's always the chance my car will be vandalized when I park it on the city streets. I have to park on the streets because it would cost me $200 a month to park my car in a parking garage.

Nonetheless, I've decided to leave my car at my cousin Brent's house in the suburbs. Otherwise, I'll end up going broke paying for parking and a course in memory improvement. My car will have a good home, and I'll use it just for longer trips. When I'm in the city, though, I'll take the bus or the tram, otherwise I'll walk. They say you can meet some interesting people on the bus. Maybe I'll find the love of my life. My only problem will be remembering which bus to take.

STEP 4 COMMUNICATION PRACTICE

EXERCISE 6 LISTENING

19|02 **A** **Listen to the excerpt from a memory training workshop. Check (✓) the two things that are true.**

☐ The workshop visitor says he's from Hawaii.
☐ The visitor has a Hawaiian name.
☐ The visitor is wearing a tuxedo.
☐ The visitor is wearing brown shoes.

19|02 **B** **Listen again. Complete the sentences. Circle the correct answers.**

1. The workshop leader says clients like to be called by their names; therefore, _____.
   a. it's polite to do that **(b.)** it's good business to do that
2. To get names into your short-term memory, first, the leader says that you should _____.
   a. call clients by their names **b.** notice particular things about clients
3. A visitor interrupts the workshop, claiming that money has been stolen. However, _____.
   a. the thief is never identified **b.** the story about the theft wasn't real.
4. One participant knows the visit wasn't real because the visitor wasn't in uniform. In addition, _____.
   a. the leader didn't seem surprised **b.** visitors aren't allowed to interrupt meetings
5. The leader says the participants were able to remember the visitor's first name because _____.
   a. they repeated the name out loud **b.** it's an unusual name
6. One participant was able to remember the visitor's last name because _____.
   a. the leader repeated his name **b.** it's an easy name to remember

7. The visitor said good-bye in an unusual way. Consequently, the participants ____.
   a. remembered it b. didn't understand it

8. Summing up the main points of the experience, the leader says that, most importantly, the participants ____.
   a. always need to write things down b. need to focus their attention consistently

9. The leader says the participants remembered the unusual things, but they need to work on remembering ____.
   a. the ordinary things b. the complicated things

C **Work with a partner. Discuss the questions.**

1. What are things that are relatively easy for you to remember? Why?
2. What are things that are difficult for you to remember? Why?

EXERCISE 7 FAMOUS QUOTATIONS ABOUT MEMORY

CRITICAL THINKING **Work in a group. Read the quotations about memory. Choose five quotations and discuss them. What do they mean? Do you agree with them? Why or why not? Then report your conclusions to the class.**

1. Remembrance of things past is not necessarily the remembrance of things as they were. *—Marcel Proust, author*

   EXAMPLE: A: I think it is true that we can remember a lot of things from the past, even though we sometimes don't remember them right. I think we often remember things the way we think they should have been.
   B: I agree this is sometimes the case. However, I think that if we're really honest with ourselves, our memories can be very accurate.

2. There are some things one remembers even though they may never have happened. *—Harold Pinter, author*

3. Those who cannot remember the past are condemned to repeat it. *—George Santayana, philosopher*

4. Sometimes you can't let go of the past without facing it again. *—Gail Tsukiyama, author*

5. One of the keys to happiness is a bad memory. *—Rita Mae Brown, author*

6. People have an annoying habit of remembering things they shouldn't. *—Christopher Paolini, author*

7. If you tell the truth, you don't have to remember anything. *—Mark Twain, author*

8. Remember tonight . . . for it is the beginning of always. *—Dante Alighieri, author*

9. Always carry a notebook. And I mean always. The short-term memory only retains information for three minutes; unless it is committed to paper you can lose an idea forever. *—Will Self, author and political commentator*

EXERCISE 8 HOW MUCH CAN YOU REMEMBER?

A PICTURE DISCUSSION Study the painting for two minutes. Then close your book. Write down as many details as you can remember. Then open your book again and check your memory. Note the details you were able to remember and those you were not able to remember.

First, I remembered that there were dogs in the painting. . . .
However, I didn't remember how many dogs there were. . . .

Kitchen Still Life with a Maid and Young Boy
Frans Snyders (Flemish painter, 1579–1657)

B Work in a small group. Compare the details you were able to remember best with those that the other members of the group remembered. Then discuss the questions below with the class.

1. Why do you think you were able to remember certain things in the painting better than others?
2. What is your reaction to the painting? Do you like it, dislike it, or are you neutral about it? Why?

FROM GRAMMAR TO WRITING

A BEFORE YOU WRITE You are going to write an essay about an experience that you remember well. Write a few sentences about each of the following points.

- What the memory is
- Why the memory is important to you
- Why you believe you remember it well

B WRITE Using your ideas in A, write a five-paragraph essay about the memory you have chosen. Remember to use connectors. Try to avoid the common mistakes shown in the chart. Use the example below to help you begin your essay.

EXAMPLE: One of my strongest, and most painful, memories is of my piano recital when I was thirteen years old. I had been taking piano lessons for three years. My piano teacher scheduled me for a recital. I was supposed to play two easy songs and one difficult one. My teacher had told me that I was making excellent progress; therefore, I was excited about the recital, and I practiced a lot for it. However, things didn't go at all as planned . . .

Common Mistakes in Using Connectors	
Don't confuse subordinating conjunctions with transitions. **Subordinating conjunctions** begin **dependent** clauses. **Transitions** begin **sentences** and independent clauses.	I tried hard to remember everyone's name. **However,** I forgot a few of them. NOT I tried hard to remember everyone's name. ~~Although,~~ I forgot a few of them.
Don't connect **independent clauses** with just a comma. Use a **period** or **semicolon** between independent clauses.	Mo forgot her **phone; therefore,** she couldn't call. OR Mo forgot her **phone. Therefore,** she couldn't call. NOT Mo forgot her ~~phone, therefore~~ she couldn't call.
Don't confuse *though* as a transition with *though* as a subordinating conjunction. ***Though*** as a transition normally comes at the **end** of an independent clause.	I can remember faces. I have trouble remembering names, **though**. *(transition)* **Though** I can remember faces, I have trouble remembering names. *(subordinating conjunction)*

C CHECK YOUR WORK Look at your essay. Underline the connectors. Use the Editing Checklist to check your work.

Editing Checklist

Did you . . . ?

☐ use subordinating conjunctions in dependent clauses and transitions in independent clauses
☐ use periods or semicolons between independent clauses
☐ correctly use *though* as either a subordinating conjunction or a transition

D REVISE YOUR WORK Read your essay again. Can you improve your writing? Make changes if necessary.

UNIT 19 REVIEW

Test yourself on the grammar of the unit.

A Complete the sentences. Circle the correct answers.

1. I never forget a face; and / however, I have trouble remembering names.
2. I never forget a face, besides / though I have trouble remembering names.
3. Because / Besides Hari forgot to pay his utility bill, the city turned off his water.
4. Hari forgot to pay his utility bill; and / therefore, the city turned off his water.
5. The house is too expensive for us; otherwise / besides, I don't really like it.
6. The house is too expensive for us, and / though I don't really like it.
7. You'd better get up right now, or / because you'll miss the bus.
8. You'd better get up right now; however / otherwise, you'll miss the bus.

B Add commas and semicolons to the sentences to give them correct punctuation.

1. I was exhausted so I went to bed at 8:00 p.m.
2. I've visited many exotic places for instance I've been to Bali, Marrakesh, and Tasmania.
3. We need to remember to get tickets otherwise we won't get seats.
4. Nora forgot her passport as a result she missed her flight.
5. Even though Bao has a degree he has a low-paying job.
6. As soon as I got off the train I took a taxi to the hotel.
7. You're too young to have a car besides cars are very expensive.

C Find and correct five mistakes in the conversation.

A: I heard you're taking a memory-improvement course, how's it coming along?

B: The course itself is fine. Although, it's pretty expensive. It's worth it, but.

A: I've been thinking about taking one, too, however, I wonder if I would really learn anything. Would you recommend your course?

B: Yes, I would, for why don't you sign up?

Now check your answers on page 431.

Noun Clauses

UNIT 20

Noun Clauses: Subjects, Objects, and Complements

BIRTH ORDER

UNIT 21

Direct and Indirect Speech

COMMUNICATION AND MISUNDERSTANDING

PART 8

OUTCOMES

- Form and use noun clauses as subjects, objects, and complements
- Identify key details in a psychology article
- Identify advice given in a counseling session
- Discuss the topic of birth order, responding to questions and presenting conclusions
- Write an essay on the topic of birth order

OUTCOMES

- Report what someone said, using direct and indirect speech, making necessary changes
- Identify key concepts in a transcribed interview
- Identify details in an interview
- Discuss the topic of communication, expressing opinions and reporting on what others said
- Write an essay about a past conflict

UNIT

20 Noun Clauses: Subjects, Objects, and Complements

BIRTH ORDER

OUTCOMES

- Form and use noun clauses as subjects, objects, and complements
- Identify key details in a psychology article
- Identify advice given in a counseling session
- Discuss the topic of birth order, responding to questions and presenting conclusions
- Write an essay on the topic of birth order

STEP 1 GRAMMAR IN CONTEXT

BEFORE YOU READ

Discuss the questions.

1. In your view, can people change their character, or is it basically determined at birth?
2. Do you think the order in which children are born might affect their character? Why or why not?

READ

20|01 Read this article about birth order.

Does It Matter When You Were Born?

Let's see if you can answer this question: There are two men, one named Sam and the other named Jerry. They're quite similar. Sam is a perfectionist, and so is Jerry. Jerry, always a high achiever, was president of his high school class. So was Sam. Neither man went to college, though both did become successful businessmen. Jerry has always been an innovator. This has made him a leader in most of his enterprises, just like Sam. Sam always tries to obey rules. Jerry does too. Jerry has never liked liberal ideas. Nor has Sam. The question is why they are so similar.

"Wait!" you say. "I know what the explanation is. They're identical twins. That's why they're so similar." Sorry, but that isn't it. They're not twins, or even related to each other, but they are both firstborns. Sam and Jerry are examples of what researchers call the birth-order theory. According to this theory, the order in which children are born plays a significant role in the formation of their personalities and in the way they ultimately turn out.[1] Does this sound like some crazy new idea? It isn't. It's been around for a while.

The main idea behind the birth-order theory is simple: Firstborn children enjoy a special relationship with their parents simply because they were there before any other children were. When other children come along, firstborns understand that these new arrivals represent a challenge to their special relationship. For this reason, firstborns tend to be conservative, rule-oriented, and opposed to change. They want to keep things as they are. Other children in the family have a different challenge. They must somehow adapt to the family dynamic and find a niche in their parents' affections. They sense that they have to become different from the oldest child, so they do. They learn to do whatever helps them establish their own identity.

1 *turn out:* develop in the end

One of the main supporters of the birth-order theory is Frank Sulloway, a researcher who did a twenty-six-year study of about 7,000 famous people in history and then performed a computer analysis. What he learned from the analysis led him to develop his theory that first-, middle-, and lastborns have very different characteristics. It is evident that firstborns are usually self-confident, assertive, and conscientious. They can also be jealous, moralistic, and inflexible. Winston Churchill, John Wayne, Oprah Winfrey, Saddam Hussein, and Joseph Stalin were all firstborns. Based on this idea, we might expect powerful political figures, such as U.S. presidents, to be firstborns. They often are, says Sulloway.

Sulloway observes that lastborns are usually more social, agreeable, and open to new and even revolutionary ideas. This is because, sensing the power of the already-established relationship between the oldest sibling[2] and the parents, they have to turn outward to establish their place in the world. Famous lastborns include Joan of Arc, Thomas Jefferson, and Leon Trotsky.

What about families in which there are more than two children? If there are three children in a family, the middle child is usually more flexible than the other two and often has a talent for compromise. Famous middle children include Nelson Mandela, Martin Luther King, Jr., and Jennifer Lopez.

A family in which there is only one child is the least predictable configuration, Sulloway says. An only child[3] isn't as inflexible as a firstborn. The fact that they are the sole child in the family, however, causes only children to identify with their parents as firstborns do.

Perhaps you're thinking this is all just too much of a generalization. That there are exceptions to the birth-order theory is clear. A child's temperament has a great deal to do

2 *sibling:* brother or sister
3 *only child:* the single child in a family

with how he or she turns out. Shy children, for example, may not become leaders even if they are firstborns. Sulloway notes that there have been famous firstborns who became revolutionaries as well as laterborns who became conservatives. Still, the theory of birth order is compelling even if its accuracy is controversial.

If we assume that there is some validity to the birth-order theory, how can parents achieve the best possible relationships with their children? What they should do, Sulloway says, is give each child unique time and attention. Whether or not they can significantly change the influences of birth order is an open question, but they will maximize the quality of those relationships.

AFTER YOU READ

A VOCABULARY Complete the sentences with words from the box.

compelling	conscientious	innovator	sole
configuration	enterprises	niche	temperament

1. A person's ________________ are his or her plans, businesses, and accomplishments.
2. A person who introduces something new is called a(n) ________________.
3. A(n) ________________ situation is one that attracts strong interest or attention.
4. A child who finds a(n) ________________ in his or her parents' affections finds a suitable place.
5. A(n) ________________ person is one who gives great attention or dedication to something.
6. The arrangement of children in a family is termed its ________________.
7. The ________________ child in a family is the only child in that family.
8. A child's ________________ is his or her nature.

B COMPREHENSION Read the statements. Check (✓) *True* or *False*.

	True	False
1. Both Sam and Jerry are firstborns.	☐	☐
2. The birth-order theory appeared very recently.	☐	☐
3. Firstborns tend to be conservative.	☐	☐
4. Powerful political figures are often lastborns.	☐	☐
5. Middle children are usually rebellious.	☐	☐
6. A family with only one child is the least predictable of the types.	☐	☐
7. According to Sulloway, there are no exceptions to the birth-order theory.	☐	☐
8. According to Sulloway, parents should give each child attention.	☐	☐

C DISCUSSION Work with a partner. What forces do you think influence a person's character and personality? Discuss.

STEP 2 GRAMMAR PRESENTATION

NOUN CLAUSES: SUBJECTS, OBJECTS, AND COMPLEMENTS

Noun Clauses Introduced by *That*

Subject
That he fits the category is obvious.
That they give the children so many gifts is unfortunate.

Object
You can see **(that) she loves her children**.
She knows **(that) they love her too**.

Complement	
Subject Complement	The problem was **(that) their son was a rebel**.
Adjective Complement	It is important **(that) people learn responsibility**.

Noun Clauses with Question Words

Subject
What I should tell her is obvious.
Why he did that wasn't evident.

Object
I wonder **what I should tell her**.
Can you explain **why he did that**?

Complement	
Subject Complement	The question is **why there are so many exceptions**.
Adjective Complement	It's interesting **who the exceptions are**.

Noun Clauses with *Whether* or *If*

Subject
Whether she'll outgrow her rebelliousness is hard to predict.
Whether the theory is valid is an interesting question.

Object
It's hard to predict **if she'll outgrow her rebelliousness**.
I care about **whether (or not) the theory accurate**.

Complement	
Subject Complement	The issue is **whether the categories are too broad**.
Adjective Complement	He's uncertain **whether he really believes it**.

Noun Clauses with *-ever* Words

Subject	Object
Whatever you want to do is OK.	It's OK to do **whatever you want to do**.
Whoever arrives first will get the job.	We'll hire **whoever arrives first**.
Whomever you recommend will be hired.	We'll hire **whomever you recommend**.
Whichever child is born first has advantages.	The advantages go to **whichever child is born first**.
Wherever Mom wants to go will be OK with Dad.	Dad will be OK with **wherever Mom wants to go**.
Whenever you want to leave will be fine.	I'll be fine with **whenever you want to leave**.
However you decide to proceed will be all right.	I'll be all right with **however you decide to proceed**.

GRAMMAR NOTES

1 Definition of Noun Clauses

Noun clauses are **dependent** clauses that perform the **same functions** as single **nouns**.

They can act as **subjects**.	**That firstborns identify with their parents** is apparent. **What laterborns must do** is become different from their siblings.
They can act as **objects**.	Laterborns sense **that they need to find a niche in their parents' affections.** We don't know **what her children's names are.**
They can act as **subject complements.** Remember that a complement is a word or phrase that describes or adds to the meaning of a subject, object, or adjective already mentioned in a sentence.	The ***problem*** is **that I don't understand the theory.** *(describes what the problem is)*
They can act as **adjective complements.** Adjective complements describe what is meant by the adjective used.	It's ***obvious*** **that she is a rebellious person.** *(describes what is obvious)*

2 *That* + Noun Clauses

Use the word ***that*** to **introduce** certain noun clauses.

When ***that*** begins a noun clause, it is a grammatical word that simply introduces the clause. It has **no concrete meaning**.	I believe **that** the birth-order theory is accurate in general.
You can omit *that* when it introduces an **object noun clause** or a **complement noun clause**. It is frequently omitted in speaking.	Firstborns realize **(that) siblings represent a challenge**. *(object noun clause)* It is evident **(that) firstborns are often conservative.** *(complement noun clause)*
When *that* introduces a **subject noun clause, do not omit** it.	**That there are exceptions to the theory** is clear. NOT ~~There are exceptions to the theory is clear.~~
It often functions as the subject of a sentence, with the noun clause coming later. Like the word *that*, *it* is sometimes a grammatical word that has no concrete meaning.	***It***'s funny **(that) you should say that.**
IN WRITING **Subject noun clauses** beginning with ***that*** are formal and are found mostly in writing.	**That birth order determines personality** is a controversial claim.
BE CAREFUL! Don't confuse *that* and *what*. The word ***that*** simply introduces certain noun clauses. The word ***what*** refers to something definite. It serves as the object of a noun clause and **cannot be omitted**.	I know **(that) Maria is a middle child.** I don't know **what** (OBJECT) **her future plans** (SUBJECT) **are.** (VERB) NOT I don't know ~~her future plans are~~.

3 *The Fact That* + Noun Clauses

You can use the phrase ***the fact that*** in place of *that* in subject noun clauses. Sentences with *the fact that* are **less formal** than sentences with *that* introducing a subject noun clause.	**The fact that** Elena is rebellious might mean that she is a lastborn. *(less formal)* **That** Elena is rebellious might mean that she is a lastborn. *(formal)*
BE CAREFUL! You **must** use *the fact that* in place of *that* in noun clauses that are **objects of prepositions**.	I'm impressed **by the fact that** Bob showed up. NOT I'm impressed by ~~that~~ Bob showed up.

4 Embedded Questions

A **question** that is **changed to a noun clause** is called an **embedded question**.

Explanation	Examples
You can change both ***wh-* questions** and ***yes/no* questions** to noun clauses. Use **statement word order**, not question word order, in embedded questions.	Do you know **who their daughter is**? No, I don't know **who she is.** I don't know **if she's from around here**.
An embedded question can occur within a statement or within another question. An embedded question within a **statement** is followed by a **period**. An embedded question within another **question** is followed by a **question mark**.	I'm not sure **how many children they have.** Do you know **if Roberto is an only child?**
USAGE NOTE An embedded question is more polite than a direct question.	What time is it? *(direct)* Do you know **what time it is**? *(more polite)* What does "niche" mean? *(direct)* Do you know **what "niche" means**? *(more polite)*
BE CAREFUL! Don't use question word order in an embedded question. Use **statement word order**.	Do you know **if they have children**? NOT Do you know ~~do~~ they have children? Can you tell me **what time it is**? NOT Can you tell me what time ~~is it~~?

5 *Wh-* Question Words + Noun Clauses

Explanation	Examples
The *wh-* question words ***what***, ***who***, ***whom***, ***when***, ***where***, ***which***, ***why***, and ***how*** introduce noun clauses (embedded questions) that are **formed from direct questions**.	Do you know **who their daughter is**? I'm not sure **when their son was born.**
The subject of an embedded *wh-* question takes a **singular verb**.	I'm not certain **who *is* going** with us.
BE CAREFUL! Don't use *do*, *does*, or *did* in embedded questions.	I have no idea **what she meant.** NOT I have no idea what ~~did she mean~~.

6 *If* and *Whether (or Not)* + Noun Clauses

Use the words *if* and ***whether (or not)*** to introduce noun clauses (embedded questions) that are **formed from *yes/no* questions**.	Do you know **if they have any children**? Who knows **whether (or not) they have any children**? I have no idea **whether they have children**.
If and *whether (or not)* are similar in meaning and can be used interchangeably in many constructions.	We're not sure **if** Bob is married. We're not sure **whether** Bob is married **or not**.
Whether . . . or not can replace ***whether*** in all noun clauses.	We don't know **whether** Maria has any siblings. We don't know **whether** Maria has any siblings **or not**.
If . . . or not can replace ***whether*** in most clauses.	We don't know **if** Maria has any siblings **or not**.
BE CAREFUL! Don't use *if* to introduce a **subject noun clause**.	**Whether (or not) she understands** the issue is questionable. NOT ~~If~~ she understands the issue is questionable.
BE CAREFUL! Don't omit *if* or *whether (or not)* in **embedded *yes/no* questions**.	I don't know **if** they are good parents. NOT I don't know ~~they are good parents~~.

7 *-Ever* Words + Noun Clauses

The *wh-* question words *what, who, whom, which, where, when,* and *how* often combine with the word ***ever*** to produce words that introduce noun clauses.	
• ***whatever***	**Whatever she does** is acceptable to her parents.
• ***whoever***	**Whoever interviews the best** will get the job.
• ***whomever***	You can invite **whomever you want** to the picnic.
• ***whichever (one)***	We can eat at **whichever restaurant you choose**.
• ***wherever***	**Wherever you want to stay** will be fine with me.
• ***whenever***	**Whenever you want to leave** will be agreeable.
• ***however***	**However you want to handle this** will be OK.
USAGE NOTE *Wherever* and *whenever* can also introduce **adverb clauses**. (See Unit 17.) *However* is also a contrast transition word. (See Unit 19.)	We run into them **wherever we go**. She makes me laugh **whenever we're together**. I find the birth-order theory interesting. **However**, I don't totally understand how it works.

REFERENCE NOTES

For information on **noun clauses used to report speech**, see Unit 21 on page 355.
For information on **noun clauses in conditional sentences**, see Unit 22 on page 377.
For information on **noun clauses using the subjunctive**, see Unit 23 on page 395.

STEP 3 FOCUSED PRACTICE

EXERCISE 1 DISCOVER THE GRAMMAR

A GRAMMAR NOTES 1–5 **Read the sentences based on the reading. Underline each noun clause. Then identify the way it is used: as *S* (a subject), *O* (an object), *SC* (a subject complement), or *AC* (an adjective complement).**

SC 1. The question is why they are so similar.

____ 2. Sam and Jerry are examples of what researchers call the birth-order theory.

____ 3. I know what the explanation is.

____ 4. They sense that they have to become different from the oldest child.

____ 5. What he learned from the analysis led him to develop his theory.

____ 6. It is evident that firstborns are usually self-confident.

____ 7. That there are exceptions to the birth-order theory is clear.

____ 8. The fact that they are the sole children in their families makes them identify with their parents.

B GRAMMAR NOTES 4–6 **Read the sentences based on the reading. Underline the embedded question in each sentence. Then, for each embedded question, write the direct question it was derived from.**

1. Let's see if you can answer this question.

   Can you answer this question?

2. The question is whether the theory is accurate.

   ______

3. I know what that word means.

   ______

4. What they should do is give each child unique attention.

   ______

5. Whether or not they can change the influences of birth order is an open question.

   ______

EXERCISE 2 *THAT*, *THE FACT THAT*, *WHAT* + NOUN CLAUSES

GRAMMAR NOTES 2–5 **Complete the email with the correct forms of the words in parentheses and *that*, *the fact that*, or *what*. Use contractions where possible.**

Hi, Sis,

You asked about the kids, so I thought I'd drop you an email and tell you

___what they've been doing___ (1. they / been doing). I'll start with Bruce. I think you know

________________ (2. he / be) a senior in high school now. He's doing great in school and is planning for college. He's been accepted by the university, and we just found out

________________ (3. he / have / earn) a scholarship for his freshman year.

________________ (4. he / be / going to do) well is a certainty; he's carrying a 4.00 grade point average. Mandy is a sophomore and is also doing well. She's in a college prep program, but so far she doesn't know ________________ (5. she / want / study) when she gets to college. I guess

________________ (6. she / be / typical of) most middle children; she has a lot of friends. She always thinks ________________ (7. it / be / important) to get along with everyone. And then there's Jason. Al and I can't believe ________________ (8. he / have / turn out) so differently from the other two. He's in the eighth grade, and he isn't doing well in school. It's always been clear

________________ (9. he / have) a rebellious streak, but now we're worried about

________________ (10. it / be / getting worse). We love him dearly, but we aren't totally sure

________________ (11. we / can / do) to keep him under control. We hope

________________ (12. he / mature) as time goes on.

That's all for the moment. Email or text me, please. We hope

________________ (13. you and Jaime / be) well and happy.

Love,
Melanie

EXERCISE 3 EMBEDDED QUESTIONS

GRAMMAR NOTES 4–6 **Read the following excerpt from a job interview. Then change each of the underlined questions to noun clauses that describe what the interviewer asked. Begin each clause with *if*, *whether or not*, or a *wh-* question word. Put the verbs in the embedded questions in the simple past or the past perfect. Do not use contractions.**

LOPEZ: Good afternoon, Mr. Pei. I'm Blanca Lopez. Thanks for being here for this interview.

PEI: My pleasure. I'm happy to be here.

LOPEZ: So, Mr. Pei, <u>are you married?</u> 1.

PEI: Yes, I am.

LOPEZ: <u>Do you have any children?</u> 2.

PEI: Yes, I do. My wife, Amy, and I have three children.

LOPEZ: You've indicated that you're working as a counselor. <u>How long have you been doing that?</u> 3.

PEI: I've been working in counselling for ten years.

LOPEZ: Mr. Pei, you've written a great deal about birth order and family dynamics. <u>What made you start writing?</u> 4.

PEI: I guess I just had a burning desire to communicate my ideas. The whole birth-order theory is pretty compelling.

LOPEZ: <u>How old are your children?</u> 5.

PEI: Our oldest child is a girl who's sixteen years old. Our middle child is a boy who's fourteen. Our youngest child is a girl. She's twelve.

LOPEZ: <u>Does your family fit the theories you've written about?</u> 6.

PEI: Yes, basically, they do. For example, our older girl is a typical firstborn. She's always been conscientious about doing what needs to be done.

LOPEZ: <u>What can you tell me about the others?</u> 7.

PEI: Well, our boy, the middle child, is very outgoing. Our younger girl is somewhat rebellious, or maybe we can call her free-thinking.

LOPEZ: Very interesting. <u>How do you deal with her rebelliousness?</u> 8.

W PEI: Well, it's complicated, but we limit her privileges, basically.

LOPEZ: All right. Now, Mr. Pei, <u>what do you consider your greatest strength as a counselor?</u> 9.

PEI: I think my greatest strength is my ability to listen actively.

LOPEZ: All right, Mr. Pei. Thank you. . . .

1. Ms. Lopez asked *if he was married* ________________.
2. She asked ________________.
3. She asked ________________.
4. She asked ________________.
5. She asked ________________.
6. She asked ________________.
7. She asked ________________.
8. She asked ________________.
9. She asked ________________.

EXERCISE 4 -*EVER* WORDS AND NOUN CLAUSES

GRAMMAR NOTE 7 **Complete the answers to the questions. Use the correct forms of the words in parentheses and the words from the box.**

however	whatever	~~whenever~~	wherever	whichever	whoever	whomever

1. Q: Bob, what time shall we leave for the family picnic?
   A: *Whenever you'd like to leave* (you'd like / leave) will be fine with me.
2. Q: Dad, where should we go on our vacation?
   A: ________________ (you kids and your mother / want to go) will be great.
3. Q: Mom, should I invite my school friends to the dinner?
   A: You can invite ________________ (you / want).
4. Q: Who's going to be our math teacher this year?
   A: It'll be ________________ (not / already have / a full teaching load).
5. Q: Which of these three books should I get Dad for his birthday?
   A: ________________ (you / should get / one) is the least expensive.
6. Q: Alice, how do you think we should deal with this issue?
   A: ________________ (you / want / deal with it) is OK with me.
7. Q: What would you like to do this weekend?
   A: I'll go along with ________________ (you'd / like to do).

EXERCISE 5 EDITING

GRAMMAR NOTES 1–7 Read this letter to Mr. and Mrs. Chen from their son James's teacher about his progress in school. There are ten mistakes in the use of noun clauses. The first mistake is already corrected. Find and correct nine more.

MADISON
JUNIOR HIGH SCHOOL

March 27

Dear Mr. and Mrs. Chen,

I'm writing to give you a progress report on your son James. In general, I would say ~~what~~ *that* he is doing better than previously, though he still isn't performing up to his abilities. That stands out to me is his tendency to daydream. It's clear what he is paying better attention during class activities, and that is a good sign. At this point, his two weakest subjects are math and science. This is quite surprising, given the fact what he scored highly on the recent national achievement tests in both those subjects. Currently, he is failing math and barely passing science. I am quite puzzled by that he is doing so poorly in these areas. However is preventing him from achieving success needs to be identified. I recently asked him what is his difficulty in math and science, but he did not seem to have a clear idea.

On the positive side, James is doing very well in English. He is also performing reasonably well in history and art. However, there is still the problem of missing assignments. Up until recently, I thought the fact that he wasn't doing the work. But last week I asked him did he do the work but simply forgot to submit it, and he said which was the case.

Thank you for your efforts to monitor James's study time in the evenings. Children today have so many distractions. Your son is lucky to have parents who care about his education. Please call me if you have any concerns.

Sincerely,
Paula Brand

STEP 4 COMMUNICATION PRACTICE

EXERCISE 6 LISTENING

20|02 **A** Listen to the conversation. Why are the husband and wife visiting the counselor?

____

20|02 **B** Listen to the conversation again. For each statement, check (✓) *True* or *False*.

	True	False
1. Amanda is the couple's youngest child.	☐	☑
2. Amanda is an unhappy child.	☐	☐
3. Amanda believes her parents don't care about her.	☐	☐
4. Tim and Anne can understand why Amanda feels that.	☐	☐
5. Amanda has a great many interests.	☐	☐
6. Tim and Anne's older son is successful in everything he does.	☐	☐
7. Tim and Anne have been spending a lot of time with Amanda.	☐	☐
8. The counselor feels she understands what the issue is.	☐	☐
9. The counselor says Tim and Anne should suggest an interest for Amanda.	☐	☐
10. The counselor believes that Amanda needs special attention.	☐	☐

C Work with a partner. Do you agree with the advice the counselor has given the parents? What do you think it is important that the parents do to solve Amanda's problems? Discuss.

EXERCISE 7 WHAT'S YOUR BIRTH ORDER?

A QUESTIONNAIRE Fill out this questionnaire. Of the three choices in each question, circle the one that you feel describes you most closely. Then check your answers on page 349. According to the questionnaire, are you a firstborn, middle born, or lastborn? What about in real life?

1. What do you consider yourself?
   a. liberal **b.** moderate **c.** conservative
2. How important is it to obey rules?
   a. not very **b.** sometimes **c.** almost always
3. Do you believe in a strong moral code?
   a. not particularly **b.** depends on the issue **c.** yes
4. Do you consider yourself a leader?
   a. sometimes **b.** not usually **c.** absolutely
5. Do you think your parents are usually right about things?
   a. not all that often **b.** fairly often **c.** almost always
6. Which is the most important goal?
   a. to chart my own course **b.** to get along with people **c.** to maintain traditional values
7. Which word best describes your personality?
   a. social **b.** flexible **c.** self-confident
8. How do you feel about change?
   a. I embrace it. **b.** 50/50. Sometimes I like it; sometimes I don't. **c.** I don't generally like it.
9. Are you ever jealous?
   a. not all that often **b.** seldom if ever **c.** sometimes
10. Which goal is most important?
    a. to do your own thing **b.** to compromise so that everyone gets something **c.** to win

B Work with a partner. Discuss your questionnaire results and your situation in real life.

EXAMPLE: A: I feel that I fit well into the birth-order theory. My questionnaire results show that I am a middle-born child, and I actually am a middle born.

B: Really? My questionnaire results were wrong. . . .

EXERCISE 8 WHAT'S THEIR BIRTH ORDER?

A GAME You are going to play a guessing game related to birth order. First, think about a person you know or a famous person you know about. How would you describe the person's background and personality? What is his or her birth order?

B Work in a group. Describe the person to the other members of your group. Talk about the person's background and personality, but do not reveal his or her birth order. Your group tries to guess the birth order of the person you have written about, giving reasons for their answers that are based on the birth-order theory.

EXAMPLE: A: My best friend, Samantha, is very outgoing and flexible, but she also has a rebellious streak. She does whatever she likes most of the time, and she doesn't seem to care about what other people think of her.

B: I think Samantha must be a lastborn. She's rebellious.

C: That Samantha isn't a firstborn is obvious, but I'm not sure she's a lastborn. She's flexible, and the theory says that middle borns are supposed to be flexible. . . .

C Report interesting examples to the class.

EXERCISE 9 PUTTING IT ALL TOGETHER

CRITICAL THINKING Work with a group. Use what you've learned in the readings and exercises in this unit to make determinations about the overall accuracy of the birth-order theory. Then report the conclusions of your group to the class.

EXAMPLE: A: I think it's hard to say if the birth-order theory is accurate or not. Some of the examples we've talked about fit into the theory, but some don't.

B: To me, it's obvious that the theory is wrong. None of the people that I talked to fit into it.

C: Whenever you have a theory that puts people into different categories, there are always exceptions. That doesn't mean the theory is completely wrong. . . .

Exercise 7 Questionnaire Answers

Count up the number of a., b., and c. answers. The category in which you have the greatest number of answers shows what your birth order is.

Mostly **a.** responses = You are a lastborn.
Mostly **b.** responses = You are a middle child.
Mostly **c.** responses = You are a firstborn.

FROM GRAMMAR TO WRITING

A BEFORE YOU WRITE You are going to write an essay about whether you feel you do or do not fit into the birth-order theory. Write a few sentences about each of the following points.

- Where you fit in a family structure
- What your personal characteristics are
- Why you believe you do or do not fit into the theory

B WRITE Using your ideas in A, write a five-paragraph essay about yourself or the person you have chosen. Remember to use noun clauses. Try to avoid the common mistakes shown in the chart. Use the example below to help you begin your essay.

EXAMPLE: I can't say whether the birth-order theory is true for everyone or not, but I think that I fit very well into it. In my family, there are three children, and all three of us have the characteristics of the firstborn, the middle child, and the lastborn. My older brother Roger is the firstborn; I'm the middle child; and my sister Nancy is the lastborn. That Roger is a typical firstborn person is clear. He's very conservative, and he agrees with whatever our parents say. . . .

Common Mistakes in Using Noun Clauses

Don't confuse *what* and *that*. ***What*** refers to something **specific**. ***That*** is a word that begins a clause but has **no concrete meaning**.	I'm not sure **what** she meant. NOT I'm not sure ~~that~~ she meant.
Be sure to use **statement word order** in embedded questions. Don't use question word order.	Do you know **who their daughter is**? NOT Do you know who ~~is their daughter~~?
Don't use ***do***, ***does***, or ***did*** in embedded questions.	Do you know **what "conscientious" means**? NOT Do you know what ~~does mean "conscientious"~~?
Don't use *if* to introduce a **subject noun clause**. Use ***whether*** *(or not)*.	**Whether or not** they're going to be here isn't clear. NOT ~~If or not~~ they're going to be here isn't clear.

C CHECK YOUR WORK Look at your essay. Underline noun clauses. Use the Editing Checklist to check your work.

Editing Checklist

Did you . . . ?

- ☐ avoid confusing *what* and *that*
- ☐ use statement word order, not question word order, in embedded questions
- ☐ avoid using *do*, *does*, or *did* in embedded questions
- ☐ use *whether (or not)*, not *if*, in subject noun clauses

D REVISE YOUR WORK Read your essay again. Can you improve your writing? Make changes if necessary.

UNIT 20 REVIEW

Test yourself on the grammar of the unit.

A **Circle the correct noun clause to complete each sentence.**

1. I'm not sure what the birth-order theory is / is the birth-order theory.
2. I don't know why does he always want / he always wants to be in charge.
3. I'm not sure what time does the meeting start / the meeting starts.
4. I don't remember what "configuration" means / means "configuration".
5. I don't know whether Samira / Samira enjoyed the party.
6. I have no idea that / what your daughter does for a living.
7. I'm not sure how long she's been / has she been a counselor.
8. We're not sure if or not / whether or not Danilo is really their son.

B **Complete the sentences with the correct forms of the words in parentheses and the words in the box.**

however	the fact that	what	whatever	whether or not	whomever

1. Did you have any idea ______________________ (Mary / mean)?
2. We're not sure ______________________ (Jama / be coming).
3. ______________________ (you / want) to do is fine with me.
4. ______________________ (Allison / love / Kahlil) is obvious.
5. Invite ______________________ (you / want) to the dinner.
6. ______________________ (you / want / proceed) is acceptable to me.

C **Find and correct six mistakes.**

A: Do you know who are our new neighbors?

B: Yes, I run into them whoever I go out in the yard.

A: Oh, yeah? What do you think are they like?

B: They seem really nice. I know what they both work.

A: Hmm. I wonder they have children.

B: They have three. I'm happy about that their daughter is the same age as Maria.

Now check your answers on page 432.

UNIT 21

Direct and Indirect Speech

COMMUNICATION AND MISUNDERSTANDING

OUTCOMES
- Report what someone said, using direct and indirect speech, making necessary changes
- Identify key concepts in a transcribed interview
- Identify details in an interview
- Discuss the topic of communication, expressing opinions and reporting on what others said
- Write an essay about a past conflict

STEP 1 GRAMMAR IN CONTEXT

BEFORE YOU READ

Discuss the questions.

1. Do you sometimes have misunderstandings with other people? In your experience, what kinds of misunderstandings are the most difficult to deal with?
2. How can misunderstandings best be avoided?

READ

21|01 Read this interview with an expert on communication.

Understanding Misunderstandings

NESS: Hello, everyone. I'm Ann Ness. Please welcome today's guest—communication expert Ellen Sands.

SANDS: Thanks for having me. You know, Ann, I think we're seeing a lot more verbal conflict these days than in the past. There seems to be a lot more rancor and a lot less civility. Today I want to talk about ways to avoid verbal conflict, or at least minimize it.

NESS: Sounds good, Ellen. Tell us more.

SANDS: All right. First, people need to listen actively to each other. We hear things, but often we don't really listen. A couple of weeks ago, I was at a restaurant in Los Angeles, sitting near an Indian couple being served by an American waitress. The service was slow, and the couple seemed distressed. When the waitress brought the check, the man said, "The bill seems very high. Did you include the service in it? How much is the service?" The waitress said, "You have to pay the tax." The man said, "The service was very slow. We have never waited so long to be served. We will pay the bill, but we won't pay for service." Then they left angrily. The waitress just glared at them and didn't say anything. It wasn't a good situation, mainly because the waitress didn't listen actively.

NESS: Let me see if I understand. When the waitress brought the check, the man said the bill seemed very high. He asked how much the service was. The waitress said they had to pay the tax. The man said the service had been very slow and they had never waited so long to be served. He said they would pay the bill but they wouldn't pay for service. Now, what did the waitress do wrong?

SANDS: She didn't listen carefully. The man asked if she had included the service in the bill. Unfortunately, she never answered his question. That was the key thing he wanted to know.

NESS: Did she do anything else wrong?

SANDS: She didn't address his concern about the slow service. She could have said something like, "Yes, I'm really sorry about the service. We're short-handed[1] today."

NESS: Very interesting. Now, what's another way to avoid verbal conflict?

SANDS: Another really good strategy is to state things positively instead of negatively. Recently, I was sitting in as a consultant at a school board meeting. Right at the start, the chair gave instructions in an arbitrary way: "We're on a very tight schedule. Make your reports brief; no one will be allowed to take more than three minutes. And no one will be allowed to interrupt the person who's speaking. No one will ask any questions." It wasn't a good meeting. You could have cut the silence with a knife.

NESS: How could the chair have done better?

SANDS: He told them to make their reports brief, but he could have asked them to try to limit their reports to three minutes. He said no one would be allowed to interrupt the person who was speaking. He also said no one would ask any questions. He had a rigid manner, spoke with a self-righteous tone, and basically treated the attendees like schoolchildren instead of like adults. That's a good way to inhibit any kind of productive discussion. He could have asked them to hold their questions for the duration of the speeches. The bottom line is this: You don't have to sugarcoat[2] your statements, but people will respond much better if you put a positive spin[3] on things.

NESS: All right. Thanks, Ellen. We'll be back shortly, after this commercial break.

---

1 *short-handed:* without enough help

2 *sugarcoat:* make something appear or sound nicer than it really is

3 *spin:* interpretation

AFTER YOU READ

A VOCABULARY **Match the words in bold with their meanings.**

_____	**1.** You should treat people with civility, not with **rancor**.	**a.** time something lasts
_____	**2.** The couple seemed **distressed**.	**b.** unreasonable
_____	**3.** The waitress didn't **address** the couple's concern.	**c.** stiff, inflexible
_____	**4.** The chair gave instructions in an **arbitrary** way.	**d.** discourage
_____	**5.** He spoke in a **rigid** manner.	**e.** angry feelings
_____	**6.** The chair's tone was **self-righteous**.	**f.** properly deal with
_____	**7.** That is a good way to **inhibit** a productive discussion.	**g.** upset
_____	**8.** The audience had to hold their questions for the **duration**.	**h.** sure that one is right

B COMPREHENSION **Complete the sentences based on the reading.**

1. Ellen Sands is a(n) ________________ expert.

2. Sands believes there is ________________ rancor in communication today than in the past.

3. She also believes there is ________________ civility today than previously.

4. Sands says that a key aspect of good communication is ________________ listening.

5. In her first example, the couple from India thought the service was too ________________.

6. In her second example, Sands talks of the need to state things in a(n) ________________ manner.

7. The chair in her second example treated the attendees like ________________.

8. Sands suggests that in a discussion, people should be treated like ________________.

C DISCUSSION **Work with a partner. Compare and justify your answers in B. Then discuss this question: Do you agree with Ellen Sands's advice on how to minimize verbal conflict? What strategies do you use to avoid conflict in your own life?**

STEP 2 GRAMMAR PRESENTATION

DIRECT AND INDIRECT SPEECH

Statements: Direct Speech

Subject	Reporting Verb	Direct Statement
He	said,	"The food **is** delicious."
		"The bill **includes** service."
		"The service **was** ridiculously slow."

Statements: Indirect Speech

Subject	Reporting Verb	Noun/Pronoun	Indirect Statement	
He	said	Ø*	(that)	the food **was** delicious.
	told	Miriam/her		the bill **included** service.
				the service **had been** slow.

*Ø: not used.

Yes/No Questions: Direct Speech

Subject	Reporting Verb	Direct Question
The chair	asked,	"**Have you finished** your report?"
		"**Do you think we are going** to have time to finish?"

Yes/No Questions: Indirect Speech

Subject	Reporting Verb	Noun/Pronoun	Indirect Question	
The chair	asked	(Marta)	**if**	**she had finished** her report.
		(her)	**whether (or not)**	**she thought they were** going to have time to finish.

Wh- Questions: Direct Speech

Subject	Reporting Verb	Direct Question
The customer	asked,	"**What time does the manager arrive**?"
		"**Who is the manager**?"

Wh- Questions: Indirect Speech

Subject	Reporting Verb	Noun/Pronoun	Indirect Question	
The customer	asked	(the waitress)	**what time**	**the manager arrived**.
		(her)	**who**	**the manager was**.

Verb Changes in Indirect Speech

Direct Speech			
		Verb	
He said,	"I	**report**	the news."
		am reporting	
		reported	
		have reported	
		had reported	
		will report	
		can report	
		should report	

Indirect Speech			
		Verb	
He said	(that) he	**reported**	the news.
		was reporting	
		had reported	
		would report	
		could report	
		should report	

Other Changes in Indirect Speech

	Direct Speech	Indirect Speech
Pronouns	"Andy, are **you** listening?" Mary asked.	Mary asked Andy if **he** was listening.
Possessives	The boss said, "Sue, bring **your** camera."	The boss told Sue to bring **her** camera.
This	"Can I have **this** film?" Sam asked.	Sam asked if he could have **that** film.
Here	Mrs. Brown asked, "Will you be **here**?"	Mrs. Brown asked if I would be **there**.
Ago	"We came a year **ago**," Jim said.	Jim said (that) they had come a year **previously / before**.
Now	Bob asked, "Are you leaving **now**?"	Bob asked if I was leaving **then**.
Today	"I need to work **today**," Jack said.	Jack said (that) he needed to work **that day**.
Yesterday	The reporter asked, "Did you call **yesterday**?"	The reporter asked if I had called **the previous day / the day before**.
Tomorrow	"Are you arriving **tomorrow**?" Sarah asked.	Sarah asked if we were arriving **the next day**.

GRAMMAR NOTES

1 Direct vs. Indirect Speech

We can report speech in two ways: with **direct speech** and with **indirect speech**.

Direct speech (also called **quoted speech**) is the **exact words** (or thoughts) of someone speaking (or thinking). It is enclosed in quotation marks. Use a **reporting verb** such as *say*, *tell*, and *ask* to introduce direct speech.

Ellen Sands said, **"I want to talk about ways to avoid verbal conflict."**
"Asha is really angry at me," I thought.

To report direct speech, use a **comma** followed by **quotation marks** at the **beginning** of the quotation. Use a **question mark** or an **exclamation point** at the **end** of a question or exclamation, followed by quotation marks.

John said, **"Tell me what's really bothering you."**
The man asked, **"Does the bill include service?"**
He said, **"We won't pay for the service!"**

In direct speech, the quoted part of the sentence can come either at the **beginning** or at the **end** of the sentence.

"Turn in your exams now," the teacher said.
The teacher said, **"Turn in your exams now."**

If a quotation is interrupted by a reporting verb, do not capitalize the first word in the second part of the quotation.

"Mr. Gomez," Kayoko asked, **"*may* I talk to you about my grades in this class?"**

Indirect speech (also called **reported speech**) is someone's **report** of direct speech. It does not contain the exact words of a speaker and is not enclosed in quotation marks. Indirect speech reports what a speaker said in a **noun clause** or **phrase** introduced by a reporting verb.

NOUN CLAUSE
She said **(that) she wanted to talk about ways to avoid verbal conflict.**

To report a statement, you can use *that* to introduce the noun clause. The word *that* can also be omitted. To report a question, use *if*, ***whether (or not)***, or a ***wh-*** question word to introduce the noun clause.

NOUN CLAUSE
The man asked ***if* the bill included service.**

BE CAREFUL! Don't use quotation marks in indirect speech.

He said **(that) he would be there.**
NOT John said ~~"he would be there."~~

2 Reporting Verbs

The verbs ***say***, ***tell***, and ***ask*** are the most common reporting verbs. Other reporting verbs include *claim*, *reply*, *state*, and *wonder*. We usually use the **simple past** forms of these verbs in both direct and indirect speech.	Hal **said**, "Martha, we have to leave." Hal **told** Martha they had to leave. Hal **asked** Martha if she was ready to leave.
USAGE NOTE *Say* and *tell* have similar meanings, but they are used differently. We ***say something*** but ***tell someone something***. Normally, *tell* must be followed by an object.	Andy **told Freda** (that) she shouldn't worry. Andy **said** (that) Freda shouldn't worry.
USAGE NOTE We often use ***tell*** when the listener is mentioned. Use ***say*** if the listener is not mentioned.	The chair **told us** to pay attention. The chair **said** to pay attention.
BE CAREFUL! Don't use *tell* when the listener is *not* mentioned. Don't use *say* immediately before an object. Use ***say*** **+ *to* + object**.	Ms. Tanaka **said** (that) she was going to the meeting. NOT Ms. Tanaka ~~told~~ (that) she was going to the meeting. Mr. Egiofor **told us** (that) he'd be lecturing. Mr. Egiofor **said to us** (that) he'd be lecturing. NOT Mr. Egiofor ~~said~~ us (that) he'd be lecturing.

3 Reporting *Yes/No* Questions

To **report indirect questions**, we normally use ***ask*** in its simple past form.	The director asked, "Do you want to talk about the issue?" The director ***asked* if we wanted to talk about the issue.**
Use **statement word order**, not question word order, to report *yes/no* questions.	I asked if **we would** know the answer soon. NOT I asked ~~would we~~ know the answer soon.
USAGE NOTE Use ***if*** or ***whether (or not)***, not *that*, to introduce an **indirect *yes/no* question**. *If* and *whether (or not)* are similar in meaning and are often used interchangeably.	Bob asked, "Do you think she'll take the job?" Bob asked **if** I thought she would take the job.
We often use *whether (or not)* to emphasize alternatives or different possibilities.	Bob asked **whether (or not)** I thought she would take the job.
BE CAREFUL! Indirect questions end with a **period**, not a question mark.	Sue asked Helen **if she had talked with her boss.** NOT Sue asked Helen if she had talked with her boss~~?~~
BE CAREFUL! Don't use ***do***, ***does***, or ***did*** in an indirect question. Use the simple present, simple past, or past perfect.	Ahmed asked Mandy **if she got** along well with her boss. NOT Ahmed asked Mandy ~~did she get~~ along well with her boss.

4 Reporting *Wh-* Questions

Use **question words** to introduce **indirect *wh-* questions**.	The man asked, "**How much** is the service?" The man asked ***how much*** **the service was**. "**Which** entrée do you prefer?" the waiter asked. The waiter asked ***which*** **entrée I preferred**.
The **predicate** of a sentence is the part that makes a statement about the subject. Use **statement word order** to **report indirect questions** about a predicate.	My daughter asked, "Why **didn't he take** our order?" My daughter asked why **he hadn't taken** our order.
We also use **statement word order** to report indirect questions about the **subject**.	"Who **is going to do** the dishes?" Mom asked. Mom asked who **was going to do** the dishes.

5 Changes in Verbs

If the reporting verb is in the simple past, the **verb in the noun clause** often **changes**.

• imperative → infinitive	The teacher said, "**Open** your books." The teacher told us **to open** our books.
• simple present → simple past	Bill said, "I **invest** in the stock market." Bill said (that) he **invested** in the stock market.
• present progressive → past progressive	Mary asked, "John, **are** you **studying** math?" Mary asked John if he **was studying** math.
• simple past → past perfect	"Priscilla **made** a delicious meal," Mark said. Mark said (that) Priscilla **had made** a delicious meal.
• present perfect → past perfect	"Sam, **have** you ever **eaten** at that café?" Jack asked. Jack asked Sam if he **had** ever **eaten** at that café.

6 Verbs That Don't Change

In spoken English, we sometimes **do not change verbs** in indirect speech, especially if what we are reporting happened a **short time ago**.	Lu just said, "Jack **didn't come** to work." Lu just said Jack **didn't come** to work. OR Lu just said Jack **hadn't come** to work.
Even in more formal English, we often do not change verbs to past forms if **general truths** are reported.	"**Does** it **snow** here in the winter?" Kenny asked. Kenny asked if it **snows** here in the winter. OR Kenny asked if it **snowed** here in the winter.
When the reporting verb is in the **simple present**, **present progressive**, **present perfect**, or **future**, the verb in the noun clause does not change.	Betty says, "I'**m going to** buy a new car." Betty says she'**s going to** buy a new car.

7 Reporting Modals

Certain **modals change** in indirect speech. Other modals do not change.

• *can* → *could*	"Sam, **can** you come by at 6:00 p.m.?" Ann asked. Ann asked Sam if he **could** come by at 6:00 p.m.
• *may* → *might*	"I **may** be able to," Sam said. Sam said he **might** be able to.
• *must* → *had to*	"I absolutely **must** leave at 6:15," Ann said. Ann said she absolutely **had to** leave at 6:15.
• *shall* → *should*	"**Shall** I drive you to the airport?" Sam asked. Sam asked if he **should** drive her to the airport.
• *will* → *would*	"I **won't** need a ride," Ann replied. Ann replied that she **wouldn't** need a ride.
Could, *had better*, *might*, *ought to*, *should*, and *would* **do not change** in indirect speech.	I said, "Helen, I **might** attend the conference." I told Helen (that) I **might** attend the conference. "Sarah, you **should** be more careful," Dad said. Dad told Sarah (that) she **should** be more careful.

8 Other Changes in Indirect Speech

In addition to verbs, certain **other words change** in indirect speech.

• pronouns/possessive adjectives → other forms	Jeremy said, "**My** boss just promoted **me**." Jeremy said (that) **his** boss had just promoted **him**.
• *this* → *that* and *these* → *those*	Don asked, "Have you read **this** book?" Don asked if I had read **that** book.
• *here* → *there*	"Please be **here** for the meeting," Sally asked. Sally asked me to be **there** for the meeting.
• *now* → *then*	Mac said, "Alan's just arriving **now**." Mac said (that) Alan was just arriving **then**.
• *ago* → *before/previously*	Julie said, "I got the job three years **ago**." Julie said (that) she had gotten the job three years **previously**.
• *yesterday* → *the day before/the previous day*	Mickey said, "I called **yesterday**." Mickey said that he had called **the day before**.
• *today* → *that day*	"Hans, are you coming **today**?" Abdul asked. Abdul asked Hans if he was coming **that day**.
• *tomorrow* → *the next day/the following day*	"I can see you **tomorrow**," said Kayoko. Kayoko said (that) she could see me **the next day**.

REFERENCE NOTES

For information on **reporting statements and questions in conditional sentences**, see Unit 22 on page 377.

For a list of **reporting verbs**, see Appendix 25 on page 421.

STEP 3 FOCUSED PRACTICE

EXERCISE 1 DISCOVER THE GRAMMAR

A GRAMMAR NOTES 1–8 **Read the direct speech sentences based on the reading and the reports of those sentences in indirect speech. Is the change to indirect speech correct (*C*) or incorrect (*I*)?**

__C__ 1. She said, "I want to talk about ways to avoid verbal conflict."
REPORT: She said she wanted to talk about ways to avoid verbal conflict.

____ 2. The man said, "The bill seems very high."
REPORT: The man said the bill seems very high.

____ 3. The man asked the waitress, "Did you include the service in the bill?"
REPORT: The man asked the waitress did she include the service in the bill.

____ 4. The waitress said, "You have to pay the tax."
REPORT: The waitress said they had to pay the tax.

____ 5. The man told the waitress, "We won't pay for service."
REPORT: The man told the waitress we wouldn't pay for service.

____ 6. The waitress could have said, "I'm really sorry about the service."
REPORT: The waitress could have said she was really sorry about the service.

____ 7. The chair said, "We're on a very tight schedule.
REPORT: The chair said they were on a very tight schedule.

____ 8. The chair said, "Make your reports brief."
REPORT: The chair said them to make their reports brief.

____ 9. The chair said, "We might need to have another meeting tomorrow."
REPORT: The chair said they might need to have another meeting the next day.

____ 10. The chair said, "No one will ask any questions."
REPORT: The chair said no one will ask any questions.

B GRAMMAR NOTES 5, 7 **Each of the following direct speech sentences has been changed to indirect speech. Identify how the verb has changed in each item.**

1. The chair said, "Make your reports brief." → The chair told them to make their reports brief.

   CHANGE: *imperative → infinitive*

2. The waitress said, "You have to pay the tax." → The waitress told them they had to pay the tax.

   CHANGE: ______________________________

3. The waitress could have said, "I'm really sorry about the service." → The waitress could have said she was really sorry about the service.

   CHANGE: ______________________________

4. The man asked the waitress, "Did you include the service in the bill?" → The man asked the waitress if she had included the service in the bill.

   CHANGE: ______________________________

5. The customer said, "I have never eaten such terrible food." → The customer said he had never eaten such terrible food.

CHANGE: ______________________________

6. The chair said, "No one will ask any questions." → The chair said no one would ask any questions.

CHANGE: ______________________________

7. The man from India asked his wife, "Shall we leave?" → The man from India asked his wife if they should leave.

CHANGE: ______________________________

8. The man asked the waitress, "Can you explain the bill?" → The man asked the waitress if she could explain the bill.

CHANGE: ______________________________

EXERCISE 2 DIRECT SPEECH TO INDIRECT SPEECH

GRAMMAR NOTES 5–7 Put the headlines into indirect speech. Add any necessary articles.

1 Divorced Man's Children Won't Speak to Him

2 Famous Actress Says She's Leaving Her Husband for the Third Time

3 Couple Is Going to Sue Restaurant Because of Rude Waiters

4 Congress Says President Vetoed Health Bill Because of Miscommunication

5 Woman's Sister Refuses to Invite Her to Her Wedding

6 Legislature Says Governor Lied about His Intentions to Sign Tax Bill

7 Rock Star and Band Are No Longer Performing Together

8 High School Students Will Soon Be Required to Take Communication Course to Graduate

1. The headline said (that) a divorced man's children wouldn't speak to him.

____

2. A famous actress said ______________________________

____

3. The headline said ______________________________

____

4. Congress said ______________________________

____

5. The headline said ______________________________

____

6. The legislature said ______________________________

____

7. The headline said ______________________________

____

8. The headline said ______________________________

____

EXERCISE 3 INDIRECT SPEECH TO DIRECT SPEECH

GRAMMAR NOTES 3–4 **A substitute teacher, Ms. Wong, had some communication difficulties with the students in her class. The students asked Ms. Wong questions. Read Ms. Wong's indirect speech answers to the questions. Then write the students' questions in direct speech.**

1. One student, Mia, asked, *"Who are you?"*
   Ms. Wong told the class she was Ms. Wong, their substitute teacher.
2. Mia asked, ______________________________
   She told the class their regular teacher was out of town.
3. Another student, Jordan, asked, ______________________________
   She said she would be with them for at least a month.
4. Jordan asked, ______________________________
   Ms. Wong told the class she was going to teach them how to do algebra.
5. Another student, Brianna, asked, ______________________________
   She answered that algebra is a type of math that uses letters and other signs to show numbers.
6. Brianna was still confused. She asked, ______________________________
   She told Brianna that yes, she could explain that again.
7. Another student, Caden, asked, ______________________________
   Ms. Wong told the class that yes, they would have to do homework.
8. Caden asked, ______________________________
   She said that they would have to do homework every week.

9. Caden said that that wasn't fair. He asked, ______________________________

____

Ms. Wong said that Caden had misunderstood. She wasn't going to make them do homework every night.

10. Another student, Lucas, asked, ______________________________

The teacher said that yes, she really did have a teaching degree.

EXERCISE 4 PUNCTUATION OF DIRECT SPEECH

GRAMMAR NOTE 1 Read Linh's narrative about a time when she felt she was insulted. Punctuate the sentences that are direct speech.

"So what happened?" I asked.

Well Linh said we were all seated in the living room. There were about twelve people there. Several of them were high-society types.

What were you doing with a bunch of high-society people I asked.

Good question Linh answered. Actually, I was visiting my cousin, and I was her guest.

So what went wrong I asked.

Well, a woman asked me where I was going to school. I said I was attending a community college. Then the woman's husband asked me if I was going to a real college after that. That made me pretty mad, and I got red in the face Linh said. I guess I raised my voice.

Oh, wow I said. Then what?

Well, Linh said my cousin came to the rescue. She explained to the man that a community college education can be just as good as a university education, and it's cheaper. It turned out that the man and his wife were from a European country, and they didn't understand our system. He said he hadn't understood and was sorry.

How did you feel about the whole thing I asked.

Embarrassed at first Linh answered. But it all turned out OK because of my cousin. It's great when there's someone who can smooth things over.

EXERCISE 5 MULTIPLE CHANGES TO INDIRECT SPEECH

GRAMMAR NOTES 3–7 **Read the conversation. Then complete the father's account of the conversation with indirect speech forms. The number in parentheses indicates how many words are needed in each case.**

SALLY: Dad, can you help me with my homework?
DAD: Yes, I can. What do you need?
SALLY: I have to write a report for my communications class. It's on a quotation.
DAD: OK. What's the quotation?
SALLY: It's by William Mizner, and it says, "A good listener is not only popular everywhere, but after a while he gets to know something."
DAD: What do you think it means?
SALLY: Well, maybe it means that people will like you if you're a good listener.
DAD: Good. That's part of it. Do you think it means anything else?
SALLY: Well, maybe that you can learn something if you listen.
DAD: Very good! You understand the quotation really well.

My daughter Sally asked me ___*if I could help her with her*___ (1. seven words) homework. I told her ______ (2. two words) and asked her ______ (3. three words). She said ______ (4. four words) a report on a quotation for ______ (5. one word) communications class. I asked her ______ (6. four words). She said ______ (7. two words) by William Mizner and went like this: "A good listener is not only popular everywhere, but after a while he gets to know something." I asked her ______ (8. five words). She said she thought maybe ______ (9. two words) that people ______ (10. two words) you if you were a good listener. I told her that ______ (11. one word) part of it and asked ______ (12. five words) anything else. She said she thought maybe it meant you ______ (13. two words) something if you listened. I told her ______ (14. two words) the quotation really well.

EXERCISE 6 EDITING

GRAMMAR NOTES 1–8 **Read the letter. It has nine mistakes in the use of direct and indirect speech. The first mistake is already corrected. Find and correct eight more.**

To: EmilyL@yoohoo.com
Fr: CharlesM@yoohoo.com

Dear Emily,

I just wanted to fill you in on Tim's school adventures. About two months ago, Melanie said she ~~feels~~ *felt* we should switch Tim to the public school. He'd been in a private school for several months, as you know. I asked her why did she think that, and she said, "He's miserable where he is, and I don't think the quality of education is good there. He tells he doesn't feel like he can communicate with the teachers and that no one understands him. He also doesn't think he has many friends." She said she thought we can move him to the local high school, which has a good academic reputation. I told to her that I agreed with her, but that we should ask Tim. The next morning, we asked Tim if he wanted to stay at the private school. I was surprised at how strong his response was. He said me that he hated the private school and didn't want to go there any longer. So we moved him. He's been at the new school for a month now, and he's doing well. Whenever I ask him does he have his homework done, he says, "Dad, I've already finished it." He's made several new friends. Every now and then, he asks us why didn't we let him change schools sooner. He says people are treating him as an individual now. I'm just glad we moved him when we did.

Not much else is new. Oh, yes—I do need to ask are you coming for the holidays. Email soon and let us know. Or call.

Love,
Charles

STEP 4 **COMMUNICATION PRACTICE**

EXERCISE 7 LISTENING

▶21|02 **A** Listen to the next part of the interview with Ellen Sands about communication and misunderstanding. What method of minimizing verbal conflict does Sands discuss here?

____

▶21|02 **B** Listen again. Then answer each question in a complete sentence.

1. What did Sands say that speaking about yourself instead of the other person involves?
   She said that it involves focusing on how the other person's statements are affecting you.
2. What did she say about how people should respond to anger?
   ____
3. What did the host ask Sands to give?
   ____
4. What did Sands say the two women were arguing about?
   ____
5. What did Rosa say about Alicia?
   ____
6. What did Alicia say in response to Rosa?
   ____
7. What is the first thing Alicia could have said?
   ____
8. What is the second thing Alicia could have said?
   ____

C Work with a partner. Discuss this question: Do you agree with what the communication expert said about not returning anger for anger? Why or why not? Give personal examples.

EXERCISE 8 WHAT REALLY HAPPENED?

A ROLE PLAY **You are going to perform a role play. First, work in a group of five students. Look at the picture. Discuss what happened to cause the accident. Who is most likely to give the most objective report of what happened, and why?**

EXAMPLE: I think that neither driver is likely to give an objective report. The bystander is likely to give an objective report because . . .

B **Invent conversations for the two police officers, the two drivers, and the bystander. Then perform them as a role play.**

EXAMPLE: POLICEMAN 1: What happened here?
DRIVER 1: Well, the accident wasn't my fault. The other driver was speeding. I wasn't . . .

C **Perform your role-play conversation for the class.**

EXERCISE 9 A TIME OF MISUNDERSTANDING

A DISCUSSION You are going to have a discussion about a misunderstanding. First, think of an example of a time when you experienced a conflict or a misunderstanding in your life. For example, think of a time when you were hurt or insulted by what someone said to you. How did you react? Did you resolve the situation satisfactorily, or not?

B Work in a group. Tell the members of your group about your experience. Did you and the other person return anger for anger? Did you listen actively? Did you state things positively or negatively?

EXAMPLE: A: Once someone I thought was my friend told me I was stupid.
B: What did you do?
A: Well, I was furious at first. I got really angry. After a while, though, I calmed down, and I told the friend that . . .

EXERCISE 10 GET WHAT THEY SAID RIGHT

A GAME You are going to play a reporting game. First, work with a partner. Work together to write a short dialogue in direct speech about communication and misunderstanding. The dialogue should be no longer than six sentences.

JOMO: My girlfriend isn't speaking to me.
MARIA: Why isn't she speaking to you?
JOMO: She thinks that I . . .

B Work with another pair. Take turns reporting each line of your dialogue to the other pair, using indirect speech. The other pair tries to guess what the original line of the dialogue was in direct speech. Make corrections if necessary.

EXAMPLE: A: First, Jomo said that his girlfriend wasn't speaking to him.
B: This is what Jomo said: "My girlfriend wasn't speaking to me."
C: No! I said, "My girlfriend *isn't* speaking to me."

FROM GRAMMAR TO WRITING

A BEFORE YOU WRITE **You are going to write an essay about a recent misunderstanding or conflict that you witnessed or took part in, and how it was resolved. Write a few paragraphs about the incident.**

B WRITE **Using your ideas in A, write a five-paragraph essay about the incident. Remember to use both direct and indirect speech. Try to avoid the common mistakes shown in the chart. Use the example below to help you begin your essay.**

EXAMPLE: Recently, I was involved in a situation that shows how easy it is to misunderstand someone. I was at a party, and there was a major political discussion going on. Before I knew it, I was heavily involved in the discussion. Someone asked me which party I supported, and I gave him my answer. He said, "Well, you should switch parties because your party can't possibly win." This made me really angry. I thought I was being attacked, and I got angrier and angrier. . . .

Common Mistakes in Direct and Indirect Speech

Don't use **quotation marks** in indirect speech. Use them in **direct speech**.	I said, **"**Jay, you need to tell me what's wrong.**"** I told Jay **he needed to tell me what was wrong.** NOT I told Jay "he needed to tell me what was wrong."
Don't use question word order in **indirect speech**. Use **statement word order**.	I asked Hassan **what time it was.** NOT I asked Hassan what time ~~was it~~.
In indirect speech, don't use *say* if the listener is mentioned. Use ***tell***.	Mia **told** me I should call Ted. NOT Mia ~~said~~ me I should call Ted.
In indirect speech, use ***say*** if the listener is *not* mentioned.	Cherie **said** she would be coming to the party. NOT Cherie ~~told~~ she would be coming to the party.

C CHECK YOUR WORK **Look at your essay. Underline direct and indirect speech. Use the Editing Checklist to check your work.**

Editing Checklist

Did you . . . ?

- ☐ use quotation marks in direct speech but not in indirect speech
- ☐ use statement word order in indirect speech
- ☐ use *tell* if the listener is mentioned and *say* if the listener is not mentioned

D REVISE YOUR WORK **Read your essay again. Can you improve your writing? Make changes if necessary.**

UNIT 21 REVIEW

Test yourself on the grammar of the unit.

A Complete the sentences. Circle the correct answers.

1. Min-Ji told Ho-Jin it's / it was time to get up.
2. Mom told Mary she hoped she had finished / have finished her homework.
3. Rob asked Marisol are you / if she was ready to leave.
4. Dad told Tadao to be sure / be sure to feed the pets.
5. Juan told Maria don't / not to forget to turn off the TV.
6. John asked Dad would he / if he would pick him up.
7. Sally said that "she would come by" / she would come by.
8. She assured us she could / can be there by 8:00.

B Complete the sentences with the words in parentheses.

1. Marta asked José ______________________ (he / will / be) late for dinner.
2. José told Marta he ______________________ (not / will / be) late.
3. Emiko told her father, ______________________ ("I / not / feel / well.")
4. Emiko's father told her ______________________ (she / need / take) her medicine.
5. Ali asked Jihan ______________________ (she / ever / see / snow)
6. She said, ______________________ ("I / see / snow / many times.")
7. The teacher told the students ______________________ (not / write) in ink.

C Find and correct five mistakes in the conversation.

Carlos said, "Ho-Jin, why you haven't called me lately?"

Ho-Jin said, "I just haven't had time. I have to study a lot right now.

Carlos said, "You said me you were going to try to relax more."

Ho-Jin said, "No, I didn't. I told I was going to relax as much as possible."

Carlos said, "Well, OK, but are we still friends."

Ho-Jin said, "Of course we are!"

Now check your answers on page 432.

Conditionals and the Subjunctive

UNIT 22

Conditionals; Other Ways to Express Unreality

ACHIEVEMENTS AND INVENTIONS

UNIT 23

More Conditions; The Subjunctive

ADVICE

PART 9

OUTCOMES

- Describe hypothetical results of a present or past situation, using present and past conditionals
- Express wishes, sadness, or regret with *wish*, *hope*, and *if only*
- Identify key information in an article and academic discussion
- Discuss hypothetical situations in the present and past
- Write an essay about the impact of a technological development or invention

OUTCOMES

- Express hypothetical situations and their results with implied and inverted conditions and the subjunctive
- Identify key details from an advice column and a conversation
- Participate in group discussions, giving advice and responding to suggestions
- Write an essay about a time when you took good or bad advice

UNIT

22

Conditionals; Other Ways to Express Unreality

ACHIEVEMENTS AND INVENTIONS

OUTCOMES

- Describe hypothetical results of a present or past situation, using present and past conditionals
- Express wishes, sadness, or regret with *wish*, *hope*, and *if only*
- Identify key information in an article and academic discussion
- Discuss hypothetical situations in the present and past
- Write an essay about the impact of a technological development or invention

STEP 1 GRAMMAR IN CONTEXT

BEFORE YOU READ

Discuss the questions.

1. What do you think is one of the greatest scientific achievements of all time?

2. What do you consider the most significant invention of the last 150 years?

READ

22|01 Read this article about famous achievements and inventions.

How Would Our World Be Different?

What causes people to make remarkable discoveries or invent remarkable devices? How would our world be different if certain remarkable discoveries or inventions hadn't been made? The experiences of Isaac Newton and Henry Ford, both of whom showed great determination, can shed some light on these questions.

Sometimes chance plays a role in scientific and technological advancement. In 1666, according to legend, young scientist Isaac Newton was sitting under an apple tree in his orchard. He looked up and saw an apple fall to the ground. This was a major historical moment: We could say that if Newton hadn't seen the apple fall, he wouldn't really have understood the force of gravity, and he probably wouldn't have formulated his famous theories. The apple did fall, though, and Newton did see it. Determined to understand this force, he theorized that two objects attract and mutually influence each other. If an apple, for example, falls from a tree, the much greater mass of the earth will attract and pull the apple to the ground.

Isaac Newton's theory of gravitation was first sparked by a chance occurrence, but it was realized through his strong dedication and determination. After the scientist's death, his French author friend Voltaire said that Newton had never had any deep relationships with other people. Newton never married, perhaps feeling that if he started a family, he wouldn't be able to devote his life to achieving his real passion: the advancement of science. Newton may even have died for science before his time. Upon his death, toxic levels of mercury were found in his body. If he hadn't exposed himself to mercury in chemical experiments, he might have lived much longer than he did. It seems clear that if Newton hadn't made such sacrifices, he might not have had such a powerful impact on the development of mathematics, optics, and physics during the next centuries. If it hadn't been for Newton, we might not have many of the inventions that characterize our time—e.g., high-powered telescopes, airplanes, rockets, or the space station.

Fast forward to 1908, when Henry Ford introduced his Model T Ford in Detroit, an action which was to change the world. Ford didn't invent the car; that accomplishment is generally attributed to German inventor Karl Benz. However, Ford was instrumental in bringing the automobile to the masses.[1] Before 1908, cars were complicated machines, difficult to operate and repair, and expensive to own. Ford utilized the assembly line in his factories to efficiently produce an automobile that the average person could afford to buy and maintain. In his own way, Ford was as determined as Newton. Before he succeeded as an automaker, Ford had persuaded wealthy businessmen to finance two other businesses to produce "horseless carriages"—i.e., cars. Both businesses failed, but Ford was undeterred.[2] In 1903, he started a new business, once again gaining the support of wealthy financiers. This time, his business was wildly successful. If Ford hadn't persisted, the revolutionary Model T might never have been produced.

Today, the car is ubiquitous, but what would our world be like if Ford hadn't been so determined to make it available to the common person? There would probably be fewer cars on the roads and fewer, if any, traffic jams. Car ownership might still be restricted to the wealthy. We probably wouldn't have as many suburbs as we presently do because the car makes it possible to live outside central cities. We can argue that if Ford hadn't marketed his Model T and made it widely available, someone else would have. But the result would have been vastly different. Ford was in the right place at the right time, and his efforts have changed the world. There are those today who wish that Ford had never popularized the gasoline-burning auto. There are even those who wish gasoline-powered cars would just disappear. "If only all cars were electric-powered," they might say. The car is here to stay, though, and it will continue to evolve.

Inventor Thomas Edison said that genius is one percent inspiration and ninety-nine percent perspiration. This seems an oversimplification. We might restate Edison's idea in this way: Genius is thirty-three percent inspiration, thirty-three percent perspiration, and thirty-four percent motivation. If Newton, Ford, and countless others hadn't been determined to forge ahead[3] with their enterprises, today's world would undoubtedly be quite different. Will the efforts of future innovators will be as far-reaching? That remains to be seen.

---

1 *the masses:* the working class, the common people

2 *undeterred:* not discouraged or stopped from taking action

3 *forge ahead:* move forward in a strong and powerful way

AFTER YOU READ

A VOCABULARY Choose the answer that is closest in meaning to the word in **bold**.

1. If he hadn't seen the apple fall, Newton probably wouldn't have **formulated** his theory.
   a. announced b. changed c. developed
2. Newton theorized that objects attract and **mutually** influence each other.
   a. both b. partially c. strongly
3. The invention of the car is generally **attributed to** Karl Benz.
   a. praised by b. credited to c. sent to
4. Ford **utilized** the assembly line in his factories.
   a. bought b. replaced c. used
5. Today the car is **ubiquitous**.
   a. limited b. everywhere c. expensive
6. Ford started a project to produce horseless carriages—**i.e.**, automobiles.
   a. for example b. whereas c. that is
7. If it hadn't been for Newton, we might not have many of the inventions that characterize our time—**e.g.**, rockets and the space station.
   a. for example b. in other words c. above all
8. The car is here to stay, and it will continue to **evolve**.
   a. increase in size b. change gradually c. be important

B COMPREHENSION Read the statements. Check (✓) *True* or *False*.

	True	False
1. Sometimes technological advances happen partly by chance.	☐	☐
2. Isaac Newton understood gravity before he saw the apple fall in 1666.	☐	☐
3. Newton had a minimal impact on the development of the sciences.	☐	☐
4. Henry Ford invented the automobile.	☐	☐
5. The automobile has influenced the growth of suburbs.	☐	☐
6. Cars were quite cheap before Ford introduced the Model T.	☐	☐
7. Ford had two successful businesses before 1903.	☐	☐
8. The article concludes that motivation is at least as important as perspiration in scientific or technological achievement.	☐	☐

C DISCUSSION Work with a partner. What do you think genius consists of? Do you agree more with Edison's statement or with the conclusions of the article? Discuss.

STEP 2 GRAMMAR PRESENTATION

CONDITIONALS; OTHER WAYS TO EXPRESS UNREALITY

Present and Future Real Conditionals

Present Conditionals

If Clause	Result Clause
If scientists **are** motivated,	they often **achieve** great things.
If an object **falls**,	gravity **pulls** it to the earth.

Future Conditionals

If Clause	Result Clause
If you **show** determination,	you **will be** successful.
If a scientist **perfects** a new invention,	the world **will** probably change.

Present Unreal Conditionals

Actual Situations	Conditionals: *If* Clause	Conditionals: Result Clause
It **is** rarely easy to invent something new.	If it **were** easy,	it **would be** unusual.
Inventors **are** often frustrated at first.	If they **weren't** frustrated,	
A new invention rarely **works** perfectly at first.	If it **worked** perfectly at first,	
It usually **takes** a long time to perfect an invention.	If it **didn't take** a long time,	

Past Unreal Conditionals

Actual Situations	Conditionals: *If* Clause	Conditionals: Result Clause
He **stopped** working on his invention, so he **lost** his funding.	If he **hadn't stopped**,	he **wouldn't have lost** his funding.
He **didn't stop** working on his invention, so he **didn't lose** his funding.	If he **had stopped**,	he **would have lost** his funding.
His colleague **encouraged** him, so he **was able** to start again.	If his colleague **hadn't encouraged** him,	he **wouldn't have been able** to start again.
His colleague **didn't help** him, so he **wasn't able** to start again.	If his colleague **had helped him**,	he **would have been able** to start again.

"Mixed" Conditionals

Actual Situations
Most cars **have been** gasoline-powered from the beginning.
Even today, many people **are not committed** to reducing pollution.

Conditionals	
If Clause	Result Clause
PAST If cars **had been** electric-powered from the beginning,	PRESENT there **wouldn't be** as much pollution today.
PRESENT If people **were** really **committed** to reducing pollution,	PAST we **might have done** something to address the problem sooner.

Other Ways to Express Unreality

Actual Situations
Cars are essential, but they cause pollution.
Some people can barely afford to buy gasoline.
Cars were gasoline-powered from the beginning.

Wish/If only Statement
Some people **wish** (that) all cars **were** electric-powered. **If only** they **were** all electric-powered.
I **wish** (that) I **could afford** gasoline. **If only** I **could afford** gasoline.
Some people **wish** (that) cars **had never been invented**. **If only** they **had never been invented**.

GRAMMAR NOTES

1 Definition of Conditionals

Conditional sentences describe situations that occur (or do not occur) because of certain **conditions**.

Conditional sentences consist of two clauses, a **dependent condition clause** (also called the *if*-clause) and an **independent result clause**.

CONDITION / DEPENDENT CLAUSE — RESULT / INDEPENDENT CLAUSE
If people **work** hard, they **are** often successful.

CONDITION / DEPENDENT CLAUSE — RESULT / INDEPENDENT CLAUSE
If I **were** a scientist, I **would try** to help the world.

There are two types of conditional sentences, **real** and **unreal**.

Real (also called **factual**) **conditionals** are sentences that describe situations that:

- occur **regularly**

  If people use cars, the air **becomes** polluted. *(present)*

- are **likely or possible** in the present and the future

  If it **snows** today, we'**ll close** the lab. *(present and future)*

CONTINUED ▶

Unreal conditionals are sentences that describe situations that are:	
• **untrue** in the present or past	**If** Maryam **worked** here, she **could help** us.
• **unlikely** in the present or past	**If** I **could afford** a new cell phone, I **could stay** in touch with people.
• **impossible** in the present or past	I **wouldn't have done** that **if I'd been** in your situation.
In conditional sentences, the clauses can come in either order, and the meaning is the same. We place a **comma** after the ***if*-clause** if it comes **first**. We don't generally place a comma after the result clause if it comes first.	**If** I **had** a computer**,** I **could get** my homework done. I **could get** my homework done **if I had** a computer.
Either or both clauses can be **negative**.	I **wouldn't buy** that computer if I **were** you. I **wouldn't have bought** that car if I **hadn't gotten** a good deal.
Form conditional **questions** in the usual way.	A: **Would** you **have become** a scientist if you**'d known** how difficult it would be? B: Yes, I certainly **would**.

2 Present Real Conditionals

Use **present real conditionals** to talk about general truths, scientific facts, or habits and repeated events.

Use **present-time verbs** in both the ***if*-clause** and the **result clause**. Most commonly, the present-time verbs are in the simple present.	Plants **die** if they **don't get** enough water. People with diabetes **can control** their disease if they **take** insulin regularly.
You can also use the present progressive in the *if*-clause.	If **I'm flying**, I always **feel** nervous.
In **future-time situations**, use the simple present or the present progressive in the *if*-clause and the **future** with *will* or *be going to*, *may*, *might*, *can*, *could*, or *should* in the **result clause**.	If Barry **passes** the final exam, he **might pass** his calculus course.
In addition to *if*, you can also use other subordinating conjunctions in the *if*-clause. These include ***unless*** and ***in case***.	***Unless*** he **studies** hard, however, he **won't pass** the final exam. We**'ll repeat** the experiment ***in case*** it **fails**.
BE CAREFUL! Use the **simple present** in the ***if*-clause** even if the time referred to is future.	I'll contact you as soon I **get** the lab results. NOT I'll contact you as soon as ~~I'll get~~ the lab results.

3 Present Unreal Conditionals

Use the **present unreal conditional** to talk about present unreal, untrue, imagined, or impossible conditions and their results.

Use the simple past form of the verb in the *if*-clause. If the verb is *be*, use ***were*** for all persons. Use *could*, *might*, or *would* + the base form of the verb in the result clause.	If he **were** really motivated, he **would be working** on his invention. We **wouldn't stay up** so late if we **weren't doing** these experiments. If I **were** you, I **wouldn't accept** the offer. I **might clean** up my lab if I **had** the day off.
USAGE NOTE The simple past verb in the *if*-clause is past in form only. It is **not past in meaning**.	If I ***had*** a million dollars, **I'd give** it to scientific research. *(I don't have a million.)*
USAGE NOTE Use ***were*** for all forms of the past of ***be*** in conditional sentences to describe situations that are **impossible** or **improbable**. In other conditional sentences, ***was*** is correct in the singular.	If I **were** you, I'd buy a new computer. *(an impossible situation; I'm not you.)* If my computer **wasn't** working properly, I would get it fixed. *(not impossible or improbable)*
BE CAREFUL! Don't use *would* in the *if*-clause in present unreal conditional sentences.	I would build a new lab if I **had** the money. NOT I would build a new lab if I ~~would have~~ the money.

4 Past Unreal Conditionals

Use the **past unreal conditional** to talk about past unreal, untrue, imagined, or impossible situations and their results.

Use the **past perfect** in the *if*-clause. Use ***would***, ***might***, or ***could*** + ***have*** + past participle in the result clause.	If I **had listened** to you, I **wouldn't have made** that mistake. Ali **might have accepted** your offer if you**'d asked** him in time.
We often use the past unreal conditional to express **regret** about a situation that actually happened in the past.	I **would have lent** you money if I **had known** you wanted to go to college.
BE CAREFUL! Don't use *would have* in the *if*-clause in past unreal conditional sentences. Use ***would have*** only in the **result** clause.	I would have lent you money if I **had known** you wanted to go to college. NOT I would have lent you money if I ~~would have known~~ you wanted to go to college.

5 Mixed Conditionals

The times of the *if*-clause and the result clause are sometimes different. Present unreal and past unreal conditional forms can be **"mixed"** in the same sentence. The time in the *if*-clause can be past, while the time in the result clause is present.	PAST ACTION / PRESENT RESULT If I **hadn't gone** to college, I**'d** be unemployed now.
Similarly, the time in the *if*-clause may be present, while the time in the result clause is past.	PRESENT ACTION / PAST RESULT If Sam **were coming**, he **would have arrived** by now.

6 *Wish* and *Hope* + Noun Clause

We often use unreal conditionals to express regret or sadness. In a similar way, we use ***wish*** **+ noun clause** to express **sadness** or a **desire** for a **different situation**.

Use:	
• ***wish*** + ***could/would*** + base form to express a wish about the future	I **wish** (that) you ***would*** **change** your mind about working for us.
• ***wish*** + **simple past** to express a wish about the present	My wife **wishes** (that) I ***didn't work*** such long hours.
• ***wish*** + **past perfect** to express a wish about the past	My son **wishes** (that) he ***hadn't taken*** that job.
USAGE NOTE Don't confuse ***wish*** with ***hope***. Use ***wish*** to express regrets about things that are **unlikely** or are **impossible to change**. Use ***hope*** + simple present/future to express a desire about **events** that are **possible** or **probable**.	I ***wish*** (that) she **would join** our team. *(I don't think she will.)* I ***hope*** (that) she **accepts** our job offer. *(It's possible or probable that she will.)*

7 *If Only* + Noun Clause

If only has a meaning similar to that of *wish*. *If only* is followed by a noun clause **without** ***that***.

Use the **simple past** after *if only* to express a wish about something that is contrary to fact at the **present** time.	I **wish** (that) I ***had*** a car. **If only** I ***had*** a car. **If only** cars ***were*** cheaper.
Use the **past perfect** after *if only* to express a wish that something had happened differently in the **past**.	**If only** I ***hadn't said*** that!
BE CAREFUL! Don't confuse *if only* with *only if*.	***If only*** Jerry **studied** more. *(I wish he studied more.)* ***Only if*** Jerry **studied** more **would** he **have** a chance of passing. *(This would be the only way for him to pass.)*

STEP 3 FOCUSED PRACTICE

EXERCISE 1 DISCOVER THE GRAMMAR

A GRAMMAR NOTES 1–4 **Look at the sentences based on the reading. Identify each sentence as a *real* (*R*) or *unreal* (*U*) conditional.**

_R_ **1.** If an apple falls from a tree, gravity will pull it to the ground.

____ **2.** If Newton hadn't seen the apple fall, he probably wouldn't have formulated his theories.

____ **3.** Chance can play a role in technological development if people understand how to use new ideas.

____ **4.** If Newton hadn't exposed himself to mercury, he might have lived longer.

____ **5.** There would be far fewer cars on the road if Ford hadn't brought the car to the masses.

____ **6.** Would today's society be recognizable if there were no cars?

____ **7.** Pollution will decrease if we promote the use of electric cars.

____ **8.** People can achieve great things if they show determination.

B GRAMMAR NOTES 2–6 **Look at the sentences based on the reading. Identify each sentence as a *past*, *present*, *future*, or *mixed* (present and past) conditional.**

past **1.** If Newton hadn't been in his orchard, he wouldn't have seen the apple fall.

____ **2.** If the wind blows strongly, the apples will fall from that tree.

____ **3.** Newton might not have become a scientist if the orchard experience hadn't happened.

____ **4.** What would our world be like today if Ford hadn't produced the Model T?

____ **5.** Some people wish gasoline-powered cars would just disappear.

____ **6.** If only all cars were electric-powered.

____ **7.** If driverless cars become widespread, we won't have to drive anymore.

____ **8.** Innovators often have success if they believe in themselves.

EXERCISE 2 PRESENT AND FUTURE REAL CONDITIONALS

GRAMMAR NOTES 1–2 **Unscramble the sentences. Write the words in the correct order to create present real conditional sentences. Use correct punctuation.**

1. (decrease / we / Pollution / popularize electric cars / if / will)

Pollution will decrease if we popularize electric cars.

2. (We / develop efficient space travel / if / colonize Mars / might / engineers)

____

3. (run out of energy / don't develop alternative fuel sources / if / will / We / researchers)

____

4. (stop climate change / If / the polar ice caps / melt / could / we / don't)

____

5. (drive hybrid cars / If / people / the environment / they / help)

____

6. (current population trends continue / the world / will / If / nine billion people by 2060 / have)

____

EXERCISE 3 PRESENT AND FUTURE REAL AND UNREAL CONDITIONALS

GRAMMAR NOTES 2–3 **Complete the conversation. Circle the correct answers.**

MARISA: Hi, Fabio. Come on in.

FABIO: Hi, Marisa. Got a couple of minutes? I need to ask you about something.

MARISA: Always. What's up?

FABIO: (If I ask) / If I will ask (1.) you a question, will you give / do you give (2.) me an honest answer?

MARISA: Of course I do / I will (3.). Shoot.

FABIO: What would you be doing / would you do (4.) if someone you liked and respected takes / took (5.) credit for your work and presented it to the CEO?

MARISA: I'd report / I report (6.) it to the CEO. Why?

FABIO: Well, I wrote a new computer program that zaps most of the bugs in our programs. I told Stanley about it. He asked if he could study it for a while. I said yes. Later, I was in the CEO's office, and he showed me the program I'd written and said he was really impressed with Stanley for writing it. I was pretty shocked, and I didn't know what to do. If I go / I'd go (7.) to the CEO, I feel / I'll feel (8.) like a tattletale.

MARISA: What is it with Stanley these days, anyway? It seems like he's been acting really weird lately.

FABIO: The thing is, Stanley is my brother-in-law. He and my sister are on the verge of a divorce. I'm afraid that if I exposed / expose (9.) him, it had / it would (10.) push him over the edge.

MARISA: Fabio, you wrote this great new program. You deserve credit. I guess if I was / were (11.) you, I'd talk / I'll talk (12.) to Stanley first. Just tell him that if he won't / wouldn't (13.) go to the CEO soon, you'll have to / you had to (14.) do it yourself.

FABIO: OK. Thanks a lot, Marisa. You gave me an honest answer and not what you thought I wanted to hear.

EXERCISE 4 *WISH* AND *IF ONLY*

A GRAMMAR NOTES 6–7 Look at the photos. Using the words in parentheses, write a sentence with *wish* for each. Photos 1 and 2 go together; 3 and 4 go together; 5 and 6 go together. Make the sentences negative if necessary.

1. (drivers / be / stuck in traffic)

   The drivers wish they weren't stuck in traffic.

2. (they / take / the subway instead)

3. (he / have / a better computer)

4. (he / can afford / a new computer)

5. (people / their cell phones / work / in this area)

6. (they / have / good cell phone service)

B GRAMMAR NOTE 7 **Look at the photos in A again. Write a statement about each photo with *if only* and the words in parentheses.**

1. (someone / invent / a flying car)

   If only someone would invent a flying car.

2. (subways / not / be / noisy and crowded)

   ____

3. (researchers / invent / a computer / that would never break down)

   ____

4. (all computers / be / affordable for everyone)

   ____

5. (someone / invent / a cell phone / that could work everywhere)

   ____

6. (cell phones / not / need / cell phone towers)

   ____

EXERCISE 5 MIXED AND PAST UNREAL CONDITIONALS

GRAMMAR NOTES 4–5 **Complete the story with mixed or past unreal conditional sentences. Use the correct forms of the words in parentheses. Use contractions where possible.**

A year ago, I took a train from Montreal to Toronto. If I *hadn't missed* (1. not / miss) the bus to the train station, I ______ (2. not / take) the particular train I took, and I ______ (3. never / meet) Professor Lozano. My life ______ (4. be) very different today. Professor Lozano was rather elderly, and he was having trouble putting his suitcase on the luggage rack. If I ______ (5. not / offer) to help him, we ______ (6. never / start) talking. Professor Lozano told me that he had invented a robotic arm that is now used in the space program. I told the professor I was a science major, and it turned out that the professor taught at the same university I was attending. He told me there was an unfilled lab position in his department and that I could apply for it. If I ______ (7. not / mention) that I was a science major, the professor ______ (8. never / tell) me about the unfilled lab position, and I ______ (9. never / apply) for it. I ______ (10. not / be studying) for my doctorate in nuclear physics right now. Let's see . . . I guess it all happened because I missed that bus. I'll always be glad that I did.

EXERCISE 6 EDITING

GRAMMAR NOTES 1–7 Read the email. There are ten mistakes in the use of conditionals and related forms. The first mistake is already corrected. Find and correct nine more.

Hi, Bruce,

This has been one of those days when I wish I ~~would have~~ had stayed in bed. When I turned on my computer this morning, it crashed immediately. It's not like this has never happened before . . . but I certainly wish the computer didn't choose this day, of all days, to crash. My scholarship application was due this afternoon by 3:00 p.m., and I had almost everything ready for it. I just needed half an hour or so to put some finishing touches on it. So I was pretty desperate. As soon as my computer crashed, I took it straight to a repair shop, but it took me two hours to get there. If I got it there by 11 a.m., they probably could fix it in time for me to make the three o'clock deadline. But I didn't get there until 12.

Everything would have worked out if there wouldn't have been a major traffic jam on the freeway. I was stuck in traffic for an hour and a half. I wish I had the sense to take another highway and not the freeway. I'm also mad at myself for another reason. If I sent in the application a week ago, they would already receive it, and everything would be fine right now.

Anyway, the computer will be fixed by tomorrow. If I'll get the application emailed by the end of the day, I might still be eligible for the scholarship. If only someone invented a computer that would never crash!

Send me a text on my cell phone, which is working fine. I need some cheering up.

Elena

STEP 4 COMMUNICATION PRACTICE

EXERCISE 7
LISTENING

22|02 **A** Listen to the classroom discussion. When and why did people start using the word "bug" to indicate a computer problem?

____

____

____

22|02 **B** Read the statements. Listen again to the class discussion. For each statement, check (✓) *True* or *False*.

	True	False
1. The teacher asks the students what actions they would take if their computers had problems.	☑	☐
2. Most students in the class would take their computers to a shop if they weren't working properly.	☐	☐
3. Andrea says that a computer probably has a bug or a virus if it isn't working.	☐	☐
4. There is probably a real insect inside a computer if it isn't working properly.	☐	☐
5. Grace Harper used the term "bug" in 1947 because it hadn't been invented yet.	☐	☐
6. Before 1947, researchers would have used the term "bug" to refer to insects causing problems in machines.	☐	☐
7. If Harvard hadn't been working closely with the Navy, Grace Harper would not have written a report about the "bug."	☐	☐
8. If Grace Harper and others hadn't started using the term "bug," it might not have become the accepted term for a computer problem.	☐	☐

C Work with a partner. What problems with computer bugs have you experienced? How do you react if you discover that your computer is not working on a particular day? Are you upset? Angry? Discuss.

EXERCISE 8 WHO WOULD YOU BE IF . . . ?

GAME Form two teams. With your team, use the prompts to construct eight conditional questions, four in the present and four in the past. Then create two questions of your own. Ask the other team each question. They guess what person or thing is being referred to, choosing from the words in the box. Take turns. To check answers, see page 436.

EXAMPLE: **Prompt:** Who / been / if / formulated / the theory of gravity

TEAM A: Who would you have been if you had formulated the theory of gravity?
TEAM B: If I had formulated the theory of gravity, I would have been Sir Isaac Newton.

a blue whale	Alexander Graham Bell	Grace Harper	one of the Wright Brothers
a dinosaur	between eighty and eighty-nine	Italy	thirty years old
a mammoth	between ninety and ninety-nine	Karl Benz	thirty-five years old
Abraham Lincoln	Bill Gates	Mount Everest	Thomas Edison

Team A's Prompts:

1. Who / been / if / invent / the electric light
2. How old / have to / be / if / be / the president of the United States
3. What creature / been / if / be / an ancestor of the elephant
4. How old / be / if / be / a nonagenarian
5. Who / been / if / made / the first successful airplane flight in 1903
6. Who / been / if / invented / the car
7. What country / been from / if / been / Marco Polo
8. What mountain / climbed / if / been / with Edmund Hillary and Tenzing Norgay in 1953
9. ______________________________
10. ______________________________

Team B's Prompts:

1. How old / be / if / an octogenarian
2. Who / be / if / be / the founder of Microsoft
3. What / be / if / be / the largest mammal
4. How old / have to be / if / be / a United States senator
5. Who / been / if / been / the inventor of the telephone
6. What kind of creature / been / if / been / a stegosaurus
7. Who / been / if / popularized / the term *bug*
8. Who / been / if / been / president of the United States during the Civil War
9. ______________________________
10. ______________________________

EXERCISE 9 HENRY FORD'S ASSEMBLY LINE

INFORMATION GAP Work with a partner. Student A will follow the instructions below. Student B will follow the instructions on page 442.

STUDENT A

- The article below is missing some information. Your partner has the same article that contains your missing information. Ask your partner questions to find the missing information.

  EXAMPLE: A: What would Ford never have done if he hadn't changed the makeup of his original assembly line?
  B: He would never have achieved success with the Model T.

- Your partner's article is missing different information. Answer your partner's questions so that he or she can fill in the missing information.

  EXAMPLE: B: When did Ford introduce his Model T to the world?
  A: He introduced his Model T to the world in 1908.

The First Moving Assembly Line

HENRY FORD introduced his Model T to the world in 1908. However, he never would have ______________________ if he hadn't changed the makeup of his original assembly line. Ford knew that ordinary people wouldn't buy his cars if they were expensive. If Ford could make Model Ts cheaper than other cars, he knew that ______________________. So Ford introduced a new, more efficient method of auto production that involved division of labor.

On Ford's original assembly line, auto workers had to do several separate tasks to put each car together. If workers have to move around a lot and do many different tasks, they can't ______________________. If you divide a big job into many different smaller tasks, however, everyone can do his or her task faster. So, Ford and his staff divided the assembly process into eighty-four different steps. In this way, they minimized the motion of each worker as much as possible. There was another advantage: If each worker was responsible for only one task, he or she would also be easier to train.

In 1913, Ford introduced the moving chassis assembly line and a mechanized belt, which sped up the car assembly process a great deal. If a business makes many products quickly, it can ______________________. So, Ford's plan to make Model Ts cheaper than other cars succeeded.

If Ford hadn't figured out a way to build his cars more efficiently, it's possible that cars ______________________. However, might the world be a better place now if there were fewer cars in it? And what about the workers themselves? ______________________ if these changes hadn't been made? Could they have felt like machines who had to perform the same repetitive actions endlessly? It's difficult to say. The bottom line is that Ford achieved his goal.

FROM GRAMMAR TO WRITING

A BEFORE YOU WRITE **You are going to write an essay about a technological advance or invention that has changed the world. Write a few sentences about one of these inventions or another invention or advance of your choice.**

- television
- the telephone
- the airplane

B WRITE **Using your ideas from A, write a five-paragraph essay about the technological advance or invention you have chosen. Remember to use real and unreal conditionals in present and past time. Try to avoid the common mistakes shown in the chart. Use the example below to help you begin your essay.**

EXAMPLE: On December 17, 1903, in Kitty Hawk, North Carolina, Wilbur and Orville Wright successfully completed a flight in an airplane. They weren't the first ones to build and fly aircraft, but their successful flight set in motion the development of air travel. How would our world be different today if the Wright Brothers had never existed?

First, travel would be very different. It would take us a month to travel across the Atlantic Ocean. We'd still be traveling by ship. . . .

Second, the airline industry would never have gotten started. . . .

Common Mistakes in Using Real and Unreal Conditionals

When using the verb *be*, don't use *was* in **present unreal situations** that are contrary to fact. Use *were* in all persons.	I wouldn't buy that computer if I **were** you. NOT I wouldn't buy that computer if I ~~was~~ you.
Don't use *had* in the **result** clause in **past unreal conditional** constructions. Use ***would*** + ***have*** + **past participle**.	People wouldn't **have** bought Ford's Model T if it had been expensive. NOT People wouldn't ~~had~~ bought Ford's Model T if it had been expensive.
Don't use *would have* + past participle in the *if*-clause in **past unreal conditional** constructions. Use ***had*** + **past participle**.	**If** I **had finished** college, I would be working in a scientific laboratory now. NOT If I ~~would have~~ finished college, I would be working in a scientific laboratory now.

C CHECK YOUR WORK **Look at your essay. Underline the conditional sentences. Use the Editing Checklist to check your work.**

Editing Checklist

Did you . . . ?

- ☐ use *were* in the verb *be* in present unreal situations that are contrary to fact
- ☐ use *would have* + past participle in the result clause in past unreal conditionals
- ☐ avoid using *would have* + past participle in the *if*-clause in past unreal conditionals

D REVISE YOUR WORK **Read your essay again. Can you improve your writing? Make changes if necessary.**

UNIT 22 **REVIEW**

Test yourself on the grammar of the unit.

A **Complete the sentences. Circle the correct answers.**

1. Our world would be a lot different if the Wright Brothers didn't build / hadn't built the world's first successful airplane.
2. If it hadn't been / wouldn't have been for the Wright Brothers, the major airline companies wouldn't have arisen.
3. We won't have / wouldn't have the airline industry today.
4. It would take / will take weeks to cross the Atlantic Ocean.
5. A lot more people will be / would be traveling by ship.
6. We hadn't had / wouldn't have had the terrible plane crashes that we have had.
7. We hadn't been able / wouldn't be able to get fresh food delivered overnight.
8. If it weren't / hadn't been for the Wright brothers, the space program might not exist.

B **Complete the sentences with the correct forms of the verbs in parentheses.**

1. Bao ______________________ (wish / he / not / forget) to change the oil in his car.
2. If he had changed the oil, the engine ______________________ (not / stop) working.
3. If the engine ______________________ (not / stop) working, the car wouldn't have broken down.
4. If that hadn't happened, he ______________________ (not / have to) pay a towing bill.
5. He also ______________________ (not / have to) replace the engine.
6. He ______________________ (have) a lot more money in the bank right now.
7. If his car had still been working, he ______________________ (could / make) it to the job interview.
8. In fact, he probably ______________________ (not / be) unemployed now.

C **Find and correct four mistakes.**

A: Jim wants to market his new invention. Would you buy it if you have the money?

B: If I was Jim, I won't market it.

A: Why not?

B: Who wants a robot that drives your car? People will laugh at him.

A: You're just jealous. I'll bet you wish you would have invented it yourself.

Check your answers on page 432.

UNIT 23

More Conditions; The Subjunctive

ADVICE

OUTCOMES

- Express hypothetical situations and their results with implied and inverted conditions and the subjunctive
- Identify key details from an advice column and a conversation
- Participate in group discussions, giving advice and responding to suggestions
- Write an essay about a time when you took good or bad advice

STEP 1 GRAMMAR IN CONTEXT

BEFORE YOU READ

Discuss the questions.

1. Do you ever read advice columns? Do you think they contain useful information?
2. What is a problem that you might potentially ask a columnist about?

READ

23|01 Read these letters to an advice columnist and her responses.

Dear Rosa,

Hank and I were best friends in high school, so when he suggested we room together in college, I thought it was a great idea. Wrong! Had I known what a slob Hank really is, I never would have agreed to room with him. We have a small suite that has become a pigsty[1] because Hank thinks it's beneath him to wash a dish and is convinced the floor is the place to keep clothes. Whenever I talk to Hank about it, he just says, "Hey, Jason, you need to lighten up. You're too tense." I'm no neat freak, but I do prefer a semblance of order. I still like Hank and want to stay friends, but I'm feeling more like a doormat[2] every day. What would you recommend I do?

Jason

1 *pigsty:* a very dirty room or house
2 *doormat:* someone who is treated badly by other people

Dear Jason,

No one should have to feel like a doormat. Unfortunately, there's no easy solution to your problem. I can suggest three potential remedies: First, Hank may be unaware there's actually a problem. If so, ask him if he really likes having dirty dishes and bugs all over the place. If he doesn't, he might lend his muscles and help with the cleaning. There's a chance this approach will work, but if not, remedy two is teaching him how to clean up—he just may not be used to it. You might suggest he do the dishes one day and you the next. Should that not work, remedy three is to remind him you both have a right to a reasonably clean and orderly living space, and you feel your rights are being violated. Sometimes an appeal to a person's sense of fairness can do the trick. Whatever you do, it's important that Hank not feel criticized. Otherwise, he'll probably become resistant, so be moderate in your suggestions. Good luck.

Rosa

Dear Rosa,

Jim and I have been married for over four years now, and our marriage would be ideal were it not for the overbearing personalities of some of the people in his family. I love Jim dearly, but there are times when I feel like I'm married to his family members as well. They often drop in without letting me know they're coming, and at this point I'm spending more time with them than with Jim. Besides that, his sister Hannah constantly bombards me with requests that I do favors for her. For example, she insists I take her grocery shopping every week, even though she has her own car and is perfectly capable of doing this on her own. Even worse, his cousin Helen often requests I lend her money. At this point, Helen owes me about $750, but if I mention it she just says, "Carla, you know I'm good for it. I just need to get some bills paid off, and then I can pay you back." Rosa, I feel like I'm being manipulated by his family members. I know how important Jim's family is to him, but I'm at the end of my rope.[3] What would you suggest that I do?

Carla

Dear Carla,

You're experiencing lack of privacy, one of the most common problems faced by young married people, so don't feel you're alone. The problem sounds quite fixable. My guess is that your husband probably doesn't know what's going on and doesn't realize the depth of your frustration. Here's my advice: Have a heart-to-heart talk with Jim. First, tell him you appreciate his family but also feel you and he need more time alone together, and that without that time together, your relationship won't be able to develop as it should. Suggest these people call before they come over. Also tell him

3 *at the end of my rope:* in an almost desperate situation

you want to be helpful, but you feel his sister and cousin are asking too much of you. I'll bet he'll be willing to speak to them privately or at least mediate between you and Helen. When you're telling Jim about this, of course, it's essential that you not criticize his family members. That would probably cause resentment. Just give an honest statement of your feelings. With a little bit of extra communication with Jim, you can right the ship[4] and make your marriage stronger. Good luck, and hang in there!

Rosa

4 *right the ship:* fix the situation

AFTER YOU READ

A VOCABULARY Match the words in **bold** with their meanings.

____ **1.** Hank is really a **slob**.		**a.** stubborn
____ **2.** I do prefer a **semblance** of order.		**b.** having the ability
____ **3.** You feel your rights are being **violated**.		**c.** act as a peacemaker
____ **4.** Otherwise, he'll probably become **resistant**.		**d.** outward appearance
____ **5.** His family members are **overbearing**.		**e.** controlled and influenced
____ **6.** She is perfectly **capable** of doing that on her own.		**f.** messy or lazy person
____ **7.** I feel like I'm being **manipulated** by his family members.		**g.** disrespected
____ **8.** He might even **mediate** between you and Hannah.		**h.** trying to make others obey

B COMPREHENSION Complete the sentences based on the reading.

1. It was Hank's suggestion that he and Jason ________________ together in college.
2. Jason is not a compulsively neat person, but he likes a certain amount of ________________.
3. Jason is feeling more like a ________________ every day.
4. Rosa says Hank may just not be ________________ cleaning up.
5. Rosa suggests that appealing to Hank's sense of ________________ may help the situation.
6. Carla is bothered by the fact that some of her husband's family ________________ without letting her know they're coming.
7. Rosa says lack of privacy is a common problem faced by young ________________.
8. Rosa says Carla should suggest to Jim that his family members ________________ before they come over.

C DISCUSSION Work with a partner. Compare and justify your answers in B. Then discuss: Do you agree with the advice columnist's suggestions for Jason and Carla? Why or why not?

STEP 2 GRAMMAR PRESENTATION

MORE CONDITIONS; THE SUBJUNCTIVE

Implied Conditions

Implied Condition (= Standard Condition)	Result Clause
With a bit of luck, (If we have a bit of luck,)	we can fix the problem.
Without your help, (If you hadn't helped,)	I wouldn't have succeeded.
But for his investments, (If he didn't have investments,)	he'd have no income.
She might be lucky; **if so,** (If she is lucky,)	she'll meet some new friends.
He might get the chance; **if not,** (If he doesn't get the chance,)	he won't take the job.
She is lonely; **otherwise,** (If she weren't lonely,)	she wouldn't need company.

Inverted Conditions

Inverted Condition (= Standard Condition)	Result Clause
Were he in love, (If he **were** in love,)	he would get married.
Were he **not** in love, (If he **weren't** in love,)	he wouldn't get married.
Had I **seen** her, (If I **had seen** her,)	I would have called you.
Should we **do** it, (If we **should do** it,)	we will celebrate.

The Subjunctive in Noun Clauses

Verbs of Advice, Necessity, and Urgency + Subjunctive

Main Clause	Noun Clause
Frank's teacher **suggested**	(that) he **take** an additional class.
The boss **demanded**	(that) Rosa **arrive** at work by 9:00.
The fireman **insisted**	(that) she **leave** the burning building immediately.

Adjectives of Advice, Necessity, and Urgency + Subjunctive	
Main Clause	**Noun Clause**
It is **advisable**	(that) he **arrive** one-half hour before the appointment.
It is **mandatory**	(that) no one **enter** the building without a permit.
It is **urgent**	(that) she **call** home at once.

GRAMMAR NOTES

1 Implied Conditions

Conditions in conditional sentences are sometimes **implied** rather than stated directly in an *if*-clause.

Use these phrases to imply conditions:

but for — *otherwise*
if not — *with*
if so — *without*

Your brother may be lonely. **If so**, he should join a singles group.
(If he is lonely . . .)
Safiya may not want your advice right now. **If not**, just let her solve her own problems.
(If she doesn't want your advice . . .)

In a sentence with an implied condition, there is **no change** in the **result** clause.

Mary needs to be part of the decision. **Otherwise**, she'll never be happy.
(If she isn't part of the decision, she'll never be happy.)

As with other conditional sentences, the conditional phrase may **precede** or **follow** the result clause.

With a little extra communication, you can fix the problem.
You can fix the problem **with a little extra communication**.

IN WRITING The implied conditional *but for* is formal and generally used only in writing and formal speech.

Mei-Ling just moved here. **But for** her co-workers, she wouldn't have any friends.
(If she didn't have her co-workers . . .)

2 Inverted Conditions

We can express unreal conditions by **deleting** *if* and **inverting** the subject and the verb.

We often use the following forms in inverted conditions: *had* (past perfect), *were*, and *should*.

If I had known he was lazy, I wouldn't have roomed with him. *(past unreal conditional)*
***Had* I known** he was lazy, I wouldn't have roomed with him. *(inverted condition)*

If there is an inverted condition, there is **no change** in the **result** clause.

If I were to accept the job, **I would insist on benefits.**
Were I to accept the job, **I would insist on benefits.**

As with other conditional sentences, the inverted condition clause can **precede** or **follow** the result clause.

Were I to move, I'd have to get a new roommate.
I'd have to get a new roommate **were I to move**.

CONTINUED ▶

Sentences with inverted condition clauses have the **same meaning** as conditionals with *if*, but they are somewhat more **formal**.	**If I were** to accept the job offer, I would ask for a salary increase. **Were I** to accept the job offer, I would ask for a salary increase.
USAGE NOTE In both the normal conditional and the inverted condition with ***should***, the meaning of *should* is quite different from its normal meaning of advice or expectation. Both sentences mean that the action is relatively **unlikely to occur**.	**If you should return** before I do, start the newspaper delivery. **Should you return** before I do, start the newspaper delivery. **Should something go wrong**, we need to have a backup plan. *(It is relatively unlikely that something will go wrong, but we need to be prepared.)*
BE CAREFUL! To form negative inversion, add ***not*** after the inverted verb and the subject. Don't contract *not* and the verb.	**Had I *not* received** the phone call, I wouldn't have been able to help. NOT ~~Hadn't I~~ received the phone call, I wouldn't have been able to help.

3 Form and Function of the Subjunctive

The **subjunctive** is a verb form that expresses **unreal conditions**, **wishes**, and **possibilities**.

We often use ***were*** for all persons of the verb ***be*** in the subjunctive.	If I ***were*** you, I'd visit my parents more often. *(I'm not you, but this is what I would do.)* We could go on a picnic if it ***weren't*** raining. *(I wish it weren't raining, but it is.)*
Another form of the subjunctive occurs in **noun clauses** and uses the **base form** of the verb. In noun clauses with subjunctive constructions, we can usually omit the word ***that***.	MAIN CLAUSE / NOUN CLAUSE We recommend **(that) he *see* a lawyer**. They insist **(that) she *visit* her doctor**.
The verb in a main clause can be past, present, or future. However, the **subjunctive verb** is always the **base form**.	We **recommended** that he **see** a lawyer. We're **going to recommend** that she ***sell*** her house.
To form the **negative** of a subjunctive verb, place ***not*** before the base form.	My aunt and uncle insisted (that) we ***not* come** to visit them today.
To form a **passive subjunctive**, use *be* + the past participle.	The doctor recommends (that) Uncle John **be hospitalized**.
BE CAREFUL! Use *were* in a subjunctive construction only in present unreal conditions. **Do not use** it for **past situations**.	If I **were** there, I would help her. NOT ~~If I were there~~, I would have helped her.

4 The Subjunctive with Verbs of Advice, Necessity, and Urgency

Use the subjunctive with the base form of the verb in noun clauses following **verbs of advice**, **necessity**, and **urgency**.

The five principal verbs of advice, necessity, and urgency are ***demand***, ***insist***, ***propose***, ***recommend***, and ***suggest***.	I ***propose*** (that) we **ask** Mom and Dad about their wishes. My parents ***insisted*** (that) I **come** to visit them more often.
USAGE NOTE The verbs ***ask***, ***order***, ***require***, ***urge***, etc., can be followed by subjunctive constructions. When they occur with subjunctive constructions, the word *that* is usually not omitted. These verbs can also occur in the more usual pattern **verb + object + infinitive**. For a list of verbs that can be used in both patterns, see Appendix 26 on page 422.	I **asked that** my brothers and sisters ***be*** present. OR I **asked** my brothers and sisters ***to be*** present.
USAGE NOTE The verbs ***insist (on)***, ***propose***, ***recommend***, and ***suggest*** can also be followed by a **gerund** phrase. The meaning of this structure is essentially the same as that of a sentence with a subjunctive in a noun clause.	We **suggest *getting*** another bid for the job. They **recommended *getting*** a second opinion from another doctor.
BE CAREFUL! Don't use infinitives after ***demand***, ***insist***, ***propose***, ***recommend***, and ***suggest***.	Bi-Yun suggested **(that) we talk**. NOT Bi-Yun suggested ~~us to talk~~.

5 The Subjunctive with Adjectives of Advice, Necessity, and Urgency

Use the subjunctive with the base form of the verb in noun clauses after **adjectives** of **advice**, **necessity**, and **urgency**.

Common adjectives of advice, necessity, and urgency are: *advisable* *important* *urgent* *crucial* *mandatory* *desirable* *necessary* These adjectives + subjunctive occur in the pattern ***It* + *be* + adjective + *that*-clause**.	**It is *essential*** that elderly people **be treated** with dignity. **It is *important*** that she **understand** her options. **It was *necessary*** that my brother **see** a lawyer.
USAGE NOTE We can replace the *that*-clause with *for* + noun or object pronoun + infinitive. These are more informal constructions.	It's **important for her to understand** her options. It was **necessary for my brother to see** a lawyer.

REFERENCE NOTE

For a list of **verbs and expressions followed by the subjunctive**, see Appendix 26 on page 422.

STEP 3 FOCUSED PRACTICE

EXERCISE 1 DISCOVER THE GRAMMAR

GRAMMAR NOTES 1–5 **Read the sentences based on the reading. Look at the underlined words. Are they *implied conditionals* (*IM*), *inverted conditionals* (*IV*), or *subjunctive verb constructions* (*SV*)? Write the correct answers.**

_SV_ **1.** Hank suggested we room together in college.

_____ **2.** Had I known what a slob Hank really is, I never would have agreed.

_____ **3.** What would you recommend I do?

_____ **4.** This may work, but if not, try teaching him how to clean up.

_____ **5.** Should that not work, remedy three is to appeal to his sense of fairness.

_____ **6.** Our marriage would be ideal were it not for the overbearing personalities of his family members.

_____ **7.** Be moderate in your suggestions; otherwise, he may become resistant.

_____ **8.** It's essential that you not criticize his family.

_____ **9.** With a little bit of extra communication, you can right the ship.

EXERCISE 2 INVERTED CONDITIONS AND THE SUBJUNCTIVE

GRAMMAR NOTES 2–5 **Read the pairs of sentences. Is the second sentence a correct rewriting of the first? Check (✓) *Yes* or *No*.**

	Yes	No
1. I would have recommended she sell it a long time ago. I would have recommended her selling it a long time ago.	☑	☐
2. She's always said it's important for her to keep her independence. She's always said it's important that she keep her independence.	☐	☐
3. I propose you make a new offer on the house. I propose you to make a new offer on the house.	☐	☐
4. I'd recommend you look into joining a singles group. I'd recommend you to join a singles group.	☐	☐
5. It's essential that you understand what your job responsibilities would be. It's essential for you to understand what your job responsibilities would be.	☐	☐
6. I would like my roommate were it not for his terrible taste in music. If it weren't for my roommate's terrible taste in music, I would like him.	☐	☐

EXERCISE 3 IMPLIED CONDITIONS

GRAMMAR NOTE 1 **Read the conversation between a man and his doctor. Rewrite the six underlined conditional sentences. Replace the *if*-clauses with these phrases: *if so*, *if not*, *otherwise*, *with*, or *without*.**

DOCTOR: Bob, there are heavy circles under your eyes. You've got to get more sleep. If you don't, you'll get sick.

BOB: It's crunch time at work. The boss is insisting I work twelve hours a day right now. If I work a lot of overtime, I'll keep my job.

DOCTOR: Maybe your boss will let you cut your hours to ten a day. If he will, that would help solve your problem.

BOB: And if he won't, what can I do? He's a task master.

DOCTOR: Try to work in a nap during your lunch hour. But now, here's another thing. You told me you're drinking ten or more cups of coffee a day. You've got to cut down on it. If you don't, it might damage your kidneys.

BOB: Impossible. If I don't have coffee, I can't make it through the day.

DOCTOR: There must be a way. You can do it. Just find a buddy who's willing to monitor your coffee consumption. You have friends at work, don't you?

BOB: I sure do.

DOCTOR: Good. So, promise me you'll try to cut down.

BOB: OK. I can promise to try.

1. If you don't, you'll get sick.
   Otherwise, you'll get sick.
2. If I work a lot of overtime, I'll keep my job.
   ____
3. If he will, that would help solve your problem.
   ____
4. And if he won't, what can I do?
   ____
5. If you don't, it might damage your kidneys.
   ____
6. If I don't have coffee, I can't make it through the day.
   ____

EXERCISE 4 INVERTED AND IMPLIED CONDITIONS

A GRAMMAR NOTES 1–2 **Complete the story with words from the box.**

had Daria	if not	if so	otherwise	~~were she~~	with

Daria Allen wanted to move to St. Louis from Russellville, the small city where she had grown up and attended college. For some time, Daria had felt it was necessary for her to leave Russellville. ___Were she___ (1.) to stay there, she felt, she would just fall into a rut she would never escape from. She decided to go to the big city and start a new life. However, she needed to work. She asked her friend Hei-Rim for advice on finding a job because Hei-Rim had recently lived in a big city and knew something about job-hunting. Hei-Rim gave her two pieces of advice: first, to avoid employment agencies; and second, to regularly check online for job opportunities.

___________ (2.) known how difficult it would be to find employment, she might have stayed in her hometown. She tried to find a job for weeks but without any success. After a month had gone by, she had checked for available jobs online many times, but nothing had materialized. She needed to find employment fairly soon; ___________ (3.), she wouldn't be able to afford her apartment.

One morning, Daria decided it wouldn't hurt just to walk around downtown and see if she saw any "help wanted" signs posted in store windows. She thought that ___________ (4.) a bit of luck she might find something. A few moments later, she walked by a florist shop and saw a "help wanted" sign in the window. She didn't know how long the sign had been in the window. Maybe they were still hiring; ___________ (5.), she might get a job. ___________ (6.), she wouldn't lose anything by going in and asking. She walked right in and said, "I'm Daria Allen, and I saw your notice in the window. I was a botany major in college, and I have a lot of experience with flowers and gardening. Is the job still available?"

The manager said, "Amazing. I just put that notice up a couple of hours ago. I haven't put the ad online yet. We're expanding and need someone to work part-time. The position could become full-time eventually. Tell me more about your experience."

Daria got the job.

B Rewrite each word or phrase from A with an *if*-clause that restates the condition.

1. ______If she were______ to stay there, she felt, she would just fall into a rut she would never escape from.
2. ______________________ known how difficult it would be to find employment, she might have stayed in her hometown.
3. She need to find employment fairly soon; ______________________, she wouldn't be able to afford her apartment.
4. She felt that ______________________ a bit of luck she might find something.
5. Maybe they were still hiring; ______________________, she might get a job.
6. ______________________, she wouldn't lose anything by going in and asking.

EXERCISE 5 VERBS WITH THE SUBJUNCTIVE

GRAMMAR NOTES 3–4 Describe what is happening in each picture by completing each sentence. Use subjunctive verb forms and appropriate subjects.

1

2

3

4

5

6

1. The police officer is suggesting *(that) the woman call a towing company* ______.
2. The workers are demanding ______.
3. The wife is insisting ______.
4. The woman is proposing ______.
5. The real estate agent is recommending ______.
6. The travel agent is suggesting ______.

EXERCISE 6 ADJECTIVES WITH THE SUBJUNCTIVE

A GRAMMAR NOTE 5 **What do young people need to make a good start to adult life? Complete each sentence with the adjective in parentheses + *that* + the correct form of a verb from the box.**

communicate	find	~~have~~	make	stay	take

1. It is *desirable that they have* (desirable) good self-esteem.
2. It is ______ (necessary) responsibility for their own actions.
3. It is ______ (important) good jobs.
4. It is ______ (essential) most of their own decisions.
5. If they are in a relationship, it is ______ (crucial) with each other.
6. It is ______ (advisable) in touch with family and close friends.

B **Write six sentences in which you give your own advice for young people. Use the structure adjective + *for* + noun or object pronoun + infinitive.**

It's important for young people to find the right kind of friends.
It's essential for them to work . . .

EXERCISE 7 EDITING

GRAMMAR NOTES 1–5 Daria (see Exercise 3) has recently moved to St. Louis. Read her email to her friend Hei-Rim. It has eleven mistakes in conditions and the subjunctive. The first mistake is already corrected. Find and correct ten more.

December 10

Dear Hei-Rim,

It's time I wrote and filled you in on what's been happening since I left Russellville. I finally got a job! Remember when you suggested I ~~checked~~ check online for job offers? It was a good suggestion, but for some reason there were no available jobs being advertised. A couple of weeks ago, I was getting worried since I had spent almost all my savings. I had gotten to the point where it was absolutely essential that I found something. If so, I would have to go back to Russellville. I had known how difficult this would be, I would probably have stayed in Russellville! Anyway, I decided to just walk around downtown and see what turned up. That's when I saw a beautiful little florist's shop with a "help wanted" sign in the window. I walked right in and asked if the job was still open. Can you believe that it was? The owner said that he hadn't had time to post the job online yet. So your advice would have worked the timing had been different. The bottom line is that I'm employed!

I was really happy in my job until my boss hired a new assistant manager who has been making my life miserable. Among other things, he demands me to make coffee for him. He also insists that I'm doing other things that aren't in my job description. I took this job to work with plants, not to serve him coffee. I think it's crucial tell him where I stand. It's important that he stops treating me as his personal assistant.

I have a few days off for the holidays. Do you have some time off? If not, how about coming down here for a visit? Wouldn't that be fun? I have a spare bedroom in my apartment. If you can come, I suggest you to drive, since it isn't far. Please email or text and let me know.

Love,
Daria

STEP 4 COMMUNICATION PRACTICE

EXERCISE 8 LISTENING

23|02 **A** Listen to the conversation. Why does Nancy need advice?

____

23|02 **B** Read the questions. Listen again to the telephone conversation and answer the questions in complete sentences.

1. What did Nancy's daughter ask her to do?
   Nancy's daughter asked her mother to babysit for her kids.
2. What did the daughter almost do when Nancy said no at first?
   ____
3. Had Nancy known what her daughter was calling about, what would she have done?
   ____
4. What did Nancy have to do the last time this happened?
   ____
5. Why is the daughter asking that her mother babysit so much?
   ____
6. According to Nancy, what is it important that her daughter do?
   ____
7. What does Marge suggest Nancy do?
   ____
8. According to Marge, what can Nancy accomplish with a little firmness?
   ____

C Work with a partner. Which person in the listening do you identify with more: the mother or the daughter? Why? How much responsibility should grandparents have to assume for their grandchildren? Discuss.

EXERCISE 9 HERE'S OUR ADVICE

A CRITICAL THINKING Work in a group. Think about this problem: A young woman was awarded a scholarship, but she wants to take time off before she goes to college. If she takes time off, she may lose the scholarship. What would you advise? In small groups, work together to suggest advice for the woman. Each group member proposes a piece of advice.

EXAMPLE: A: I would suggest she give up the scholarship and take time off. She needs to be ready for college. Otherwise, she won't do well . . .
B: I recommend that she . . .

B What is the best advice? Vote on the different pieces of advice your group has proposed and justify your opinions. Count the votes and discuss the results further. Then share your results with the class.

EXERCISE 10 TRAVEL ADVICE

A PRESENTATION You are going to give a presentation in which you offer advice to someone who is going on a trip. First, look at the postcards below and on the next page. Choose one of the locations and do research on the Internet about places to visit there. Then write sentences offering travel advice. Use subjunctive verb constructions with *suggest*, *recommend*, and *it is essential that*.

B Work in a group. Give your presentation. Do the other members of your group agree with your advice?

EXAMPLE: If the person is visiting China, I suggest he or she visit the Great Wall and the Forbidden City. . . .

EXERCISE 11 CAN YOU GIVE ME SOME ADVICE?

A ROLE PLAY **You are going to role-play a conversation about a problem. First, think of a problem that needs to be solved. Write a few sentences about it.**

My roommate, Elena, is always borrowing money from me. She did it again yesterday. Without a loan, she said, she won't be able to pay the rent. . . .

B **Work with a partner. Present your problem to your partner and ask for his or her advice. Have a conversation with your partner about the problem. Then switch roles.**

EXAMPLE: A: Sergei, I'm having a problem with my roommate, Elena.
B: Oh. What's the problem?
A: Well, Elena is a great friend, but she's always short of money. I've had to lend her money to help pay our rent. I don't have much money myself. What would you recommend I do?
B: Hmm. Let's see. Well, I guess I'd recommend that, first, you sit down and explain your feelings and say why this bothers you. Then . . .

C **Present your role plays to another group. Ask for their advice on what to do about the problems.**

FROM GRAMMAR TO WRITING

A BEFORE YOU WRITE You are going to write an essay about a time when you followed either some good advice or some bad advice. Decide on the situation and write a few sentences about it.

B WRITE Using your ideas in A, write a five-paragraph essay about the good or bad advice you took. Remember to use subjunctive constructions, inverted conditions, and implied conditions. Try to avoid the common mistakes shown in the chart. Use the example below to help you begin your essay.

EXAMPLE: One of the worst pieces of advice I've ever followed was to try out for the football team in high school. My friend Mark had suggested I try to make the team. He had assured me I would be chosen for the team if I did try out. I've never been very good at football, and I knew that in the back of my mind, but because of my desire for popularity, I took Mark's suggestion. Had I known how badly the situation would turn out, I never would have done it. Here's what happened. . . .

Common Mistakes in Using Conditionals and Subjunctives

Don't use ***were*** in past-time unreal situations. Use it only in **present** time situations.	If she **were** in love with Dennis, she **would** marry him. OR If she **had been** in love with Dennis, she **would have married** him. NOT If she ~~were~~ in love with Dennis, she would have married him.
Don't use past or future time verbs in **subjunctive** constructions. Use the **base form**.	I suggest that Mary **listen** more carefully to what people say. NOT I suggest that Mary ~~listens~~ more carefully to what people say.
Don't contract ***had***, ***were***, or ***should*** + ***not*** in **inverted** conditionals.	**Had I not** put in the extra work, I wouldn't have passed the course. NOT ~~Hadn't I~~ put in the extra work, I wouldn't have passed the course.

C CHECK YOUR WORK Look at your essay. Underline the subjunctive constructions, inverted conditions, and implied conditions. Use the Editing Checklist to check your work.

Editing Checklist

Did you . . . ?

☐ avoid using *were* in past-time unreal situations
☐ use the base form of the verbs in subjunctive constructions
☐ avoid contracting *not* with *had*, *were*, and *should* in inverted conditions

D REVISE YOUR WORK Read your essay again. Can you improve your writing? Make changes if necessary.

UNIT 23 **REVIEW**

Test yourself on the grammar of the unit.

A Complete the sentences. Circle the correct answers.

1. You need to get some job retraining. With / Without it, you risk being laid off.
2. Juan may or may not go to college. If so / If not, he will have to get a full-time job.
3. I think something is wrong with the car. If so / If not, we'd better have it fixed.
4. You have to take notes; if not / otherwise, you'll forget what you learned.
5. We want to buy a house. If so / With a loan from the bank, we'll be able to.
6. I may not pass the class; if not / if so, I'll have to take it over.
7. Ana has a daughter; without / if not her daughter, she'd be all alone.
8. The traffic is heavy, but with / if a bit of luck, we'll be on time.

B Complete the sentences with words from the box.

but for	call	had I	if so	otherwise	should that	understand

1. Give me a call; ________________, I may forget the meeting.
2. ________________ not reminded Jiro of the party, he would have forgotten.
3. Hana suggested that I ________________ the airline, but I didn't.
4. I might be late. ________________ happen, go without me.
5. ________________ her pension, she would never be able to survive financially.
6. It's crucial that Linh ________________ the gravity of his situation.
7. Jae-Yong may be coming; ________________, you can ride back with him.

C Find and correct five mistakes.

A: I'm glad you suggested we hired Bob Burnham. He's done a great job.

B: Yes. I had known how good he is, I'd have recommended him sooner.

A: Do you recommend Jen Valdez for the sales position? If not, let's interview her.

B: I do, yes. However, I suggest we offered a higher salary for that position.

A: Really? Why?

B: With a salary increase, we'll never be able to hire Jen.

Check your answers on page 433.

Appendices

1 Irregular Verbs

When two or more forms are given, the first form is considered the more common.

BASE FORM	SIMPLE PAST	PAST PARTICIPLE
arise	arose	arisen
awake	awoke/awaked	awaked/awoken
be	was/were	been
bear	bore	borne/born
beat	beat	beaten/beat
become	became	become
begin	began	begun
bend	bent	bent
bet	bet	bet
bind	bound	bound
bite	bit	bitten
bleed	bled	bled
blow	blew	blown
break	broke	broken
breed	bred	bred
bring	brought	brought
broadcast	broadcast/broadcasted	broadcast/broadcasted
build	built	built
burn	burned/burnt	burned/burnt
burst	burst	burst
buy	bought	bought
cast	cast	cast
catch	caught	caught
choose	chose	chosen
cling	clung	clung
come	came	come
cost	cost	cost
creep	crept	crept
cut	cut	cut
deal	dealt	dealt
dig	dug	dug
dive	dived/dove	dived
do	did	done
draw	drew	drawn
dream	dreamed/dreamt	dreamed/dreamt
drink	drank	drunk
drive	drove	driven
dwell	dwelt/dwelled	dwelt/dwelled
eat	ate	eaten
fall	fell	fallen
feed	fed	fed
feel	felt	felt
fight	fought	fought
find	found	found
fit	fitted/fit	fitted/fit
flee	fled	fled

BASE FORM	SIMPLE PAST	PAST PARTICIPLE
fly	flew	flown
forbid	forbade/forbad	forbidden/forbid
forecast	forecast/forecasted	forecast/forecasted
forget	forgot	forgotten
forgive	forgave	forgiven
forsake	forsook	forsaken
freeze	froze	frozen
get	got	gotten/got
give	gave	given
go	went	gone
grind	ground	ground
grow	grew	grown
hang	hung/hanged*	hung/hanged
have	had	had
hear	heard	heard
hide	hid	hidden/hid
hit	hit	hit
hold	held	held
hurt	hurt	hurt
keep	kept	kept
kneel	knelt/kneeled	knelt/kneeled
knit	knit/knitted	knit/knitted
know	knew	known
lay	laid	laid
lead	led	led
leap	leaped/leapt	leaped/leapt
learn	learned/learnt	learned/learnt
leave	left	left
lend	lent	lent
let	let	let
lie (down)	lay	lain
light	lit/lighted	lit/lighted
lose	lost	lost
make	made	made
mean	meant	meant
meet	met	met
mislead**	misled	misled
pay	paid	paid
plead	pleaded/pled	pleaded/pled
prove	proved	proved/proven
put	put	put
quit	quit	quit
read	read	read
rid	rid/ridded	rid/ridded
ride	rode	ridden
ring	rang	rung

* *hung*: put an object up on a hook (**EXAMPLE:** We hung the picture carefully.)
hanged: executed by hanging (**EXAMPLE:** I wouldn't want to be hanged.)

** Note that verbs with prefixes have the same past forms as the base verb without prefixes (**EXAMPLE:** *mislead misled misled* follows the same pattern as *lead led led*.)

BASE FORM	SIMPLE PAST	PAST PARTICIPLE	BASE FORM	SIMPLE PAST	PAST PARTICIPLE
rise	rose	risen	spread	spread	spread
run	ran	run	spring	sprang/sprung	sprung
saw	sawed	sawed/sawn	stand	stood	stood
say	said	said	steal	stole	stolen
see	saw	seen	stick	stuck	stuck
seek	sought	sought	sting	stung	stung
sell	sold	sold	stink	stank/stunk	stunk
send	sent	sent	strike	struck	struck/stricken
set	set	set	strive	strove	striven/strived
sew	sewed	sewn/sewed	swear	swore	sworn
shake	shook	shaken	sweat	sweated/sweat	sweated/sweat
shave	shaved	shaved/shaven	sweep	swept	swept
shear	sheared	sheared/shorn	swell	swelled	swelled/swollen
shed	shed	shed	swim	swam	swum
shine	shone/shined*	shone/shined	swing	swung	swung
shoot	shot	shot	take	took	taken
show	showed	shown/showed	teach	taught	taught
shrink	shrank/shrunk	shrunk/shrunken	tear	tore	torn
shut	shut	shut	tell	told	told
sing	sang	sung	think	thought	thought
sink	sank/sunk	sunk	thrive	thrived/throve	thrived/thriven
sit	sat	sat	throw	threw	thrown
slay	slew/slayed	slain/slayed	thrust	thrust	thrust
sleep	slept	slept	tread	trod	trodden/trod
slide	slid	slid	upset	upset	upset
slit	slit	slit	wake	woke/waked	waked/woken
smell	smelled/smelt	smelled/smelt	wear	wore	worn
sneak	sneaked/snuck	sneaked/snuck	weave	wove/weaved**	woven/weaved
sow	sowed	sown/sowed	wed	wedded/wed	wedded/wed
speak	spoke	spoken	weep	wept	wept
speed	sped/speeded	sped/speeded	wet	wetted/wet	wetted/wet
spell	spelled/spelt	spelled/spelt	win	won	won
spend	spent	spent	wind	wound	wound
spill	spilled/spilt	spilled/spilt	withdraw	withdrew	withdrawn
spin	spun	spun	withhold	withheld	withheld
spit	spat/spit	spat/spit	wring	wrung	wrung
split	split	split	write	wrote	written

* *shone*: intransitive (**EXAMPLE:** The sun shone brightly.)
shined: transitive (**EXAMPLE:** He shined his shoes.)

** *wove/woven*: created a fabric (**EXAMPLE:** She wove a rug.)
weaved: moved in and out or side to side (**EXAMPLE:** The driver weaved from one lane to another on the freeway.)

2 Non-Action Verbs

EXAMPLES: She **seems** happy in her new job.
I **have** a terrible headache.
The food **smells** good.
Mary **owes** me money.

APPEARANCE
appear
be
concern
indicate
look
mean *(signify)*
parallel
represent
resemble
seem
signify *(mean)*

EMOTIONS
abhor
admire
adore
appreciate
care
desire
detest
dislike
doubt
empathize
envy
fear
hate
hope
like
love
regret
respect
sympathize
trust

MENTAL STATES
agree
amaze
amuse
annoy
assume
astonish
believe
bore
care
consider
deem
deny
disagree
disbelieve
entertain *(amuse)*
estimate
expect
fancy
favor
feel *(believe)*
figure *(assume)*
find *(believe)*
guess
hesitate
hope
imagine
imply
impress
infer
know
mean
mind
presume
realize
recognize
recollect
remember
revere
see *(understand)*
suit
suppose
suspect
think *(believe)*
tire
understand
wonder

SENSES AND PERCEPTION
ache
feel
hear
hurt
notice
observe
perceive
see
sense
smart
smell
sound
taste

POSSESSION
belong
have
own
pertain
possess

WANTS AND PREFERENCES
desire
need
prefer
want
wish

OTHER
cost
include
lack
matter
owe
refuse
suffice
weigh

3 Non-Action Verbs Sometimes Used in the Progressive

EXAMPLES: The students **are being** silly today.
We**'re having** dinner right now. Can I call you back?
Mary **is smelling** the roses.

ache
admire
agree
amuse
annoy
assume
be
bore
consider
deny
disagree
doubt
empathize
entertain
expect
favor
feel
figure
find
guess
have
hear
hesitate
hope
hurt
imagine
imply
impress
include
indicate
lack
look
notice
observe
perceive
presume
realize
refuse
represent
see
sense
smell
sympathize
taste
think
wonder

4 Irregular Noun Plurals

SINGULAR FORM	PLURAL FORM
alumna	alumnae
alumnus	alumni
amoeba	amoebae
analysis	analyses
antenna	antennae/antennas*
appendix	appendices
axis	axes
basis	bases
businessman	businessmen
businesswoman	businesswomen
cactus	cacti
calf	calves
—	cattle
child	children
crisis	crises
criterion	criteria
datum	data
deer	deer
dwarf	dwarves
elf	elves
elk	elk
fish	fish
foot	feet
genus	genera
goose	geese
half	halves
index	indices
knife	knives
leaf	leaves
life	lives
loaf	loaves
louse	lice
man	men
millennium	millennia
money	monies
moose	moose
mouse	mice
octopus	octopi
ox	oxen
paramecium	paramecia
people**	peoples
person	people
phenomenon	phenomena
—	police
policeman	policemen
policewoman	policewomen
protozoan	protozoa
radius	radii
series	series
sheaf	sheaves
sheep	sheep
shelf	shelves
species	species
thesis	theses
tooth	teeth
vertebra	vertebrae
wife	wives
woman	women

* *antennae*: insects' feelers
antennas: devices to receive radio or television signals

** *a people*: an ethnic group

5 Non-Count Nouns

ABSTRACTIONS
advice
anarchy
behavior
capitalism
chance
consent
decay
democracy
determination
energy
entertainment
evil
falsehood
freedom
fun
good
grief
happiness
hate
hatred
honesty
inertia
integrity
intelligence
love
luck
momentum
motivation
oppression
peace
pollution
responsibility
sadness
slavery
socialism
spontaneity
stupidity
time
totalitarianism
truth
violence

ACTIVITIES
badminton
baseball
basketball
biking
billiards
bowling
boxing
canoeing
cards
conversation
cycling
dancing
football
golf
hiking
hockey
judo
karate
reading
rowing
sailing
singing
skating
skiing
soccer
surfing
tae kwon do
talking
tennis
volleyball
wrestling

DISEASES
AIDS
appendicitis
bronchitis
cancer
chicken pox
cholera
diabetes
diphtheria
flu (influenza)
heart disease
malaria
measles
mumps
pneumonia
polio
smallpox
strep throat
tuberculosis (TB)

FOODS
barley
beef
bread
broccoli
cake
candy
cereal
chicken
corn
dessert
fish
meat
oats
pasta
pie
rice
salad
wheat

GASES
carbon dioxide
helium
hydrogen
neon
nitrogen
oxygen

LIQUIDS	NATURAL PHENOMENA	OCCUPATIONS	PARTICLES	SOLID ELEMENTS	SUBJECTS	OTHER
coffee	air	banking	dust	aluminum	accounting	clothing
gasoline	cold	computer technology	gravel	calcium	Arabic	equipment
juice	electricity	construction	pepper	carbon	art	film
milk	fog	dentistry	salt	copper	astronomy	furniture
oil	hail	engineering	sand	gold	biology	news
soda	heat	farming	spice	iron	business	play
tea	ice	fishing	sugar	lead	chemistry	work
water	lightning	law		magnesium	civics	
	mist	manufacturing		platinum	computer science	
	rain	medicine		plutonium	economics	
	sleet	nursing		radium	English	
	slush	retail		silver	geography	
	smog	sales		sodium	history	
	smoke	teaching		tin	linguistics	
	snow	therapy		titanium	literature	
	steam	writing		uranium	mathematics	
	thunder			zinc	music	
	warmth				physics	
	wind				psychology	
					science	
					sociology	
					Spanish	
					speech	
					writing	

6 Ways of Making Non-Count Nouns Countable

ABSTRACTIONS
a matter of choice
a piece of advice
a piece/bit of luck
a type/form of entertainment
a unit of energy

ACTIVITIES
a badminton game/a baseball game, etc.
a game of badminton/baseball/basketball/cards/football/golf/soccer/tennis, etc.

FOODS
a cut/piece/slice of beef
a grain of barley
a grain of rice
a loaf of bread
a piece of cake
a piece/wedge of pie
a portion/serving of . . .

LIQUIDS
a can of oil
a can/glass of soda
a cup of coffee, tea, cocoa
a gallon/liter of gasoline
a glass of milk, water, juice

NATURAL PHENOMENA
a bolt/current of electricity
a bolt/flash of lightning
a clap of thunder
a drop of rain
a ray of sun/sunshine

PARTICLES
a grain of pepper, salt, sand, sugar
a speck of dust

SUBJECTS
a branch of accounting/art/astronomy/biology/chemistry/economics/geography/linguistics/literature/mathematics/music/physics/psychology/sociology, etc.

OTHER
an article of clothing/jewelry
a news item/an item of news/a piece of news
a period of time
a piece of equipment/luggage
a piece/article of furniture/machinery

7 Non-Count Nouns Not Usually Made Countable

anger	courage	happiness	intelligence	patience	safety	violence
baldness	feedback	hospitality	knowledge	peace	shopping	warmth
chaos	foliage	humidity	leisure	precision	softness	weather
cholesterol	fun	importance	melancholy	progress	traffic	wildlife
conduct	gravity					

8 Nouns with Non-Count and Count Meanings

NON-COUNT MEANING	COUNT MEANING
Cancer is a dread disease.	There is **a cancer** on the presidency.
Cheese is a healthy food.	Brie is **a** soft **cheese** produced in France.
We eat **chicken** at least once a week.	I saw **a chicken** running down the road.
Coffee helps me wake up.	Please bring us two **coffees**.
Exercise is essential for good health.	Alice did some **exercises** in her grammar book.
Experience is a good teacher.	We had **a** fascinating **experience** at the game.
Film is my favorite art form.	Steven has directed a great many **films**.
We always eat **fish** on Fridays.	My son caught **a** big **fish** yesterday.
Maria has just gotten her **hair** curled.	There's **a hair** in my soup!
History has always been my favorite subject.	Stephanie is writing **a history** of World War I.
Light is essential for plants to grow.	Do you see **a light** in the distance?
Pasta is a popular food.	Lasagna is **an** Italian **pasta**.
People need times of work and times of **play**.	We're going to see the new **play** tonight.
Elena doesn't drink much **soda**.	Please bring us three **sodas**.
Space is sometimes called the final frontier.	There's **an** empty **space** in that row.
There's **talk** of building a skyscraper on that lot.	Indira and I had **a** good **talk** last night.
We drink **tea** every evening.	Earl Gray is **a** well-known **tea**.
I never have enough **time** to finish things.	I've told you that three **times**.
Work should be fulfilling.	Asha's painting is truly **a work** of art.

9 Nouns Often Used with the Definite Article

the air
the Arab League
the atmosphere
the authorities
the Bhagavad Gita
the Bible
the cosmos
the Creator
the earth
the economy
the Empire State Building
the environment
the European Union
the flu
the gross national product (the GNP)
the Internet
the King
the Koran
the measles
the Milky Way (galaxy)
the moon
the movies
the mumps
the ocean
the police
the President
the Prime Minister
the Queen
the radio
the sky
the Solar System
the stock market
the stratosphere
the sun
the Taj Mahal
the theater
the *Titanic*, etc.
the tropics
the United Nations
the universe
the Vatican
the world

10 Countries Whose Names Contain the Definite Article

the Bahamas
the Cayman Islands
the Central African Republic
the Channel Islands
the Comoros
the Czech Republic
the Dominican Republic
the Falkland Islands
the Gambia
the Isle of Man
the Ivory Coast
the Leeward Islands
the Maldives (the Maldive Islands)
the Marshall Islands
the Netherlands
the Netherlands Antilles
the Philippines
the Solomon Islands
the Turks and Caicos Islands
the United Arab Emirates
the United Kingdom (of Great Britain and Northern Ireland)
the United States (of America)
the Virgin Islands

11 Geographical Features with the Definite Article

GULFS, OCEANS, SEAS, AND STRAITS

the Adriatic Sea
the Aegean Sea
the Arabian Sea
the Arctic Ocean
the Atlantic (Ocean)
the Baltic (Sea)
the Black Sea
the Caribbean (Sea)
the Caspian (Sea)
the Coral Sea
the Gulf of Aden
the Gulf of Mexico
the Gulf of Oman
the Indian Ocean
the Mediterranean (Sea)
the North Sea
the Pacific (Ocean)
the Persian Gulf
the Philippine Sea
the Red Sea
the Sea of Japan
the South China Sea
the Strait of Gibraltar
the Strait of Magellan
the Yellow Sea

MOUNTAIN RANGES

the Alps
the Andes
the Appalachians
the Atlas Mountains
the Caucasus
the Himalayas
the Pyrenees
the Rockies (the Rocky Mountains)
the Urals

RIVERS

All of the following can contain the word *River.*

the Amazon
the Colorado
the Columbia
the Congo
the Danube
the Don
the Ebro
the Euphrates
the Ganges
the Huang
the Hudson
the Indus
the Jordan
the Lena
the Mackenzie
the Mekong
the Mississippi
the Missouri
the Niger
the Nile
the Ob
the Ohio
the Orange
the Orinoco
the Po
the Potomac
the Rhine
the Rhone
the Rio Grande
the Seine
the St. Lawrence
the Tagus
the Thames
the Tiber
the Tigris
the Ural
the Uruguay
the Volga
the Yangtze
the Zambezi

OTHER FEATURES

the Arctic Circle
the Antarctic Circle
the Atacama (Desert)
the equator
the Far East
the Gobi (Desert)
the Kalahari (Desert)
the Middle East
the Near East
the North Pole
the Occident
the Orient
the Panama Canal
the Sahara (Desert)
the Sonoran (Desert)
the South Pole
the Suez Canal
the tropic of Cancer
the tropic of Capricorn

12 Passive Verbs Followed by a *That*-Clause

EXAMPLE: It **is alleged that** he committed the crime.

allege
assume
believe
claim
fear
feel
hold
postulate
predict
say
theorize
think

13 Stative Passive Verbs + Prepositions

EXAMPLE: The island of Hispaniola **is divided into** two separate nations.

be bordered by
be composed of
be comprised of
be connected to/with/by
be covered by/with
be divided into/by
be filled with
be found in/on, etc.
be intended
be joined to
be known as
be listed in/as
be located in/on, etc.
be made (out) of
be made (up) of
be measured by
be placed near/in
be positioned near/in
be related to
be surrounded by

14 Verbs + Gerunds

EXAMPLE: Jane **enjoys playing** tennis.

abhor
acknowledge
admit
advise
allow
anticipate
appreciate
avoid
be worth
can't help
celebrate
confess
consider
defend
delay
deny
detest
discontinue
discuss
dislike
dispute
dread
endure
enjoy
escape
evade
explain
fancy
fear
feel like
feign
finish
forgive
give up *(stop)*
imagine
keep *(continue)*
keep on
mention
mind *(object to)*
miss
necessitate
omit
permit
picture
postpone
practice
prevent
put off
recall
recollect
recommend
report
resent
resist
resume
risk
shirk
shun
suggest
support
tolerate
understand
urge
warrant

15 Verbs + Infinitives

EXAMPLE: The Baxters **decided to sell** their house.

afford	claim	endeavor	incline	plan	resolve	threaten
agree	come	expect	intend	prepare	say	turn out
appear	consent	fail	learn	pretend	seek	venture
arrange	dare	get	manage	profess	seem	volunteer
ask	decide	grow (up)	mean	promise	shudder	wait
attempt	demand	guarantee	need	prove	strive	want
beg	deserve	hesitate	neglect	refuse	struggle	wish
care	determine	hope	offer	remain	swear	would like
chance	elect	hurry	pay	request	tend	yearn
choose						

16 Verbs + Gerunds OR Infinitives; No Change in Meaning

EXAMPLES: Martha **hates to go** to bed early.
Martha **hates going** to bed early.

begin	can't stand	hate	love	propose
can't bear	continue	like	prefer	start

17 Verbs + Gerunds OR Infinitives; Change in Meaning

forget
I'd almost **forgotten meeting** him. *(I was hardly able to remember meeting him.)*
I almost **forgot to meet** him. *(I almost didn't remember to meet him.)*

go on
Jack **went on writing** novels. *(Jack continued to write novels.)*
Carrie **went on to write** novels. *(Carrie ended some other activity and began to write novels.)*

quit
Ella **quit working** at Sloan's. *(She isn't working at Sloan's anymore.)*
Frank **quit to work** at Sloan's. *(He quit another job in order to work at Sloan's.)*

regret
I **regret telling** you I'm taking the job. *(I'm sorry that I said I would take the job.)*
I **regret to tell** you I'm taking the job. *(I'm sorry to tell you that I'm taking the job.)*

remember
Velma **remembered writing** to Bill. *(Velma remembered the previous activity of writing to Bill.)*
Melissa **remembered to write** to Bill. *(Melissa didn't forget to write to Bill. She wrote to him.)*

stop
Hank **stopped eating**. *(He stopped the activity of eating.)*
Bruce **stopped to eat**. *(He stopped doing something else in order to eat.)*

try
Martin **tried skiing**. *(Martin sampled the activity of skiing.)*
Helen **tried to ski**. *(Helen attempted to ski but didn't succeed.)*

18 Adjective + Preposition Combinations

These phrases are followed by nouns, pronouns, or gerunds.

EXAMPLES: I'm not **familiar with** that writer.
I'm **amazed at** her.
We're **excited about** going.

accustomed to
afraid of
amazed at/by
angry at/with
ashamed of
astonished at/by
aware of
awful at
bad at
bored with/by
capable of
careful of
concerned with/by
content with
curious about
different from
excellent at
excited about
familiar with
famous for
fascinated with/by
fed up with
fond of
furious with/at
glad about
good at
good with
guilty of
happy about
incapable of
intent on
interested in
intrigued by/at
mad at *(angry at/with)*
nervous about
obsessed with/about
opposed to
pleased about/with
poor at
ready for
responsible for
sad about
safe from
satisfied with
shocked at/by
sick of
slow at
sorry for/about
suited to
surprised at/about
terrible at
tired from
tired of
used to
weary of
worried about

19 Verbs Followed by Noun or Pronoun + Infinitive

EXAMPLE: I **asked Sally to lend** me her car.

advise
allow
ask*
cause
choose*
convince
encourage
expect*
forbid
force
get*
hire
invite
need*
order
pay*
permit
persuade
remind
require
teach
tell
urge
want*
warn
would like*

*These verbs can also be followed by the infinitive without an object.

EXAMPLES: I **want** Jerry **to go**.
I **want to go**.

20 Adjectives Followed by the Infinitive

EXAMPLE: I was **glad to hear** about that.

advisable*
afraid
alarmed
amazed
angry
anxious
ashamed
astonished
careful
crucial*
curious
delighted
depressed
desirable*
determined*
difficult
disappointed
distressed
disturbed
eager
easy
ecstatic
embarrassed
encouraged
essential*
excited
fascinated
fortunate
frightened
furious
glad
good
happy
hard
hesitant
important*
impossible
interested
intrigued
likely
lucky
mandatory*
necessary*
nice
obligatory*
pleased
possible
prepared
proud
ready
relieved
reluctant
right
sad
scared
shocked
sorry
surprised
touched
unlikely
unnecessary*
upset
willing
wrong

*These adjectives can also be followed with a noun clause containing a subjunctive verb form.

EXAMPLES: It's **essential to communicate**.
It's **essential** that she **communicate** with her parents.

21 Sentence Adverbs

EXAMPLES: **Clearly**, this is the best course of action.
This is **clearly** the best course of action.
This is the best course of action, **clearly**.

absolutely
actually
amazingly
apparently
basically
certainly
clearly
definitely
essentially
evidently
fortunately
frankly
generally
happily
honestly
hopefully
importantly
mainly
maybe
mercifully
obviously
overall
perhaps
possibly
probably
significantly
surely
surprisingly
thankfully
understandably
unfortunately

22 Words and Phrases That Begin Dependent Clauses

SUBORDINATING CONJUNCTIONS (To Introduce Adverb Clauses)

after
although
anywhere
as
as if
as long as
as many as
as much as
as soon as
as though
because
because of the fact that
before
despite the fact that
due to the fact that
even if
even though
even when
everywhere
if
if only
in case
in spite of the fact that
inasmuch as
no matter if
no matter whether
now that
on account of the fact that
once
only if
plus the fact that
provided (that)
providing (that)
since
so . . . that (in order to)
so that
such . . . that
though
till
unless
until
when
whenever
where
whereas
wherever
whether (or not)
while

PRONOUNS (To Introduce Adjective Clauses)

that
when
where
which
who
whom
whose

OTHERS (To Introduce Noun Clauses)

how
how far
how long
how many
how much
however (the way in which)
if
that
the fact that
what
what color
whatever
what time
when
where
whether (or not)
whichever (one)
whoever
whomever
why

23 Transitions to Connect Sentences

TO SHOW ADDITION	TO SHOW A CONTRAST	TO SHOW AN EFFECT/RESULT	TO SHOW TIME AND SEQUENCE
additionally	actually	accordingly	after this/that
along with this/that	anyhow	as a result	afterwards
also	anyway	because of this/that	an hour later (several hours later, etc.)
alternatively	as a matter of fact	consequently	at last
as a matter of fact	at any rate	for this/that reason	at this moment
besides	despite this/that	hence	before this/that
furthermore	even so	in consequence	from now on
in addition	however	on account of this/that	henceforth
indeed	in any case	otherwise	hitherto
in fact	in contrast	then	in the meantime
in other words	in either case	therefore	just then
in the same way	in fact	this/that being so	meanwhile
likewise	in spite of this/that	thus	next
moreover	instead (of this/that)	to this end	on another occasion
plus (the fact that)	nevertheless		previously
	nonetheless		then
	on the contrary		under the circumstances
	on the other hand		until then
	rather		up to now
	still		
	though		

24 Transitions to Connect Blocks of Text

all in all	in short	most importantly	to conclude
another reason/point, etc.	in sum	second(ly)	to resume
finally	in summary	the most important reason/factor, etc.	to return to the point
first(ly)	last(ly)	third(ly), fourth(ly), etc.	to summarize
in conclusion			

25 Reporting Verbs

EXAMPLES: "This is the best course of action," Jack **added**.
Rhonda **said**, "I don't agree with your proposal."

add	ask	confess	murmur	point out	respond	tell
allege	claim	exclaim	note	query	say	wonder
allow	comment	maintain	observe	report	shout	yell

26 Verbs and Expressions Followed by the Subjunctive

EXAMPLES: We **demand** (that) he **do** it.
It is **essential** (that) he **do** it.
The professor **suggested** (that) we **buy** his book.

AFTER SINGLE VERBS		AFTER *IT* + ADJECTIVE + NOUN CLAUSE	
ask*	recommend	it is advisable that	it is necessary that
demand	request*	it is crucial that	it is obligatory that
insist	require*	it is desirable that	it is reasonable that
order*	suggest	it is essential that	it is required that
prefer*	urge*	it is important that	it is unnecessary that
propose		it is mandatory that	it is unreasonable that

*These verbs also take the form verb + object pronoun + infinitive.

EXAMPLES: We **asked** that she **be** present.
We **asked her to be** present.

27 Pronunciation Table

A|01 These are the pronunciation symbols used in this text. Listen to the pronunciation of the key words.

VOWELS				CONSONANTS			
SYMBOL	KEY WORD	SYMBOL	KEY WORD	SYMBOL	KEY WORD	SYMBOL	KEY WORD
i	**bea**t, **fee**d	ə	b**a**n**a**na, **a**mong	p	**p**ack, ha**pp**y	z	**z**ip, plea**s**e, goe**s**
ɪ	b**i**t, d**i**d	ɚ	sh**ir**t, m**ur**d**er**	b	**b**ack, ru**bb**er	ʃ	**sh**ip, ma**ch**ine, sta**t**ion, spe**c**ial, discu**ss**ion
eɪ	d**a**te, p**ai**d	aɪ	b**i**te, cr**y**, b**uy**, **eye**	t	**t**ie		
ɛ	b**e**t, b**e**d	aʊ	ab**ou**t, h**ow**	d	**d**ie	ʒ	mea**s**ure, vi**s**ion
æ	b**a**t, b**a**d	ɔɪ	v**oi**ce, b**oy**	k	**c**ame, **k**ey, **qu**ick	h	**h**ot, **wh**o
ɑ	b**o**x, **o**dd, f**a**ther	ɪr	b**eer**	g	**g**ame, **g**uest	m	**m**en
ɔ	b**ough**t, d**o**g	ɛr	b**are**	tʃ	**ch**urch, na**t**ure, wa**tch**	n	su**n**, **kn**ow, **pn**eumonia
oʊ	b**oa**t, r**oa**d	ɑr	b**ar**	dʒ	**j**u**dg**e, **g**eneral, ma**j**or	ŋ	su**ng**, ri**ng**i**ng**
ʊ	b**oo**k, g**oo**d	ɔr	d**oor**	f	**f**an, **ph**otogra**ph**	w	**w**et, **wh**ite
u	b**oo**t, f**oo**d, st**u**dent	ʊr	t**our**	v	**v**an	l	**l**ight, **l**ong
ʌ	b**u**t, m**u**d, m**o**ther			θ	**th**ing, brea**th**	r	**r**ight, **wr**ong
				ð	**th**en, brea**the**	y	**y**es, **u**se, m**u**sic
				s	**s**ip, **c**ity, **ps**ychology	ţ	bu**tt**er, bo**tt**le

Glossary of Grammar Terms

action verb A verb that describes an action.

James **exercises** three days a week.

active sentence A sentence in which the subject acts upon the object.

William Shakespeare wrote **Hamlet**.

adjective A part of speech modifying a noun or pronoun.

The **blue** sofa is **beautiful**, but it's also **expensive**.

adjective clause A clause that identifies or gives additional information about a noun.

The man **who directed the film** won an Oscar.

adjective phrase A phrase that identifies or gives additional information about a noun.

In that movie, the actress **playing the heroine** is Penélope Cruz.

adverb A part of speech modifying a verb, an adjective, another adverb, or an entire sentence.

Ben drives his **incredibly** valuable car **very carefully**.

adverb clause A dependent clause that indicates how, when, where, why, or under what conditions things happen; or which establishes a contrast. An adverb clause begins with a subordinating conjunction and modifies an independent clause.

We're going to leave for the airport **as soon as Jack gets home**.

adverb / adverbial phrase A phrase that indicates how, when, where, why, or under what conditions things happen. An adverb phrase modifies an independent clause.

We learned a great deal of Spanish **while traveling in Mexico**.

An adverbial phrase performs the same functions as an adverb phrase but does not contain a subordinating conjunction.

Having had the professor for a previous class, I knew what to expect.

auxiliary (helping) verb A verb that occurs with and "helps" a main verb.

Did Mary contact you? She **should have** called at least.

base form The form of a verb listed in a dictionary. It has no endings (*-s*, *-ed*, etc.).

It is mandatory that Sally **be** there and **participate** in the discussion.

causative A verb construction showing that someone arranges for or causes something to happen. ***Get*** and ***have*** are the two most common causative verbs.

We **got** Martha to help us when we **had** the house remodeled.

clause A group of words with a subject and a verb that shows time. An **independent clause** can stand by itself. A **dependent clause** needs to be attached to an independent clause to be understood fully.

INDEPENDENT	DEPENDENT
We'll go out for dinner	when Mom gets back from the bank.

comma splice An error resulting from joining two independent clauses with only a comma.

I understand the point he made; however, I don't agree with it.

NOT I understand the point he made, however, I don't agree with it. *(comma splice)*

common noun A noun that does not name a particular thing or individual.

We bought a **turkey**, cranberry **sauce**, mashed **potatoes**, and **rolls** for the special **dinner**.

complement A noun or adjective (phrase) that describes or explains a subject or direct object.

Hal is **a man with unusual tastes**. He painted his house **orange**.

compound modifier A modifier of a noun that is composed of more than one word. A compound modifier is usually hyphenated when it precedes a noun.

My **five-year-old** daughter can already read.

conditional sentence A sentence containing a dependent clause showing a condition and an independent clause showing a result. The condition may or may not be fulfilled.

CONDITION	RESULT
If I had enough time,	I would visit Morocco.

coordinating conjunction A word connecting independent clauses or items in a series. The seven coordinating conjunctions are ***and***, ***but***, ***for***, ***nor***, ***or***, ***so***, and ***yet***.

> Mom had forgotten to buy groceries, **so** we had a supper of cold pizza, salad, **and** water.

count noun A noun that can be counted in its basic sense. Count nouns have plural forms.

> The **students** in my **class** all have at least one **sibling**.

definite article The article ***the***; it indicates that the person or thing being talked about is unique or is known or identified to the speaker and listener.

> China is **the** most populous nation in **the** world.

definite past The simple past form; it shows an action, state, or event at a particular time or period in the past.

> I **lived** in Spain in the '90s and **visited** there again last year.

dependent clause A dependent clause is a group of words that cannot stand alone as a sentence. It requires a main (independent) clause for its meaning.

MAIN CLAUSE	DEPENDENT CLAUSE
They saw the movie star,	who was wearing sunglasses.

direct object A noun or pronoun that receives the action of a verb.

> Martin discovered a large **dog** in his yard.

direct (quoted) speech The exact words (or thoughts) of a speaker, which are enclosed in quotation marks.

> **"Barry,"** Phyllis said, **"I want you to tell me the truth."**

embedded question A question that is inside another sentence.

> He didn't know **what he should buy for his mother**.

focus adverb An adverb that focuses attention on a word or phrase. Focus adverbs come before the word or phrase they focus on.

> **Even** I don't support that idea. It's too radical.

fragment A group of words that is not a complete sentence. It is often considered an error.

> He's asking for our help because he doesn't know what to do about the situation.
> NOT ~~Because he doesn't know what to do about the situation.~~ *(fragment)*

future in the past A verb construction showing a state, action, or event now past but future from some point of time in the past.

> We **were going to help** Tim move but couldn't. Sam said he **would help** instead.

generic Referred to in general; including all the members of the class to which something belongs.

> **The computer** has become essential in today's world.
>
> **Whales** are endangered.
>
> **An orangutan** is a primate living in Borneo and Sumatra.

gerund A verbal noun made by adding ***-ing*** to a verb.

> Dad loves **cooking**, and we love **eating** what he cooks.

identifying (essential) clauses and phrases Clauses and phrases that distinguish one person or thing from others. They are not enclosed in commas.

> The student **who is sitting at the end of the second row** is my niece.
>
> The film **starring Johnny Depp** is the one I want to see.

***if* clause** The clause in a conditional sentence that states the condition.

> **If it rains**, they will cancel the picnic.

implied condition A condition that is suggested or implied but not stated fully. Implied conditional sentences use expressions such as *if so*, *if not*, *otherwise*, *with*, and *without*.

> You may be able to get the item for half price. **If so**, please buy one for me as well. *(if you are able to get the item for half price)*

indefinite article The articles ***a*** and ***an***; they occur with count nouns and indicate that what is referred to is not a particular or identified person or thing.

> In the last year I have bought **an** old **house** and **a** new **car**.

indefinite past The present perfect; it shows a past action, event, or state not occurring at any particular or identified time.

We **have seen** that movie several times.

indirect object A noun or pronoun that shows the person or thing that receives something as a result of the action of the verb.

Martin gave **Priscilla** an autographed copy of his new novel. He also gave **her** a DVD.

indirect (reported) speech A report of the words of a speaker. Indirect speech does not include all of a speaker's exact words and is not enclosed in quotation marks.

Phyllis told Barry **that she wanted him to tell her the truth.**

infinitive *To* + the base form of a verb.

Frank Jones is said **to be** the author of that article.

inverted condition The condition of a conditional sentence, stated without the word *if*. Inverted conditions occur with the verbs *had*, *were*, and *should*, which come first in the sentence and are followed by the subject.

Had I known that would happen, I never would have agreed.

main (independent) clause A clause that can stand alone as a sentence.

MAIN CLAUSE	DEPENDENT CLAUSE
They saw the movie star,	who was wearing sunglasses.

mixed conditional A conditional sentence that shows the hypothetical present result of a past unreal situation or the hypothetical past result of a present unreal situation.

If I had taken that job, I **would be living** in Bucharest now.

Sam **would have arrived** by now **if he were planning** to come.

modal (auxiliary) A type of helping verb. ***Can***, ***could***, ***had better***, ***may***, ***might***, ***must***, ***ought to***, ***shall***, ***should***, ***will***, and ***would*** are modals. They each have one form and no endings.

You certainly **can** do that; the question is whether you **should** do it.

modal-like expression An expression with a meaning similar to that of a modal. Modal-like expressions have endings and show time.

Russell **has to** find a new job.

non-action (stative) verb A verb that in its basic sense does not show action.

It **seems** to me that Joe **has** a problem.

non-count noun A noun that in its basic sense cannot be counted.

Smoke from the **fire** filled the **air**.

nonidentifying (nonessential) clauses and phrases Clauses and phrases that add extra information but do not distinguish one person or thing from others. They are enclosed in commas.

Henry**, who is a member of the hockey team,** is also a star basketball player.

noun clause A dependent clause that performs the same function as a noun. Noun clauses function as subjects, objects, objects of prepositions, and complements.

What I want to do is spend a week relaxing on the beach.

noun modifier A noun that modifies another noun.

What did you buy, **milk** chocolate or **chocolate** milk?

parallelism (parallel structure) The placing of items in a series in the same grammatical form.

Marie loves **hiking**, **riding** horses, and **collecting** artifacts.

participial adjective An adjective formed from present and past participial forms of verbs.

The **bored** students were not paying attention to the **boring** speaker.

passive causative A verb structure formed with ***have*** or ***get*** + **object** + **past participle**. It is used to talk about services that you arrange for someone to do for you.

I usually **have my dresses made** by Chantal.

passive sentence A sentence that shows the subject being acted upon by the object.

Hamlet was written by **William Shakespeare**.

perfect forms Verb constructions formed with the auxiliary verbs ***had***, ***has***, and ***have*** and a past participle. They include the **past perfect**, **present perfect**, and **future perfect**.

I **had** never **been** to Brazil before 1990. Since then **I've been** there eight times. By this time next year, **I'll have been** there ten times.

phrase A group of related words without a subject or a verb showing time.

Relaxing in the hammock, I pondered my future.

proper noun The name of a particular individual or thing. Proper nouns are capitalized.

Stella and I both think that **Rio de Janeiro** and **Paris** are the world's two most beautiful cities.

quantifier A word or phrase showing the amount or number of something.

Ken earned **a lot of** money selling books. I bought **a few of** them myself.

relative pronoun A pronoun used to form adjective clauses. ***That***, ***when***, ***where***, ***which***, ***who***, ***whom***, and ***whose*** are relative pronouns.

The fairy tale **that** always scared me when I was a child was "Rumpelstiltskin."

reporting verb A verb such as ***said***, ***told***, or ***asked***, which introduces both direct and indirect speech. It can also come after the quotation in direct speech.

The mayor **said**, "I've read the report." or "I've read the report," the mayor **said**.

result clause The clause in a conditional sentence that indicates what happens if the condition occurs.

If it rains, **they'll cancel the picnic.**

run-on sentence An error resulting from the joining of two independent clauses with no punctuation.

She is a good student. Her grades are always excellent.

NOT She is a good student, ~~her grades are always excellent~~. *(run-on sentence)*

sentence adverb An adverb that modifies an entire sentence. It can occur at the beginning, in the middle, or at the end of a sentence.

Fortunately, Sarah was not hurt badly in the accident.

stative passive A passive form used to describe situations or states.

North and South America **are connected by** the Isthmus of Panama.

subjunctive A verb form using the base form of a verb and normally following a verb or expression showing advice, necessity, or urgency. The verb *be* has the special subjunctive form *were*, which is used for all persons.

We always **insist** that our daughter **do** her homework before watching TV.

If I **were** you, I would pay off my mortgage as soon as possible.

subordinating conjunction A connecting word used to begin an adverb clause.

We were relieved **when** Jack finally called at 1 a.m.

tag question A statement + tag. The **tag** is a short question that follows the statement. Tag questions are used to check information or comment on a situation.

She's an actor, **isn't she?**

topic sentence A general sentence that indicates the content of a paragraph.

There are several things to keep in mind when you visit a Japanese home.

transition A word or phrase showing a connection between sentences or between larger blocks of text.

Climate change is a serious problem. **However,** it is not as serious as the problem of poverty.

unreal conditional sentence A sentence that talks about untrue, imagined, or impossible conditions and their results.

If I were you, I would study a lot harder.

zero article The absence of a definite or indefinite article. The zero article occurs before unidentified plurals or non-count nouns.

Whales are endangered.
Water is necessary for survival.

Unit Review Answer Key

UNIT 1

A
1. we're doing
2. loves
3. he takes
4. I'm getting
5. They seem
6. attends
7. she's making
8. she texts

B
1. have been living
2. has directed
3. has been working
4. have owned
5. have been remodeling
6. has been running

C My neighbor Jeff is a teacher. His job is going ~~good~~ *well* in general, and he likes it. But sometimes he sounds ~~angrily~~ *angry* when he talks about it. He feels ~~frustratedly~~ *frustrated* because a few students in his class behave ~~bad~~ *badly*. They pretend to listen to him, and they look ~~quietly~~ *quiet* and innocent in class. But they don't take their studies ~~serious~~ *seriously*. Instead, they surf the Internet and text each other during class.

UNIT 2

A
1. got
2. have done **or** 've done
3. have been **or** 've been
4. have visited **or** 've visited
5. was
6. went
7. wanted
8. have never known **or** 've never known

B
1. came
2. met
3. didn't know
4. didn't speak
5. had lived
6. had learned
7. was

C Solange grew up in Brazil, and she misses it. When she was a teenager, she ~~didn't used to~~ *didn't use to* study very hard at school. Instead, she ~~will~~ *would* go to the beach every day and have fun with her friends. Solange has ~~been being~~ *been* married to Ty, who is American, for ten years. Solange and Ty have two children, Ava and Jacob. Solange wants to show her homeland to her family. They ~~would~~ *were going to* go to Brazil last year, but unfortunately, they had to call off the trip, though they *had* been planning it for months. Solange hopes that they can go next year instead.

UNIT 3

A
1. have to
2. 'll be **or** 'm going to be **or** will be **or** am going to be
3. 'll call **or** will call
4. lets
5. 'll stop by **or** will stop by
6. come

B
1. Sam and I are taking
2. Our flight leaves
3. we get
4. we'll have been flying
5. We'll be
6. We're spending **or** We'll be spending **or** We're going to be spending
7. We'll send
8. we're

C

A: Hey, Cheryl! How are you doing?

B: Good! I've been traveling all over the country for work. By the time the summer is over, I'll have ~~visiting~~ *visited* ten cities, and I'll have been ~~traveled~~ *traveling* for three months straight!

A: Wow! That's a lot! ~~Do you come~~ *Are you coming* **or** *Will you be coming* to New York, too?

B: Yes! Actually, ~~I'll come~~ *I'm coming* **or** *I'm going to come* to New York next week! Can we get together?

A: Sure! Call me when ~~you're getting~~ *you get* to town. It'll be great to see you!

B: ~~I~~ *I'll* call you as soon as I arrive at my hotel!

UNIT 4

A
1. weren't supposed to
2. didn't have to
3. shouldn't have
4. could
5. We'd better not
6. must have
7. Chie's got to
8. aren't allowed to
9. could have
10. Hadn't we better

B **1.** must
2. should
3. may not **or** cannot **or** can't
4. must
5. Should (you)

C A: Did you see the email? All employees ~~is~~ *are* to attend the good-bye party for our CEO, Brent Chang.

B: Yes, I did see it. His wife was invited too, but she ~~must~~ *had to* decline because she is going on a trip.

A: Since it's a good-bye party, we ~~don't have to~~ *mustn't* **or** *must not* forget to buy him a present. We had better ~~to~~ get him something nice. We ought *to* buy him something useful, too.

B: I agree.

UNIT 5

A	**1.** must	**6.** ought not to
	2. might	**7.** had to
	3. might	**8.** has got to be
	4. couldn't	**9.** must have been
	5. should	**10.** must

B **1.** Jeremy might have **or** Jeremy may have **or** Jeremy could have
2. Mari must have
3. They couldn't have **or** They can't have
4. We should **or** We ought to
5. You could have gotten

C A: Hi, Jack. I'm glad you finally made it to the party! But where's Gina? Do you think she might have forgotten about the party, or could she *have* had to work late?

B: I think Gina ~~must to~~ *must* be sick. She didn't look good earlier today.

A: That's too bad. What about Al and Lisa?

B: Al told me to tell you that he couldn't get here by 7:00, but he ~~should to~~ *should* make it by 8:00. I don't know about Lisa. I suppose she could be ~~work~~ *working* late, but she didn't say anything to me about it.

A: I guess she might ~~been~~ *be* on her way here right now. I hope so!

UNIT 6

A	**1.** is being constructed	**5.** has been
	2. had his car serviced	**6.** being
	3. were caught	**7.** been
	4. died	**8.** by noon

B	**1.** is reported	**5.** was being reported
	2. is being reported	**6.** had been reported
	3. has been reported	**7.** will be reported
	4. was reported	**8.** will have been reported

C The Turkish city of Trabzon has just ~~being~~ *been* hit by a tsunami. The tsunami ~~got~~ *was* caused by an earthquake centered in the Black Sea. At this time last year, international talks were ~~been~~ *being* held on how to protect countries from tsunamis, but no significant decisions were agreed upon. U.N. officials said, "We must get these talks ~~start~~ *started* again."

UNIT 7

A	**1.** is bordered by	**5.** by
	2. as	**6.** is located in
	3. is claimed	**7.** is thought
	4. is believed to be	**8.** are alleged

B **1.** are thought to have come
2. It is said
3. is claimed by witnesses
4. is assumed by experts to date
5. is believed to have been

C Hawaii is regarded ~~by~~ *as* one of the most beautiful places in the world. It is composed ~~from~~ *of* a number of islands, some large and some small. An island is an area of land that ~~surrounds~~ *is surrounded* on all sides by water, so Hawaii is not bordered ~~of~~ *by* any other country. It is ~~claiming~~ *claimed* by some that mythical creatures live in Hawaii. For example, the Menehune ~~say~~ *are said* to be very small people who live deep in the forests there. They are ~~allege~~ *alleged* to have lived in Hawaii since before the Polynesians arrived from Tahiti many centuries ago.

UNIT 8

A
1. not smoking
2. making
3. Emiko's
4. giving
5. having
6. seeing
7. being awakened
8. not having been invited

B
1. Mary's inviting
2. Being invited
3. not having called
4. children's not having
5. have trouble understanding
6. used to being assigned

C A: Going to that movie was a good idea; it's definitely worth ~~to see~~ *seeing*.

B: I agree! It was great. So, how's it going at work these days? Are you excited about having ~~hiring~~ *hired* your friend Jack to work with you?

A: Well…no! I thought I'd enjoy ~~to work~~ *working* with him, but I'm kind of upset with him right now. First of all, he has trouble ~~finish~~ *finishing* his work on time. And sometimes he's rude. At a meeting yesterday, I was bothered by ~~he~~ *his* coming in without asking permission. Also, he seems to hate *being* told what to do; he prefers making his own decisions.

UNIT 9

A
1. to do
2. to accept
3. to give up
4. smoking
5. to lock
6. locking
7. to confront
8. to be criticized

B
1. not to put off
2. allowed to choose
3. not to have happened
4. to have been hit
5. tired to finish
6. to have forgotten

C I decided *to* buy an apartment last year. My friends warned *me* not to procrastinate. They told me ~~buying~~ *to buy* the apartment as soon as possible before prices went up. But there are occasionally good reasons *to* postpone things. I found an apartment I liked on the beach, but it wasn't ~~enough cheap~~ *cheap enough* to buy. So I procrastinated… and the prices went down! I'm lucky to *have* gotten my apartment for a very low price.

UNIT 10

A
1. C
2. NC
3. NC
4. C
5. NC
6. C
7. NC

B
1. a. exercise
   b. exercises
2. a. pieces of advice
   b. advice
3. a. grain of rice
   b. Rice
4. a. Cheese
   b. a cheese

C Many people ~~needs~~ *need* to lose weight these days. I do too. My doctor gave me ~~an advice~~ *advice* **or** *some advice* **or** *a piece of advice* to help me lose weight. He said I should improve my diet. But it takes ~~a work~~ *work* to prepare a nutritious meal. Also, I dislike cauliflower, carrots, beans, and most other ~~vegetable~~ *vegetables*. And I like to drink a can of ~~sodas~~ *soda* with every meal. What can I do?

UNIT 11

A
1. G
2. N
3. D
4. G
5. G
6. D
7. N
8. N

B
1. the
2. a
3. the
4. an
5. the
6. Ø
7. Ø

C One of the most famous animals in the history of Earth is ~~a~~ *the* dinosaur. The extinction of the dinosaurs is still a matter of debate in *the* scientific community. Why did they die out? Many scientists now believe that *a* giant meteorite flew through ~~the space~~ *space* and hit our planet very hard. This changed ~~an~~ *the* earth's climate, making it too cold for dinosaurs to survive.

UNIT 12

A
1. Most
2. amount
3. any
4. a lot of
5. a couple of
6. number
7. many
8. little
9. plenty of
10. no

B
1. many **or** a great many
2. much **or** a great deal of **or** lots of
3. a lot of **or** lots of
4. a number of
5. a lot of **or** lots of **or** a great many
6. Every

C On the whole, I have a lot of fun at my new job. I earn less money than I used to, but I have a lot ~~fewer~~ less stress. Most of my co-workers are responsible and work hard, but a few of them do ~~a little~~ little if any work. The majority of my colleagues have a lot of experience, so I can ask them for advice and help. The only real negative about my new position is the ~~number~~ amount of traffic on the roads in the morning and afternoon.

UNIT 13

A
1. sweltering, humid summer
2. challenging five-hour job
3. new striped cotton
4. handsome young Asian
5. last World Cup soccer
6. dirty, little old

B
1. an eleven-year-old son
2. an unexpected pleasure
3. a surprising new experience
4. six fifty-five-minute periods
5. a voter-initiated proposal
6. a forty-five-story building
7. a Chinese ivory statue
8. a heavy gray cat

C Over the weekend, I attended a ~~film wonderful~~ wonderful film festival. As I expected, the films were excellent in general, with one major exception. This one exception was a ~~horror terrible~~ terrible horror movie with a lot of ~~special silly~~ silly special effects and ~~strange looking~~ strange-looking creatures. The best film overall, surprisingly, was a digitally remastered version of *Gone with the Wind*. I'd seen it previously and wasn't all that excited about seeing it again. I was pleasantly surprised. Even though it's a nearly ~~four hours long~~ four-hour-long movie, it never gets boring. Everyone should see this awesome, exciting movie at least once.

UNIT 14

A
1. who
2. where
3. whom
4. whose
5. which
6. when
7. likes
8. who

B
1. no commas
2. no commas
3. Mrs. Ching, whose dog is always barking, is very wealthy.
4. no commas
5. no commas
6. Ms. Voicu, who is a student, is from Romania.
7. Tumba, whose children are very energetic, is always exhausted.

C Last week in my psychology class, we took a personality test ~~who~~ that **or** which is designed to determine what kind of person you are. The test, ~~that~~ which I found interesting, took a couple of hours to complete. Today I got my results, ~~whose~~ which were pretty much what I expected. I have many friends ~~whom~~ who **or** that mean a lot to me, so it's not surprising that I'm classified as an extrovert. I would recommend that everyone who **or** that wants to find out more about himself or herself should take a test like this.

UNIT 15

A
1. whom
2. whose
3. whom
4. which
5. who
6. interested
7. born
8. including

B
1. whom
2. which
3. whom
4. which
5. whose
6. who **or** that
7. that **or** which

C Newcomers to a country who **or** that begin to suffer from culture shock often develop communication problems. They may be acquainted with many people, most of ~~which~~ whom they were previously able to talk with easily. Now they find it difficult to talk to these people. Moreover, aspects of the new culture, most of ~~whom~~ which used to seem interesting and exciting, now begin to seem boring and unappealing. These newcomers may begin to experience negative emotions, ~~included~~ including anger, hostility, and depression. Fortunately, this is only a temporary attitude that **or** which is soon replaced by gradual acceptance.

UNIT 16

A 1. just don't
2. had we
3. he even thinks
4. only members can
5. don't just
6. even he can
7. does Eva
8. comes the train

B 1. are kangaroos found
2. Clearly, something has to change. **or** Something clearly has to change. **or** Something has to change, clearly.
3. Not only should education be available to everyone
4. Seldom does our team lose.
5. Only citizens can vote;
6. Here is the money
7. There goes the plane.

C Ben is my partner on our debate team, and he's one of my best friends, but sometimes he irritates me. Not only ~~he is~~ *is he* often late for debates, but I never know if he's going to be prepared. Rarely ~~he will~~ *will he* accept criticism, and at times ~~even he won't~~ *he won't even* listen. I ~~never just~~ *just never* know what kind of mood he's going to be in. He's an excellent debater, fortunately. So, if his heart is in the debate*,* we usually win it.

UNIT 17

A 1. unless
2. Even though
3. in case
4. As
5. Once
6. now that
7. wherever
8. when

B 1. whenever
2. As soon as
3. Unless
4. Because
5. Only if
6. Although **or** While
7. While **or** Although

C A: As soon as Mom ~~will get~~ *gets* here, we can leave for the game.

B: You mean Mom is coming with us to the game? She won't understand what's going on even *if* we give her a long explanation.

A: ~~Unless~~ *If* we explain it slowly and carefully, she'll get the basic idea.

B: I'm not so sure. Only if we can take an hour or so to explain it ~~she'll~~ *will she* get the overall picture.

A: Even though she might not understand everything*,* she'll enjoy being with us.

UNIT 18

A 1. Not knowing
2. Caught cheating
3. Having gotten the tickets
4. before leaving
5. On realizing
6. Relaxing
7. Having visited
8. being given

B 1. Hearing
2. while doing
3. Having eaten
4. Upon finishing
5. Having been
6. after being taken
7. Given

C ~~When~~ *On* **or** *Upon* arriving at the Cairo airport, I was certain I had plenty of time to make the connection for my next flight. Not ~~eating~~ *having eaten* on the plane and ~~feel~~ *feeling* very hungry, I stopped at a restaurant to get some food. ~~Lost~~ *Losing* track of time, I enjoyed my meal. Then I glanced at my boarding pass and saw I had fifteen minutes to make it to my flight gate. I had a lot of heavy bags, so I grabbed them and started running toward the gate, ~~known~~ *knowing* I'd never make it on time. Just then, out of the blue, a man I'd never met took a couple of my suitcases and got me to the gate with five minutes to spare. I wish I could have returned the favor.

UNIT 19

A 1. however
2. though
3. Because
4. therefore
5. besides
6. and
7. or
8. otherwise

B 1. I was exhausted, so I went to bed at 8:00 p.m.
2. I've visited many exotic places; for instance, I've been to Bali, Marrakesh, and Tasmania.
3. We need to remember to get tickets; otherwise, we won't get seats.
4. Nora forgot her passport; as a result, she missed her flight.
5. Even though Bao has a degree, he has a low-paying job.
6. As soon as I got off the train, I took a taxi to the hotel.
7. You're too young to have a car; besides, cars are very expensive.

C A: I heard you're taking a memory improvement ~~course, how's~~ *course; how's* **or** *course. How's* it coming along?

B: The course itself is fine. ~~Although~~ *However,* it's pretty expensive. It's worth it, ~~but~~ *though*.

A: I've been thinking about taking one, ~~too, however~~ *too; however,* **or** *too. However,* I wonder if I would really learn anything. Would you recommend your course?

B: Yes, I would, ~~for~~ *so* why don't you sign up?

UNIT 20

A
1. the birth order theory is
2. he always wants
3. the meeting starts
4. "configuration" means
5. whether Samira
6. what
7. she's been
8. whether or not

B
1. what Mary meant
2. whether (or not) Jama is coming **or** whether Jama is coming (or not)
3. Whatever you want
4. The fact that Allison loves Kahlil
5. whomever you want
6. However you want to proceed

C A: Do you know ~~who are our new neighbors~~ *who our new neighbors are*?

B: Yes, I run into them ~~whoever~~ *whenever* I go out in the yard.

A: Oh, yeah? What do you think ~~are they~~ *they are* **or** *they're* like?

B: They seem really nice. I know ~~what they~~ *that they* **or** *they* both work.

A: Hmm. I wonder *if* they have children.

B: They have three. I'm happy ~~about that~~ *about the fact that* **or** *that* their older daughter is the same age as Maria.

UNIT 21

A
1. it was
2. had finished
3. if she was
4. to be sure
5. not to
6. if he would
7. she would come by
8. could

B
1. if he would be
2. would not be
3. "I don't feel well."
4. she needed to take
5. if she had ever seen snow
6. "I've seen snow many times."
7. not to write

C Carlos said, "Ho-Jin, why ~~you haven't~~ *haven't you* called me lately?"

Ho-Jin said, "I just haven't had time. I have to study a lot right now*."*

Carlos said, "You ~~said~~ *told* **or** *said to* me you were going to try to relax more."

Ho-Jin said, "No, I didn't. I ~~told~~ *told you* **or** *said* I was going to relax as much as possible."

Carlos said, "Well, OK, but are we still ~~friends.~~ *friends?*"

Ho-Jin said, "Of course we are!"

UNIT 22

A
1. hadn't built
2. hadn't been
3. wouldn't have
4. would take
5. would be traveling
6. wouldn't have had
7. wouldn't be able
8. hadn't been

B
1. wishes he hadn't forgotten
2. wouldn't have stopped
3. hadn't stopped
4. wouldn't have had to
5. wouldn't have had to
6. would have had **or** 'd have had
7. could have made
8. wouldn't be

C A: What do you think of Jim's new invention? He's thinking of marketing it. Would you buy it if you ~~have~~ *had* the money?

B: If I ~~was~~ *were* Jim, I ~~won't~~ *wouldn't* market it.

A: Why not?

B: Who wants a robot that drives your car? People will laugh at him.

A: You're just jealous. I'll bet you wish you ~~would have~~ *had* invented it yourself.

UNIT 23

A
1. Without
2. If not
3. If so
4. otherwise
5. With
6. if not
7. without
8. with

B
1. otherwise
2. Had I
3. call
4. Should that
5. But for
6. understand
7. if so

C
A: I'm glad you suggested we ~~hired~~ *hire* Bob Burnham. He's done a great job.

B: Yes, he has. ~~I had~~ *Had I* known how good he is, I'd have recommended him sooner.

A: Do you recommend Jen Valdez for the sales position? If ~~not~~ *so*, let's interview her.

B: I do, yes. However, I suggest we ~~offered~~ *offer* a higher salary for that position.

A: Really? Why?

B: ~~With~~ *Without* a salary increase, we'll never be able to hire Jen.

Games and Pronunciation Answer Key

UNIT 3

EXERCISE 8

Team A's prompts and the answers:

1. We'll be landing in the capital of Egypt in half an hour. (Cairo)
2. We're going to arrive in the largest country in South America in three hours. (Brazil)
3. We're arriving in the largest city in Canada in an hour. (Toronto)
4. We're going to cross the longest river in Europe in two hours. (the Volga)
5. We leave for **or** We're leaving for the largest city in the United States at 8 p.m. tonight. (New York)
6. We'll be in the world's most populous country tomorrow. (China)
7. We'll see Africa's highest mountain when we land. (Mount Kilimanjaro)
8. We're arriving **or** We'll be arriving in the Eternal City in forty-five minutes. (Rome)

Team B's prompts and the answers:

1. We'll be landing in the capital of Iran in forty-five minutes. (Tehran)
2. We're going to arrive in the largest country in North America in an hour and twenty minutes. (Canada)
3. We're arriving **or** We'll be arriving in the largest city in India in an hour and a half. (Mumbai)
4. We're going to cross the longest river in Africa in four hours. (the Nile)
5. We leave for **or** We're leaving for the largest city in South Africa tomorrow night. (Johannesburg)
6. We'll be **or** We'll be in the world's smallest continent tomorrow morning. (Australia)
7. We'll see **or** We're going to see the highest waterfall in the world when we land. (Angel Falls)
8. We're arriving **or** We'll be arriving in the City of Love in ninety minutes. (Paris)

UNIT 7

EXERCISE 8

Team A's prompts and the answers:

1. Which island is composed of the nations of Haiti and the Dominican Republic? (Hispaniola)
2. Which Central American country is bordered by Panama and Nicaragua? (Costa Rica)
3. Which people are considered by some to be the descendants of Atlanteans? (the Basque people)
4. Which legendary creature is thought to live in the Himalayas? (the yeti)
5. Which man is claimed to have been the greatest playwright ever? (William Shakespeare)
6. Which individuals are regarded as great humanitarians? (Albert Schweitzer and Mother Teresa)

Team B's prompts and the answers:

1. Which Caribbean nation is composed of many islands? (the Bahamas)
2. Which Caribbean nation is located about 90 miles south of Florida? (Cuba)
3. Which forest creature is said to live in the Pacific Northwest? (Bigfoot)
4. Which lost continent is thought to have been located in the Atlantic Ocean? (Atlantis)
5. Which planet was thought to be the center of the universe before Copernicus? (Earth)
6. Which two presidents are regarded as the greatest American presidents? (George Washington and Abraham Lincoln)

UNIT 10

EXERCISE 9

A

a. film
b. advice
c. talk
d. baldness
e. a work
f. a tan
g. traffic
h. cancer
i. a space
j. a criterion
k. sunblock
l. cholesterol
m. criteria
n. fast food
o. news
p. lightning
q. the police
r. rice
s. work
t. people
u. a film
v. thunder
w. a people
x. space
y. a talk

UNIT 11

EXERCISE 8

2. What is a bank?
3. Who are the poor?
4. What is poaching?
5. What is plastic?
6. What are wolves?
7. What is a humpback whale?
8. What is the brain?
9. Who are the rich?
10. What is the telephone?

11. What is a species?
12. What is an elk?
13. What is a silverback?
14. What is the sun?
15. What is water?
16. What is the post office?

UNIT 13

EXERCISE 5

1. She's going to wear her new red silk dress.
2. Everyone expected that ugly, strange, old building to be torn down.
3. The trip we took was an expensive, silly, miserable waste of time.
4. She was upset by her disappointing, terrible test scores.
5. My intelligent, gracious twenty-five-year-old sister just got engaged.
6. My parents just bought an attractive old condo.

UNIT 22

EXERCISE 8

Team A's prompts and the answers:

1. Who would you have been if you had invented the electric light? (Thomas Edison)
2. How old would you have to be if you were the president of the United States? (thirty-five years old)
3. What creature would you have been if you were an ancestor of the elephant? (a mammoth)
4. How old would you be if you were a nonagenarian? (between ninety and ninety-nine)
5. Who would you have been if you had made the first successful airplane flight in 1903? (one of the Wright brothers)
6. Who would you have been if you had invented the car? (Karl Benz)
7. What country would you have been from if you had been Marco Polo? (Italy)
8. What mountain would you have climbed if you had been with Edmund Hillary and Tenzing Norgay in 1953? (Mount Everest)

Team B's prompts and the answers:

1. How old would you be if you were an octogenarian? (between eighty and eighty-nine)
2. Who would you be if you were the founder of Microsoft? (Bill Gates)
3. What would you be if you were the largest mammal? (a blue whale)
4. How old would you have to be if you were a United States senator? (thirty years old)
5. Who would you have been if you had been the inventor of the telephone? (Alexander Graham Bell)
6. What kind of creature would you have been if you had been a stegosaurus? (a dinosaur)
7. Who would you have been if you had popularized the term *bug*? (Grace Harper)
8. Who would you have been if you had been president of the United States during the Civil War? (Abraham Lincoln)

Information Gaps, Student B

UNIT 2

EXERCISE 9 WHAT'S THE STORY?

A INFORMATION GAP **Work with a partner. Student B will follow the instructions below. Student A will follow the instructions on** **page 31.**

STUDENT B

- **The story below is missing some information. Your partner has the same story that contains your missing information. Ask your partner questions to find the missing information.**

  EXAMPLE: B: How long would he stay on the road?
  A: He would stay on the road for . . .

- **Your partner's story is missing some information. Answer your partner's questions so that your partner can fill in his or her missing information.**

  EXAMPLE: A: What kind of company did he use to work for?
  B: He used to work for a company that . . .

Jack Strait's life is quite different now from the way it used to be. He used to work for a company that sold carpets and flooring. His job required him to do a lot of traveling. He would stay on the road for ______________________. It was always the same: As soon as he pulled into a town, he would look for a cheap motel to stay in.

The next morning, he'd ______________________ at a lot of different establishments, hoping that someone would agree to see him. If he'd been lucky enough to arrange an appointment in advance, he'd show them his samples. Occasionally they would order ______________________; most often they wouldn't.

Jack's marriage began to suffer. His wife had come to the United States from Russia to marry him. She didn't know anyone in their town, and her family was back in Russia. She was lonely. He missed his wife a lot, but there wasn't much he could do about the situation. And when he was on the road, he hardly ever saw his children. He would try to call them in the evenings if he had a spare moment. Usually, however, it was so late that they had already gone to bed. The children were growing up without him.

Finally, Ivana laid down the law, saying, "Why should we even be married if we're never going to see each other? I didn't come to this country to be a job widow." Jack decided she was right. He took a risk. He quit his job and started his own business. Things were difficult at first, but at least the family was together.

That was five years ago. Things have changed a lot since then. Jack and his family used to live ______________________. Now they own a house. Life is good.

UNIT 4

EXERCISE 8 THE KINDNESS OF STRANGERS

INFORMATION GAP Work with a partner. Student B will follow the instructions below. Student A will follow the instructions on page 65.

STUDENT B

- The story below is missing some information. Your partner has the same story that contains your missing information. Ask your partner questions to find the missing information.

EXAMPLE: B: What should the couple have gotten?
A: They should have gotten . . .

- Your partner's story is missing different information. Answer your partner's questions so that he or she can fill in the missing information.

EXAMPLE: A: Where were the married couple supposed to stay?
B: They were supposed to stay at . . .

A married couple was traveling in Europe and had just entered a new country. They had been having a wonderful time, but now everything was going wrong. The first problem was finding accommodations. They were supposed to stay at the Grand State Hotel, but when they got to the hotel, there was no record of their reservation. The wife said they should have gotten ______________________. They hadn't, unfortunately, so they had to spend the night at the train station. The next day, they finally found a room at a hotel far from the center of town. There were two rooms available: a large one and a tiny one. Since they were on a tight budget, they decided they had better ______________________.

The second problem was communication. They were starving after spending hours looking for accommodations, so they went into a restaurant. A waiter brought them a menu, but they couldn't understand it. The husband said they should have brought along a phrasebook. They hadn't done that, though, so they didn't know what to order.

Time passed. Other people were being served, but they weren't. Frustrated, they decided ______________________. But what? They noticed that a boy about eleven years old seemed to be listening to their conversation. Soon the boy came over to their table. "Excuse me," he said. "You have to pay for your meal first. Then they'll take your order." The husband and wife were both astonished but grateful. The wife said, "You speak our language very well. Did you study it somewhere?" The boy said, "I lived in Australia for three years. I learned English there." He asked, "______________________? I can translate the menu."

When the couple got back home, their friends asked them what they had liked best about the trip. The wife said, "Well, the best part was visiting that country where everything went wrong, and that boy helped us. He could have ______________________, but he didn't. It's wonderful when strangers help you. It made me realize that we should all be ready to help others when the need arises."

UNIT 6

EXERCISE 9 WHO STOLE THE PAINTING?

INFORMATION GAP Work with a partner. Student B will follow the instructions below. Student A will follow the instructions on page 101.

STUDENT B

- The story below is missing some information. Your partner has the same story that contains your missing information. Ask your partner questions to find the missing information.

  EXAMPLE: B: When was the *Mona Lisa* stolen from the Louvre Museum in Paris?
  A: It was stolen from the Louvre Museum on August 21, 1911.

- Your partner's story is missing different information. Answer your partner's questions so that he or she can fill in the missing information.

  EXAMPLE: A: What has been called the world's most famous painting?
  B: The *Mona Lisa* has been called the world's most famous painting.

The *Mona Lisa*, which has been called the world's most famous painting, was stolen from the Louvre Museum in Paris on ______________________. Amazingly, the theft was not even noticed until the day after the theft. ______________________ was eventually discovered to be the thief. Peruggia had been hired by the museum to build glass cases. How did he manage to steal the painting? He first hid in a closet overnight. After the museum had been closed for the day, Peruggia ______________________. He then hid it under his coat and walked out of the building. No one stopped him because at this time, security was not given much attention by museum authorities. Also, the actions of the police investigating the crime were unimpressive, to say the least. Peruggia was named a suspect and was questioned ______________________ before it became clear that he had perpetrated the crime. Famous painter Pablo Picasso was even treated as a suspect for a time. Two years later, after he tried to sell the *Mona Lisa*, Peruggia ______________________ in a successful police operation. He was finally arrested and was sentenced to ______________________ of jail time, and the painting was returned to the Louvre.

EXERCISE 7 THE MOUNTAIN GORILLA

INFORMATION GAP Work with a partner. Student B will follow the instructions below. Student A will follow the instructions on page 189.

STUDENT B

- The article below is missing some information. Your partner has the same article that contains your missing information. Ask your partner questions to find the missing information.

  EXAMPLE: B: What kind of ape is the mountain gorilla?
  A: It is the largest of the great apes.

- Your partner's story is missing different information. Answer your partner's questions so that he or she can fill in the missing information.

  EXAMPLE: A: What is the mountain gorilla?
  B: The mountain gorilla is a great ape.

THE MOUNTAIN GORILLA is a great ape; in fact, it is ______________________________ apes. Mountain gorillas inhabit national parks in three countries in central Africa: Uganda, Rwanda, and the Democratic Republic of the Congo.

Mountain gorillas have thick fur, a characteristic that enables them to live in cold, mountainous areas. An adult male is called ______________________________ and can grow as tall as 6 feet 3 inches, or 1.9 meters. Adult males can weigh up to 430 pounds or 195 kilograms. Mountain gorillas live together in social groups dominated by adult silverbacks. A group is composed mainly of ______________________________ and several females and young gorillas. The mountain gorilla is ______________________________; silverbacks can often remove the traps left by poachers. Since these animals are ______________________________, they need a good deal of food daily in order to support their great bulk.

The mountain gorilla is a critically endangered species. There are two principal causes of its endangerment: poaching and loss of habitat. Mountain gorillas are sometimes hunted for food, and they are pursued by poachers for their fur and for sale to zoos. It is clear that ______________________________ and encroachment on locales where mountain gorillas have traditionally lived has split their habitat into widely separated areas. There were only 254 mountain gorillas in 1981, and there are now about 880. This sounds positive, but since particular groups of mountain gorillas are not able to interact with other gorilla groups, the result is lack of genetic diversity within the species. This is ______________________________.

UNIT 12

EXERCISE 10 STUDY SKILLS

INFORMATION GAP Work with a partner. Student B will follow the instructions below. Student A will follow the instructions on page 208.

STUDENT B

- The article below is missing some information. Your partner has the same article that contains your missing information. Ask your partner questions to find the missing information.

  EXAMPLE: B: Who is at their best late at night?
  A: A few people are at their best late at night.

- Your partner's article is missing different information. Answer your partner's questions so that he or she can fill in the missing information.

  EXAMPLE: A: Who feels most alert early in the morning?
  B: Many people feel most alert early in the morning.

Want to be the best student you can be? Here are several suggestions.

- Do your studying when you are the most awake and alert. Many people feel most alert early in the morning. ______________________, however, are at their best late at night. Identify your own particular characteristics.
- Take plenty of good notes in class. ______________________ prefer just to listen to a lecture, believing that note-taking distracts them from what the professor is saying. Relatively few people, however, learn effectively by following this strategy. You interact with the course material when you take notes about it, and that kind of active learning is highly beneficial.
- Review your notes regularly. Do this ______________________ if possible. You don't have to spend a lot of time doing this. Going over your notes for ______________________ daily can really help you to learn and retain information.
- Examine your lifestyle and make improvements in it if necessary. According to a well-known English proverb, "All work and no play makes Jack a dull boy." You need to work hard, but your life will be dull indeed if you never have ______________________. Build in time for entertainment and socializing. And while you're at it, make sure you eat healthy food and get enough sleep. You'll have ______________________ if you do.
- Finish whatever you start. Once you start something, keep working at it until you've made a visible ______________________. Then stay with the project until it's done. If you don't do this, you'll simply waste a great deal of time. Don't worry if this takes a long time. Rome wasn't built in a day, but it did get built.

UNIT 22

EXERCISE 9 HENRY FORD'S ASSEMBLY LINE

INFORMATION GAP Work with a partner. Student B will follow the instructions below. Student A will follow the instructions on page 389.

STUDENT B

- The article below is missing some information. Your partner has the same article that contains your missing information. Ask your partner questions to find the missing information.

EXAMPLE: B: When did Ford introduce his Model T to the world?
A: He introduced his Model T to the world in 1908.

- Your partner's article is missing different information. Answer your partner's questions so that he or she can fill in the missing information.

EXAMPLE: A: What would Ford never have done if he hadn't changed the makeup of his original assembly line?
B: He never would have achieved success with the Model T.

The First Moving Assembly Line

HENRY FORD introduced his Model T to the world in ________________________. However, he never would have achieved success with the Model T if he hadn't changed the makeup of his original assembly line. Ford knew that ordinary people wouldn't buy his cars if they ________________________. If Ford could make Model Ts cheaper than other cars, he knew that people would buy them. So Ford introduced a new, more efficient method of auto production that involved division of labor.

On Ford's original assembly line, auto workers had to do several separate tasks to put each car together. If workers have to move around a lot and do many different tasks, they can't produce as much. If you divide a big job into many different smaller tasks, however, everyone can ________________________. So, Ford and his staff divided the assembly process into eighty-four different steps. In this way, they minimized the motion of each worker as much as possible. There was another advantage: If each worker was responsible for only one task, he or she ________________________.

In 1913, Ford introduced the moving chassis assembly line and a mechanized belt, which sped up the car assembly process a great deal. If a business makes many products quickly, it can charge less for each one. So, Ford's plan to make Model Ts cheaper than other cars succeeded.

If Ford hadn't figured out a way to build his cars more efficiently and cheaply, it's possible that cars would never have become popular with the masses. However, might the world be a better place now if ________________________? And what about the workers themselves? Might they not have been happier if these changes hadn't been made? Could they have ________________________ who had to perform the same repetitive actions endlessly? It's difficult to say. The bottom line is that Ford achieved his goal.

Index

This index is for the full and split editions. All entries are in the full book. Entries for Volume A of the split edition are in black. Entries for Volume B are in blue.